FREEDOM AND HISTORY *and Other Essays*

FREEDOM AND HISTORY *and Other Essays*

Richard McKeon

An introduction to the thought
of Richard McKeon

Edited by Zahava K. McKeon, *with an*
Introduction by Howard Ruttenberg

The University of Chicago Press · *Chicago and London*

At the time of his death in 1985, *Richard McKeon* was the Charles F. Grey Distinguished Service Professor Emeritus in Philosophy and Greek at the University of Chicago, where he had taught since 1935. During his career he served as advisor to the United States Delegations at the first three sessions of UNESCO and was a founding member of UNESCO's International Institute of Philosophy. A prolific author, McKeon wrote eleven books and over 150 journal articles.

The University of Chicago Press, Chicago 60637
The University of Chicago Press, Ltd., London
© 1990 by the University of Chicago
All rights reserved. Published 1990
Printed in the United States of America

99 98 97 96 95 94 93 92 91 90   5 4 3 2 1

Library of Congress Cataloging-in-Publication Data

McKeon, Richard Peter, 1900–1985
    Freedom and history and other essays : an introduction to the
thought of Richard McKeon / Richard McKeon ; edited by Zahava K.
McKeon ; with an introduction by Howard Ruttenberg.
      p.   cm.
    Includes index.
    ISBN 0-226-56028-7 (alk. paper) ; — ISBN 0-226-56029-5
(pbk. : alk. paper)
    1. Liberty. 2. History—Philosophy. 3. Philosophy. I. McKeon,
Zahava Karl. II. Title.
B824.4.M39 1990   89-5056
191—dc20   CIP

Contents

To the Memory of Peter McKeon

Preface

The publication of this introductory volume of Richard McKeon's essays is the first step in an enterprise that will afford access to the work of a great scholar, teacher, and philosopher, and, in so doing, will pay tribute to a remarkable man whose career spanned the greater part of the twentieth century. Richard McKeon was born on 26 April 1900, in Union Hill, New Jersey. After a brief stint in the Navy during the first world war, he returned to graduate work at Columbia University in 1919, studying with Frederick J. E. Woodbridge and John Dewey. He earned an M.A. in philosophy in 1920, then wrote a Ph.D. dissertation on Spinoza.

In 1922 McKeon left for Paris to study with the great teachers of the day, Brunschvicq, Robin, and Gilson, returning to teach at Columbia in 1925. During the decade following he established medieval philosophy, long considered essentially theology, as a serious part of the philosophy curriculum. In 1935 Robert Maynard Hutchins persuaded him to come to the University of Chicago to participate in its great experiment in education, and McKeon taught there until his retirement in 1974.

Behind these brief biographical details lie extraordinary contributions to the intellectual lives of several generations of students, to philosophy, and to international relations. Richard McKeon believed that "philosophy is not only a form of knowledge; it is also an expression of cultures . . . a preliminary study of the relations of cultures as expressions of values, divergent in form but possibly identical with each other in fundamental character, . . . [they] reproduce, when they are stated formally, differences on which philosophers have been engaged ever since Socrates brought philosophy down from the skies."*

*From "A Philosopher Meditates on Discovery," in *Moments of Personal Discovery*, ed. R. M. MacIver (New York: Jewish Theological Seminary, 1952), 132.

This concern with the clashes of cultures seems to have been a major force in the development of his ideas. After World War II, he served as adviser to the United States Delegations at the first three sessions of UNESCO, in 1946, 1947, and 1948. In the first essay of the present volume he discusses these activities in some detail. It was UNESCO that gave birth to the International Institute of Philosophy, of which McKeon was one of the founding members, and in which he was active for the rest of his life.

As a teacher Richard McKeon was unforgettable. Studying with him was often frustrating and difficult—he presented no doctrine a student could master once and for all; moreover, he demanded that the student learn to recognize and to formulate a genuine philosophic problem, one mark of which was that it could not be resolved simply by interpreting what others had said. The student who persisted was willing to tolerate ambiguity, to explore and to believe that exploration valuable even if certainty remained elusive.

For to study with him was always exciting, an adventure in ideas; and on a one-to-one basis he had an extraordinary gift of discernment. The student would speak at length of his or her confusion, of an inability to formulate coherently what he or she wanted to work on. When the thoughts ran dry, McKeon could formulate what the student had been struggling to express, and help him or her begin a productive period of research and writing. And, by no means a minor virtue in a teacher, he was always available, reading papers and dissertation chapters thoroughly and promptly.

But finally, the educator who was a major participant in inaugurating, with Robert Maynard Hutchins, a college curriculum that was a unique achievement in American education, the teacher who never failed his students as long as they sought to do the best that they could do, the citizen who used his great learning to serve his country and an ideal of cultural exchange—Richard McKeon was, above all, a scholar and philosopher.

He was a classical scholar whose introductions to Aristotle and essays on ancient Greek philosophy earned him a lifetime reputation as an "Aristotelian," which he was not. He was a medievalist whose essays in that field are landmark contributions. His doctoral dissertation on Spinoza remains an important study in seventeenth-century philosophy six decades after its publication.

As impressive as his scholarship was, however, his contribution to philosophy in the twentieth century was even more significant. The two, indeed, are inextricably linked. McKeon's intellectual range and interests were remarkably extensive, and they remained so throughout a long and productive life. He wrote important essays in aesthetic theory and literary criticism; he was a scholar of classical antiquity; and his seminal essay, "Rhetoric in the Middle Ages," inaugurated the serious study of medieval and Renaissance rhetoric that has blossomed in the second half of the twentieth century. In 1976–77 the University of Chicago Press published his and Blanche Boyer's definitive edition of the *Sic et Non* of Peter Abelard. He studied Indian philosophy, and with N. A. Nikam edited *The Edicts of Asoka,* first published in Bombay in 1962.

McKeon took very seriously the philosophers he studied, seeking to understand them on their own terms. The profound knowledge of the scholar combined with the reflections of the philosopher led him to propose philosophic pluralism as the only philosophical stance that made sense of the history of philosophy, and the conflicts among cultures and ideas. McKeon argued that controversial opposition among philosophers is a function of a complex set of variables, and it is so whether the thinkers are contemporaries or worlds or ages apart. He constructed a semantic schematism for analyzing systems of thought with great precision. Language is finite and consequently ambiguous, and this schematism made it possible to appreciate the philosophy of the past without taking sides. One can appreciate and enjoy Plato and Aristotle, Hume and Kant, and one needn't be a Platonist or an Aristotelian, a Humean or a Kantian; instead, one can learn what philosophers have to teach, and try to "do" philosophy, to solve genuine philosophic problems. On a theoretic level, the decision to decline adherence to any dogma was central to McKeon's thought; he went further in declining to produce any dogma of his own. His commitment to pluralism was not exclusively theoretical, however. He was convinced that the mechanisms of controversial opposition as they operated in professional philosophy were equally present in practical life— in political and social life, national and international. But the consequences were more than theoretical. The variables that determine meaning in philosophy are ubiquitous. In every argument in which facts are alleged and structured coherently, in which conclusions are reached, there is embedded an orientation to reality, principles of organization, and a characteristic method of argument. Because of this, whereas it is possible in practical life for persons to share a goal, sometimes they do so for totally different reasons. Unless they are willing to accept that to have disagreements "in principle" is quite reasonable as long as they agree on the goal to be reached—unless, in fact, they acknowledge the legitimacy of pluralism—they will be endlessly embattled and/or paralyzed with respect to cooperating to produce desirable social or political action.

McKeon's semantic schematism facilitates the interpretation of texts and the exchange of ideas in discussion, to be sure. But in itself it is more than that; it is the affirmation of a universe so multifaceted that no one philosophy can encompass its complex variety, including the schematism which illuminates it. Great philosophies are never obsolete, nor are the philosophies that seem to refute them. The history of ideas is an ongoing conversation, productively ambiguous.

Philosophic pluralism was by no means a popular position in McKeon's last years. Just as philosophies may be seen as doctrinaire and dogmatic, pluralism is vulnerable to the charge that it is simply "relativism." McKeon's patience and good humor seldom failed the task of explaining that to claim that truth shows itself in many guises, and that "reality" is many rather than one, is not to claim that any intellectual construct or statement is as true as any other. The many arguments and statements of principle and allegations of facts in a many-sided world can be held to the canons of rational argument. However, to judge an idea wanting solely because it stems from premises alien to our own is to deny ourselves the full richness of available thought.

The present volume begins with an essay in intellectual autobiography, "Spiritual Autobiography," in which the philosopher reflects on his thought in a narrative mode. The next two papers, "Philosophy and History in the Development of Human Rights" and "The Development and the Significance of the Concept of Responsibility" both explore the principles of rights and responsibility, and the fourth, "Communication, Truth, and Society," deals with the way in which communication of what is perceived as truth is related to the community communication makes. "Dialogue and Controversy in Philosophy" discusses those two modes of philosophizing. The sixth essay, "Has History a Direction?" presents McKeon's essay, his oral treatment of the topic at a meeting, and his responses to queries, objections, and discussion of the essay and the speech. It is especially interesting in showing how McKeon tried to transform controversial opposition so that discussion could replace it, and how he countered objections to pluralism.

"Freedom and History," the title essay, discusses the concepts of freedom and history, their interrelation over time, and how that interrelation depends on the semantic orientations of philosophers and historians. First published as a monograph in 1952, "Freedom and History" has been out of print for some time.

"Philosophic Semantics and Philosophic Inquiry," the last essay, is published here for the first time. McKeon delivered this paper at the Illinois Philosophy Conference meeting at Carbondale, Illinois, on 26 February 1966, and in it he presents in detail the semantic schematism in terms of which his explorations of the history of philosophy were conducted. McKeon's semantic schematism does not explain away philosophies and philosophers; rather, it enables us to interpret texts such that they can speak to us directly and relevantly, whatever their origins in time or in culture. Finally, the semantic schematism, in bringing philosophies to life, is more than an intellectual tool; it is simultaneously an embodiment and an affirmation of the pluralism of reality and truth and the timelessness of philosophic inquiry and philosophic thought.

When Richard McKeon died on 31 March 1985, he left behind a rich intellectual legacy. Plans are now well underway for publishing the collected works in several volumes; the present introduction to McKeon's work began to take shape when Morris Philipson suggested that *Freedom and History* ought to be reintroduced in company with appropriate selected essays.

A group of Richard McKeon's students met to discuss the project, and their advice and support have been invaluable. I would like to thank Howard Ruttenberg for his labor of love, the introduction to this volume of essays, and to acknowledge here, too, the good offices of Michael F. Buckley and King Dykeman in planning the volume. Sue Salm provided a superb archivist's bibliography of the collected works, and Thomas Stark read and reread the introduction, as did Douglas Mitchell, who has been available for discussion whenever I needed him.

Finally, I am especially grateful to William Swenson, who came to Chicago several times during the preparation of this manuscript offering technical help and editorial advice. To all of the aforementioned, my thanks for making my own labor of love a little less lonely.

15 October 1988   Zahava K. McKeon
                                                   Chicago, Illinois

Introduction

This volume is an introduction to the thought of Richard McKeon. It focuses on the complex interrelations he traces among philosophical arguments, historical accounts, and practical problems of communication and action. Current dilemmas and paradoxes, emerging in our deliberations about the relations between ideas and life, make McKeon's thought especially significant. Faith in democracy and freedom as fundamental values has increased despite deepening despair over our capacity to overcome differences and solve our own problems. Rational discussion of these problems has been inadequate to the task of finding real solutions to conflicts that threaten war or the arbitrary imposition of authority. We see no acceptable alternative to science and technology as tools for improving life, but their own logic endangers all life. The extension of scientific methods and technology to apply to the achievement of human values, once the very formula of enlightenment, now seems highly problematic. The means of communication have grown prodigiously, but tend to spread bland uniformity rather than to promote rich dialogue. Contact among cultures leads more often to conflict and war than to mutual appreciation of traditions, ideas, and values. Ideologies and philosophies abound, but the richness of alternatives promotes relativism rather than inquiry and discussion, and concern with the quality of life stimulates antiintellectualism rather than practical thinking.

Richard McKeon's writings provide a powerful antidote to the loss of confidence that the apparent intractability of these problems can induce. His profound and original interpretations of the systematic arguments of great philosophers, and his historical analyses of the emergence of problems and the concomitant development of new ideas and disciplines renew our sense of what we can accomplish. Despite the wisdom of the individuals who enrich our traditions, McKeon's account of the practical consequence of philosophy tells the story of a community of inquirers. While each participant in this community brings distinctive intellectual tools to the task, each depends on the tradition, even for the development of the most original ideas. McKeon went beyond the by now familiar and influential idea of scientific paradigms even before these appeared in the philosophical literature, with his idea of a distinctively philosophical communication among authors who do not share a paradigm. His analysis of philosophical communication eschews both the faith in a uniquely correct or adequate way of thinking, and the skepticism reductive of each approach to the preferences and unsupportable opinions of those who hold those opinions.[1] Instead, his pluralism specifies different principles, methods, and interpretations through which facts and values can be discovered and supported, while showing how agreement about facts and values can be achieved despite different ways of thinking about them. He has taken the commonplace that we can learn from each other despite our differences and without removing them, and given it a power commensurate with the power of great philosophers to analyze and solve problems.

The breadth of Richard McKeon's scholarly undertakings was unusual. His Columbia University dissertation on the unity of Spinoza's philosophy interrelated the treatise on politics, the treatise on politics and religion, the uncompleted work on method, and the *Ethics*. He wrote a dissertation in French at the University of Paris on the problem of the universal in twelfth-century philosophy. He translated two volumes of medieval philosophy on epistemological problems, wrote on scientific method as conceived by Aristotle and Spinoza, contrasted Plato and Aristotle as historians, wrote on Cicero, Maimonides, Saadia Gaon, and G. E. Moore, and on law, mathematics, physics, rhetoric, art and criticism, the liberal arts, human rights, and UNESCO,[2] all before the publication in 1953 of the centerpiece of the present volume, "Freedom and History." He wrote, edited, or collaborated on eleven books and contributed about one hundred fifty articles, some of these seventy pages long, to various scholarly journals and books. From the begin-

1. From "Communication, Truth, and Society."
2. United Nations Educational, Scientific and Cultural Organization, a specialized agency of the United Nations which seeks to further world peace by removing social, religious, and racial tensions, encouraging the free interchange of ideas and of cultural and scientific achievements, and by improving and expanding education.

ning he was interested in particular authors; not just in what they wrote, but in what their methods of analysis show us about the range of meanings of terms, the diverse uses to which devices of logic, history and rhetoric can be put, and the implications for knowledge and action of different ways of relating theory and practice.

He regarded the issue of theory and practice as more than a matter of applications. He saw it instead as dependent upon basic notions about knowledge and what it is about, and hence on the connection of knowledge to human endeavor in general. His own unusual capacity to see philosophical principles in concrete practical issues was apparent in his service to his country during World War II, and in his participation in the efforts to establish peace in its aftermath. A professor of Greek and classical languages, history, and philosophy at the University of Chicago, he participated in a program of language instruction for army intelligence officers. In that capacity, he rejected the approach that sought to convey as much information as possible about the country whose language was being taught, in favor of one which made the student familiar with the culture and values of its people. The philosopher recognized that information is infinite, and that even the native speaker must rely on knowing how to get it rather than on having a ready supply for all occasions.

If intelligence in war could not be reduced to information, then peace could not be sustained after the war by thinking in terms that reduced it to relations of power and material interests. McKeon was an American representative to UNESCO participating in its postwar effort, developing the knowledge and common values considered to be "indispensable instruments in the construction of a world community within which political institutions can operate on a worldwide basis."[3] The UNESCO Committee on the Theoretical Bases of Human Rights prepared for the General Assembley's adoption of the Universal Declaration of Human Rights. Reflecting on the work of that committee twenty years later in "Philosophy and History in the Development of Human Rights" (in this volume), McKeon rethought the issue of human rights in the light of events following the adoption of the Universal Declaration. He cited the Committee's argument that an international declaration of human rights "must be the expression of a faith to be maintained no less than a programme of actions," and thus "faces

3. From "Thirteen Americans: Their Spiritual Autobiographies."

fundamental problems concerning principles and interpretations."[4]

McKeon saw in different world cultures the same problems and conflicts treated in philosophy. Whereas the later reconciles "alternative attitudes and modes of thought" abstractly and systematically, in cultures resolution is found in "practical reconciliation in the habits of life and social institutions."[5] Cultures are not merely the expressions of different material conditions and relations of power, but neither are they unique embodiments of specific ways of philosophizing. Habits of life reconcile some modes of thought and are irreconcilable with others; indeed, some habits are irreconcilable with some forms of life. Philosophy, on the other hand, lacks practical significance when its dialogue becomes an insular, primarily technical affair, neglecting "the actual operations which define ideas . . . in cultures" and "the actual languages developed by men associated in cultures and engaged in the solution of practical and theoretic problems."[6]

Far from belying McKeon's insistence on multiple philosophic approaches, this rich interplay between forms of life and thought underscores the necessity for reconciling opposed points of view; that is, if thought is to render practical service to the cultures of the world, whose increased contact has led to new and dangerous conflicts. Reconciliation means unanimity only if only one philosophy can be true. McKeon's own work is enriched by a sense of real human aspirations and conflicts, not unlike the effect in the dialogues of Plato, which are dramatic instances of the ideas they discuss. His work reflects the influence of study with Woodbridge and Dewey at Columbia and with Brunschvicq, Gilson, and Robin in Paris. With the latter group he traced to antiquity the various relations between theory and practice that he found in the history of philosophy. Informed by an awareness of the actual circumstances of nations in our time and of the dangerous consequences for action that arise from degrading interpretations of rival theories, his pluralism yields sorely needed practical insights into the relations between ideas, communication, and community.[7]

McKeon's explications of philosophers are so clear and persuasive

4. The first quotation is cited by McKeon from *Human Rights: Comments and Interpretations, A Symposium Edited by UNESCO* (London, 1949), 258. The second is from McKeon's "Philosophy and History in the Development of Human Rights."

5. From "Freedom and History."

6. From "Thirteen Americans: Their Spiritual Autobiographies."

7. From "Freedom and History."

that they have often converted readers to positions he presents as one among many. His appreciation of alternative ways of thinking did not prevent him from espousing his own, reflected clearly in the original and distinctive philosophical character of his pluralism, and in the uses to which he put it. His lectures and articles amply demonstrate his thesis that a philosopher can make accurate statements about philosophies departing radically from his own, although usually these are distorted by a failure to recognize differences of meaning and method. McKeon delineates various ways of relating theory to practice by means of semantic distinctions. Rather than engaging in controversy and polemic, the essays in this volume examine practical and theoretical problems. "Freedom and History," a long monograph originally published in book form, focuses on the discovery of a variety of meanings of "freedom" and "history." It also specifies a number of methods by which philosophers have used different meanings to inquire into problems of freedom and history. Semantics studies what philosophers mean when they write about a subject. Inquiry, using semantic distinctions, investigates the subject itself.

Semantic distinctions are particularly important for practical purposes because differences of meaning, values, and ways of thinking are part of the problems being considered—not just ways of considering them. McKeon's philosophical semantics aims at mutual understanding, not at conversion to a single philosophy. Mutual understanding increases the possibility of agreement about common actions required to form and maintain community. It does so without insisting that the reasons informing actions, and the principles which justify the reasons, be the same for all. By contrast, semantic distinctions are useful for theoretical purposes as the means of discovering true principles rather than common actions, thus leading to more adequate solutions to problems of knowledge.

Philosophers tend to consider alternative meanings for the purpose of rejecting them as false or inadequate; indeed, philosophers are frequently in polemical rather than irenic relation to each other. Polemics in practical matters threaten to lead to the suppression of ideas and the imposition of "wise" policies by force. This threat has added significance today because of the technologically augmented capacity to influence thought and its expression. Paradoxically, knowledge has increased the power which, when used arbitrarily, inhibits the development of knowledge and its ability to solve problems and advance freedom. It has become more urgent that we distinguish between the threat to values and what are simply alternative values or ways of talking about them. The better communication of alternative values is necessary for the discovery and nurturing of those we have in common.

"Freedom" and "history" are topics, places of discussion, which have been specified in terms of a wide range of alternative values. Each topic has an ambiguous meaning that embraces different and opposed meanings determined by different ways of thinking. Thus the ambiguous formula, "freedom is the ability to act without external restraint," has been made definite by meanings of "ability" which range from spontaneity to wisdom. The ambiguous formula, "history is the account of events which promote or impede freedom and other values," yields different kinds of accounts as the meaning and value of freedom are differently specified, since means and obstacles vary according to what is sought, and according to the way in which connections are made among events. In "Freedom and History" three methods or philosophic ways of thinking are delineated: the "dialectical," the "logistic," and the "problematic."

"Freedom and History" presents one version of McKeon's semantic schematism. In it, as in many other of his essays, he uses but does not draw attention to distinctions he made in his courses at the University of Chicago. These are made explicit in "Philosophic Semantics and Philosophic Inquiry," published here for the first time. The latter presents philosophic semantics as a formal schematism. McKeon distinguishes four modes of thought: assimilation, discrimination, construction, and resolution. Each is familiar from ordinary, nonsystematic thought. To assimilate is to find likenesses among different things and to merge several positions into one which contains and transforms them; assimilation may be exemplified by the manner of Plato. To discriminate is to find the character of things to be determined by the perspective of a viewer or agent; thus John Stuart Mill in his *On Liberty* discriminates between self-regarding and other-regarding actions. Construction searches for the parts of which complex wholes are composed; for example, Descartes, in Part II of the *Discourse on Method,* illustrates this mode clearly when he says (in rule 3) that "beginning with objects which are the most simple and easy to understand," he will "rise little by little . . . to knowledge of the most complex." Finally, resolution differentiates problems and devises techniques appropriate for their solutions.[8] In *Reconstruction in Philosophy,* John Dewey solves the problem of the possibility of knowledge of the world by substituting the hypothesis of the knower as participant for the traditional concept of the mind as mere observer of the world. The modes of thought designate operations of thought, and are not simply labels for a philosopher's conclusions or cherished beliefs.

As ordinary operations of thought, these four modes are available to any thinker, including the philosopher. When thinking achieves a high level of development, one mode defines the manner in which each of several specific functions of thought is performed. The functions range from selection of data (which give the philosophy its basic vocabulary) to interpretation of fact (which provides its basic meanings) to method of warranting fact (connecting ideas in arguments and facts in coherent sequences) to principles that ground argument in basic assumptions (which systematize arguments and define a whole science or area of inquiry). Each mode of thought performs each function of thought differently, leading to disputes among philosophers as to what constitutes a fact or a good argument. For example, philosophers who employ a logistic method (construction) may use dialogue to canvas opposing views,[9] but find it inadequate for analyzing wholes into their simple components, whereas in Plato a dialogic method, dialectic (assimilation) performs all the operations necessary for inquiry. These distinctions exhaust alternative possibilities, but not the richness of particular philosophies. Part of that richness is indicated by the possibility of using different modes of thought for some or each of the functions.

McKeon argues that many of the controversial issues dividing philosophies arise from disparate modes of thinking, rather than from conclusions reached through inquiry. His schematism can help to clarify these oppositions. As an example, let us consider the interpretation of fact. It involves, initially, two possibilities: Either reality is distinct from phenomena or it is identified with them. The first possibility interprets phenomena either in terms of a reality that transcends them and exists in a state of permanent stability, or as the nature that underlies them.

8. See "Freedom and History," section 6, for brief descriptions of three of the modes of thought.

9. See McKeon's description of the logistic separation of sciences "from the disorderly mass of conjecture, superstition, and insight" which is philosophy, in "Dialogue and Controversy in Philosophy."

On the other hand, phenomena may be seen as real in themselves and knowable by the careful investigation of their many facets and structures, or as a function of agents whose viewpoints are inevitably partial and must be multiplied to achieve adequate conception of reality.

Understanding a philosopher involves detecting the mode of interpretation, method, and principle used, in order to follow the treatment provided in determining meanings and solving problems with respect to such terms as "freedom" and "history" (or "space" and "time," or "imagination" and "expression"). McKeon's approach to philosophic semantics enhances our appreciation of individual philosophers and of the function of philosophy in general. First, philosophers cease to seem merely idiosyncratic when viewed as exploring fundamental options inherent in thinking about the nature of things and their relations to human thought. One example, Plato's "ontological interpretation," according to which "to be is to be intelligible" (*Republic,* v, 477), finds the meaning of words, the objects of thought, and the nature of things to appear in unchanging, rational patterns. Plato is taken seriously and on his own terms by this approach, not as inventing bizarre entities to remove his confusions about predication, or as arbitrarily devising abstractions about justice in order to satisfy his need for political orderliness. Similarly, ideas about nature (or knowledge, or works of art) which take it to be a whole antecedent to parts which exist and function because of their places in the inclusive structure become opportunities for serious reflection, rather than remnants of archaic thinking laid to rest by modern empiricism. Philosophers are rescued, as cultures need to be, from distorted, sometimes polemical interpretations based on meanings and assumptions in opposition to the ones supposedly being clarified.

Second, philosophic semantics helps us to recognize, as a sign of the vitality of philosophy, the existence of many apparently contradictory philosophies. The polemical elimination of opposition affords only the illusion of having achieved a unique statement of the truth. The specification of common problems and alternative solutions does more for the progress of knowledge than the elimination of opposition. Pluralism provides multiple perspectives in a universe of discourse in which no one perspective can be universal or exhaustive. The reflexivity of thinking, by which it defines a philosophy's very subject matter and methods, precludes agreement about basic assumptions. But the "facts" revealed by the philosophy can be agreed upon, as long as they are not viewed with a jaundiced eye that sees in them only the rejected ways of thinking that first uncovered them. On the contrary, ambiguous facts, susceptible of diverse formulations in statement, advance thinking in any reflexively defined inquiries which consider them.

In "Freedom and History" McKeon's philosophic semantics illuminates the varieties of systematic thought that we call histories. There he characterizes the problematic approach as using reflexive principles to distinguish theoretical from practical problems. Reflexive principles define a field of inquiry distinguished by its own problems and relevant considerations. Thus we can study one text for the logic of its arguments, its insights into the nature of things, its prudential maxims, or the elegance of its expression, without reducing it to any one of these functions. A problematic practical philosophy features the resolution of difficulties that arise when conflicts of ideas and values prevent common action and cooperation. What McKeon himself does in this essay exemplifies this approach: The problematic is both one of three alternatives and the approach in terms of which they are presented. As we have seen, the essay seeks to promote mutual understanding as a precondition for agreements about what to do. McKeon uses only three methods, rather than his usual four, and conflates his distinctions between interpretation, method, and principle, in order to focus on the problem of agreement despite fundamental theoretical opposition. He uses only the distinctions needed for solution of that problem, much as Aristotle uses only four of his ten categories to discuss change in the *Physics*.

When theoretical differences cannot be removed, the practical enterprise of common action requires making theoretical obstacles irrelevant. The first step is to show that the different theories offer plausible accounts that need not be contradictory. McKeon accomplishes this by isolating ambiguous formulas for freedom and history from the specific meanings given them in dialectical, logistic, and problematic philosophies. If freedom is, ambiguously, the ability to act without external restraint, these philosophies can be read as granting different meanings to "ability" and "external." History, as an account of the facts which support or prevent the achievement of freedom, can confirm a preferred set of meanings with those facts, but only by using the meanings in the historical inquiries to determine what has occurred. If, however, pluralism is to have practical consequences, more than mutual understanding is needed. The ties between theory and action must be loosened.

The problematic approach gives us a way of thinking about this without rejecting either of the other two ways of thinking about freedom and history. Neither the dialectical nor the logistical ways of thinking about freedom and history recognize the distinction between theory and practice. One assimilates human history to universal cosmic processes, the other reduces it to the elemental natural forces that compose human nature. The problematic approach, however, separates history from any necessary or natural processes, and causes progress to depend upon the application of intelligence to problems that arise when people have different ideas and values. When practical solutions for these problems are sought without attempting a reconciliation of opposed ideas, the objective is a course of action which satisfies all those ideas.

Dialectical histories tell the story of the development in stages of the essence of man or spirit. Using the mode of assimilation, they find no ultimate difference between the processes of the mind and those of things. History itself is a kind of thinking, the "cunning of reason," as Hegel phrased it. Nor does historical knowledge differ ultimately from other kinds of knowledge. History, as events and as science, works out concretely, in the lives of actual people and communities, the same ideas that define universally the nature and development of the individual, community, and cosmos. Plato's *Timaeus* describes a universe that thinks, possessing the same virtues found to comprise justice in the *Republic*. Both the *Timaeus* and the *Critias,* which tells the story of an ancient, virtuous Athens, heroically fighting off the invaders from Atlantis, are called myths by Plato. History as myth depicts the concrete embodiment of the same dialectical connections found in philosophy. When the ideas that govern all processes, including human events, achieve internal realization as the knowledge which governs actions, human beings are free. The wisdom that defines freedom may be possible strictly speaking only for God, but human minds and communities can be governed by something approximating divine wisdom. The Idea of the Good surpasses human capacity and yet inspires the arts and sciences, which achieve their full dimensions as they are merged in dialectics. Similarly, the unlimited potential of human labor and creativity is released, according to Marx's dialectic, when human alienation is overcome in the classless society. Practice is no more distinct from theory, in dialectical thought, than virtuous action is from the wisdom governing it. Agreement between opposed ideas of action depends upon an understanding of the essence of man.

Logistic history treats man as part of nature. It identifies history with a part of natural science which is concerned with human nature or with a science that extends the experimental methods of natural to moral philosophy, as Hume's did.[10] Logistic thought defines freedom as the operation of any nature unimpeded by other natures impinging upon it. At the other extreme from dialectical freedom, which applies only to God and the wise, logistic freedom applies to all bodies insofar as they operate according to the laws of their own natures. History seeks knowledge of human nature in order to devise institutions which would protect people from interference by nature in general and each other in particular. Logistic histories tell the story of the growth of human knowledge and of the control of nature to serve human ends. Knowledge of nature also provides humanity with greater self-control by replacing the fears and superstitions which the mind creates when it lacks understanding of external things. With such knowledge the mind operates according to its own nature, rather than according to inadequate images and passions, which are the effects of external causes. Theoretical knowledge of the operations and interactions of natures yields the practical benefit of curing the deformities and inhibitions induced by external causes. Agreement between individuals and nations depends upon knowledge of their common human nature and of the means for its liberation.

Of these philosophical approaches, the problematic approach, as I have noted, makes a distinction between theory and practice. The cosmos and human nature constitute the context in which human choices realize some possibilities among many. Practical histories of what has been said and done with respect to human actions and associations are distinguished from histories appropriate to other disciplines and concerned with the other problems of nature, first philosophy, art, rhetoric, etc. In Aristotle's treatises, histories often occupy the early chapters or a whole first book, in preparation for a new treatment of the problems that define a distinct area of study. The reflexivity of thought, by which dialectical and logistic philosophies define freedom and history, is evident also in the problematic treatment. A history which gathers facts about human action distinct from the facts of nature and of the cosmos also defines freedom as something distinct from the operations of human nature and from the universal processes of all things. Freedom as

10. David Hume, *An Enquiry Concerning Human Understanding*, section I.

the exercise of choice "builds its own world of human affairs," according to R. G. Collingwood.[11]

The knowledge necessary for freedom in this sense of "self-rule" has to do with the achievement of aims chosen, including the knowledge of how to get others to agree to pursue them. Dewey refers to agreement and participation in moral ends as an actual universality, distinguished from the metaphysical universality spoken of by Plato, and the logical one of Kant's moral philosophy.[12] Freedom as self-rule tends to be associated with democracy. Aristotle limits self-rule to those capable of virtue, but even so, what is best in general and in particular circumstances he regards as a blend of democratic and oligarchic principles. John Stuart Mill thinks that most nations would be fortunate to be prepared for democracy by a benevolent despot. Dewey identifies community with democracy, on the ground that only the exercise of self-rule produces the means for the growth of understanding necessary for self-rule.

McKeon's problematic history locates ambiguous common meanings of "freedom" and "history," and traces variations on the theme that knowledge of the facts of history determines the means for achieving freedom. The semantic analysis of different meanings of freedom and restraint shows each to be the consequence of distinct principles, not necessarily in contradiction to each other. Semantic analysis supplants polemical opposition and thereby enriches the meanings that each way of thinking explores. But common action does not result from this enrichment of meanings, unless a similar enrichment of the relation of means to ends replaces the tendency for opposed meanings to be translated into competing forces. The opening up of meanings, connections, and principles to embrace those of diverse modes of thought makes possible and marks the transition from philosophic semantics to philosophic inquiry.

The unique use to which McKeon put his semantic distinctions for the resolution of problems of thought and action has often been obscured, ironically, by both the erudition and clarity of his expositions of other philosophers' ideas. In essays on topics such as responsibility, a pluralistic society, human rights, and the question of the meaning or

11. R. G. Collingwood, *The Idea of History* (Oxford, 1946), 318. Cited by McKeon in "Freedom and History."

12. John Dewey, *Reconstruction in Philosophy* (Beacon Press, 1957), 205–6.

direction of history, he develops a philosophy for the resolution of problems of action based on principles of communication.

Communication is in vogue as a value to be sought and as a means of analyzing problems. Better communication does not just offer hope of better relations between people, from couples and business associates to ethnic groups and nations. The term "communication" refers to the very activities that define these relationships, including the activities of scholars and scientists. McKeon sees in these facts something of greater significance for philosophy and history than merely a popular trend. On the one hand, he does refer to the changes in the vocabulary of philosophy as "fashions in philosophizing."[13] In calling the periodic revolutions in philosophy "fashions," he means to shock the reader out of the dogmatic assumption that philosophy can only be done fruitfully, or best, in the manner in which it is currently done. On the contrary, the pluralism expressed in McKeon's schematism includes the selection of basic vocabulary evident in philosophy as metaphysics, epistemology, or as analysis of language and action.

As McKeon depicts it, the progression of philosophy from one to the other of these in modern times reflects the very nature of philosophy as a discipline of the whole and of the fundamental, which does not allow it even the temporary agreement or common paradigm possible in other disciplines. This manifests itself periodically in the awareness that the common problems of a whole period, expressed in its basic vocabulary, have not been solved in ways convincing for all who think about them. Hume and Kant argued that metaphysical problems concerning the nature of things and their first causes had not been resolved, and could not be without a prior examination of the faculties of the mind and a critical evaluation of its capacities. When the subsequent discussion of these problems likewise failed to produce unanimity, it was natural for philosophers to take the further step of examining what it is we say and do when we think and make judgments about things; Russell, Husserl, Dewey and others did this in developing the philosophies of language, phenomenology, and pragmatism that Dewey, following Kant, called "a second Copernican Revolution." By regarding periods of philosophy in the light of the priority in analysis of things,

13. The selection of a basic vocabulary "is colored by the general selection characteristic of the philosophic communication of a period." In "Philosophic Semantics and Philosophic Inquiry."

or thoughts, or "words and deeds" (Cicero's expression), McKeon was able to locate similar revolutions in ancient and medieval thought. This enabled him to compare our own time to other periods, such as that of the late Roman republic, the age of Charlemagne, and the Renaissance, which brought rhetoric to the center of the discussion of problems of philosophy. These changes in priority are mere fashion only in the sense that there is nothing inherently prior in the analysis of things or thoughts or words. They are not fashion in that each alternative focuses on different problems. Analysis of language and action, for example, focuses on interpretation, and this makes method and principles part of the analysis of meaning. McKeon's own philosophy of meaning, his philosophical semantics, thus participates in the common discussion of problems of his age. It has the advantage over other semantics of being inclusively historical, defining alternative philosophies in terms of the problems to which they give priority (as well as in terms of the different modes of thought they use to analyze them). It is not historical in the "bad" sense of limiting history to anticipations of a favored approach. As a result, the distinctions he uses, though formally exhaustive, are the ones actually employed, not only by philosophers, but by all who engage in the discussion of theoretic and practical problems.

The ubiquity of the vocabulary of communication and action is due in part to the influence of philosophers and other thinkers, and in part it is a response to characteristic problems of the period. As McKeon points out in "Communication, Truth, and Society," "When problems are broad and complexly interrelated, the initial distinctions must be found in communication." The divergence of meanings and ways of thinking characteristic of the cultures and philosophies brought into contact by new and more powerful means of communication leaves little basis for progressive mutual understanding. Focus on the concrete, on what we say and do, does not of itself relieve the problem, since it can easily lead to the representation of certain facts and the theories which advance them as the only truth. Whereas all philosophers who seek descriptions of the concrete avoid speculation about principles, McKeon is rare in his recognition of the dependence of description on the use of philosophic principles. Dogmatism turns communication into disputation and thought contributes to the prevailing antiintellectualism and relativism. We despair of solutions coming from philosophy, just as we despair of cooperation among the warring factions of the world. When, on the contrary, principles are regarded as alternative hypotheses, they enrich common inquiry in discovering new facts.

All of the essays included in this collection address philosophy as communication and communication as the formation of community. In "Dialogue and Controversy in Philosophy" the possibility of dialogue among opposed philosophies is explored, rather than the possibility of common action—but the problem of controversy in contemporary philosophy is said to be a "symptom of what is happening in larger communications in cultural relations and political negotiations." Four methods are defined in terms of different relations between arguments, the minds which conceive and communicate them, and the objects to which they refer.

The alternatives have been exhausted. The dialectical method makes argument primary; the perspective of the viewer or individual mind is the measure of argument and object for the operational method; the logistic method removes the contribution of the knower so that arguments map the nature of things; the problematic method distinguishes and relates all three. Controversy relating arguments to objects is unavoidable, but dialogue is possible "by turning attention to problems of the relations of arguments to elucidation of minds" and to the "large regions of coincidence" where different methods "take into account the audiences to which their arguments are addressed."[14] When we look at the meanings in what others say and at the reasons for their conclusions, rather than comparing those conclusions to what we *think* we know to be the case, we at least understand what is being said. And with understanding arises the possibility of coming to agreement with others on occasions for common action, since their proposals will at least be meaningful. Some proposals, even if supported for what we take to be the wrong reasons, will be acceptable.

In "Communication, Truth, and Society," McKeon raises the question of how it is possible to function as a community despite many opposed views of truth, and the question of how truth unites people. But placing philosophy thus in the setting of society or community; i.e., as what people say and do, McKeon effects a transition to the broad sense in which all philosophy is communication. His distinction between pluralistic and unitary societies echoes the distinction of the four methods of communication, except that they are reduced to two: in a

14. From "Dialogue and Controversy in Philosophy."

unitary society the functions of communication are equated; in a pluralistic society each is independent of the others. The primary function,
to establish relations among people, requires self-expression by those
who would have relations with others (freedom). Self-expression succeeds in uniting people when communication establishes common values and overcomes false or partial views in the discovery of truth.
McKeon's essay develops the idea that in a pluralistic society communication becomes the inclusive mode of treating problems. Nothing can
be established as valuable or true or free, unless it succeeds in being
accepted by means of communication.

Communication among many opposed views depends on tenuous
agreement about principles, expressed in ambiguous terms such as
"freedom" and "democracy." That these embrace opposed ideas reveals
the operation of communication. But each idea also offers an alternative
conception of truth and how it functions in society, making people of
one mind. Ambiguity and opposition become fruitful in any communication that considers the implications of ideas rather than their oppositions. Despite opposed conceptions of how people are persuaded
to become of one mind, a unity emerges inclusive of all of those conceptions, because it has to do with individuals judging the communications of others as they bear on common problems. This unity is not
indicative of principles.

Here again McKeon advocates a method which separates different
functions and points of view, and achieves unity among them without
sacrificing their distinctness. He implicitly rejects the alternative, unitary conception of the functions of society. The term for the method of
communication proposed, the "democratic art of deliberative rhetoric,"
seems itself to contrast with the nondemocratic, authoritarian rhetoric
of the unitary society. But the paradox of his advocacy of pluralism,
that it is both one position and inclusive of all, runs deeper than that,
as his final words on the possibility of communication between a pluralistic and a unitary society show. Just as pluralism leads to society only
if it finds means for achieving common values, so unified values are
social only if they embrace differences. Communication between the
two kinds of society thus depends on the presence and cultivation of
deliberative rhetoric in each.

The same fruitful paradox informs McKeon's discussions of responsibility (in "The Development and Significance of the Concept of Responsibility") and of human rights (in "Philosophy and History in the

Development of Human Rights"). Both essays trace the transformation of traditional concepts[15] and distinctions with new ways of thinking responsive to changed circumstances. The concept of responsibility has come to embrace earlier distinctions—between imputation and accountability, and moral and political responsibility—as communication has become the inclusive mode of inquiry in treating the problem of forming new communities. Recognition of human rights likewise has been extended historically from political and civil rights to social and economic ones, and to the current emerging awareness of cultural rights. These extend and transform previously recognized rights in terms of participation in the formation of communities and the determination of their values. In both cases, the inclusive concept that emerges, linked to the idea of communication as inclusive mode of inquiry, preserves the earlier distinctions while relating them to each other. The effect of McKeon's histories, which are about actual nations and events as well as philosophies, is to show that the values opposed in the controversies of the latter are all recognized in acts and agreements of the former. While Marxists will always stress economic rights, for example, and liberal democrats will always advocate the primacy of political and civil rights, McKeon's study of events and communication shows that neither value belongs exclusively to either point of view— and that the preservation and advancement of both depend upon the pluralistic discussion of values, or cultural rights.

Philosophers were at first unaware of any new meaning or reference and used the term "responsibility" interchangeably with its predecessors, "accountability" and "imputation." Later, Mill and L. Lévy-Bruhl used it in ways indicative of the new circumstances, pointing out the need for a new concept. Prominent among these circumstances were the American and French Revolutions, for these marked a new stage in the efforts of people to form new nations, or new constitutions for existing nations. The process of seeking new foundations in thought has often been called philosophy; in the formation of a community, such thinking necessarily becomes communication. Even if the ideas that unite people originate in a single mind, to be effective they must be communicated to and accepted by others. "Responsibility" refers to

15. When McKeon wrote "The Development and Significance of the Concept of Responsibility," the earliest use of the term he had found was in *The Federalist,* no. 64 (1787). Later he found it in Madison, *Notes on the Constitutional Convention* (1787), and in the first edition of Bentham, *The Principles of Moral Legislation* (1780).

what has been done or proposed, relating actions not only to their consequences (accountability) and to the character of the person who performs them (imputation), but also to the discussion determining the values applied to them. "Accountability" and "imputation," terms in use before the concept of responsibility was invented, refer to communications applying criteria established outside of communication. They apply external restraints and impose values not determined within the process of discussion itself. Conversely, responsibility refers to a process of discussion which defines common values and thereby forms community. Persons and communities are responsible because of the way they enter into discussion, and not because of the principles they espouse. McKeon's analysis of responsibility completes the progressive understanding of this new and important idea. Such understanding provides a unique awareness of what it means to be free and to participate freely and rationally in democratic communities.

McKeon provides a history, in "Philosophy and History in the Development of Human Rights," of the recognition of civil, political, social, economic, and cultural rights, from the seventeenth century to the present, without reference to the various and opposed philosophies interpreting them during that period. Clearly, political rights are not the same for Hobbes as they are for Spinoza, nor economic rights the same for Marx as for Mill—but the philosophers and societies which adopted bills of rights, seeking to provide employment and health care for the people, agree ambiguously as to the existence and nature of these rights. The last two-thirds of the essay, however, considers a different relation between philosophy and history, such that they cannot be kept apart. The emergence of cultural rights in the twenty years after the work of the Committee on the Theoretical Bases of Human Rights, and the adoption by the U.N. of the Universal Declaration of Human Rights suggested to McKeon the need for a new approach.

Cultural rights include and transform political and social rights in the same way that responsibility includes and transforms imputation and accountability. Responsibility brings thinking about values within the compass of communication. Cultural rights extend the recognition of rights to include participation in the advances of civilization, including the arts and sciences. They do not merely add rights of cultivation of the mind to political and social rights; they put the latter in a new perspective, in which they, too, are cultural rights, values to be discovered and defined by thought and discussion. The absence of opposed philosophies of rights from McKeon's earlier history of the recognition of new kinds of rights can no longer be maintained. Because the second version is a history of cultural rights, it is one of opposed philosophies defining different values.

But it is also a history of the discovery of common values. The paradoxes and paralogisms that mark oppositions in the history of philosophy reappear in the history of the pursuit of cultural rights. This quest has become an argument embracing four formally distinct relations between right and law, defined by the four modes of thought. Plato, by way of illustration, makes transcendent rights (justice) prior to laws which are just insofar as they imitate them, whereas Hobbes defines right as whatever is not forbidden by law. The two come together, ambiguously and paradoxically, in the idea of a civil rights law that forbids interference with the pursuit of political, social, and educational values. Philosophy enters history, just as it becomes communication, as the ideas and values of people who seek to form their own communities, thereby altering the operation of the more inclusive community. Violence can be avoided in the struggle for cultural rights only if "revolution" and related terms are understood in their cultural meanings, and not rigidly opposed in terms of narrowly defined political and social rights.

McKeon develops this conception of history as an inclusive mode of inquiry in "Has History a Direction?" His written paper, talk, and responses to the questions of other participants in a symposium on the meaning of history are included here. The participants are philosophers and historians from many nations, many of whom are internationally known, such as Karl Löwith and Jean Wahl. McKeon argues that the idea of a meaning of history is peculiar to dialectical, epochal histories, which find processes of thought in the sequence of historical events. Methods which separate thought and event find meanings only in the interpretations of events by minds which think about them, as in his own, problematic approach and disciplinary kind of history. In his written paper and talk he describes four kinds of history: "epochal" (dialectic), "causal" (logistic)), "exemplary" (operational), and "disciplinary" (problematic). Exemplary history is added to the three discussed in "Freedom and History," but the operational method is one of the four discussed in "Dialogue and Controversy in Philosophy," as well as in "Philosophic Semantics and Philosophic Inquiry."

He discusses in some detail the processes by which historians select and interpret data, making arguments warranting their interpretations, in order to support his contention that the various kinds of history are complementary rather than contradictory. In their employment of the modes of thought to make arguments, all historians are philosophers. The pluralism of methods yields complementary facts and is in no way a relativism. On the contrary, the objectivity of the results of each method argues for the inclusion of these results by the others. McKeon envisions a common inquiry and new mode of thinking by historians, who "will learn the semantics of the variety of meanings," and will guide inquiry "in ways that take into account other methods and results," treating principles as hypotheses and "concentrating on facts . . . rather than on intentions and imputed meanings."[16] Each will develop a unique mode of philosophy and history, in a new way and with a cumulative effect contributing to the progress of truth.

The importance of history in McKeon's work is manifest. His conception of it as a "fundamental and inclusive mode of inquiry concerning experience and existence"[17] constitutes an original contribution to collective thought. Thus his works can be seen as striving to enrich the discussion of the concrete and the pursuit of common values with an understanding of the principles of those learned men who constitute our philosophic tradition, and who are at the same time the future tools of a new, irenic, and more fruitful community of philosophers.

Howard Ruttenberg
York College
The City University of New York

16. From "Has History a Direction?"
17. From "History and Philosophy, Art and Science, Validity and Truth," in *Verité et Historicité: Institut International de Philosophie, Entretiens de Heidelberg, 12–16 Septembre 1969,* ed. Hans-Georg Gadamer (The Hague: Martinus Nijhoff, 1972), 47.

FREEDOM AND HISTORY *and Other Essays*

1
Spiritual Autobiography

The line which divides narrative from argument is tenuous and vaguely drawn, even when the account is of actions performed publicly and of matters of record attested by independent witnesses. Soldiers who have completed their campaigns or withdrawn from them and politicans who have put policies into effect or have seen them defeated have often set down some form of history in the conviction, expressed by Thucydides, that an exact knowledge of the past is an aid to the interpretation of the future.[1] The line is tenuous, however, because history is frequently transformed into fiction under the influence of arguments constructed to square actions with principles, and the arguments are twisted by the events into sophistry. Accounts of adventures among things of the spirit are still more esoteric than military and political myths. Incidents, dates, and even protagonists, are not easily determined by external witnesses to the evolution of ideas. The narrative therefore tends to reassemble the parts of an argument in the chronological sequence of their development, and the agents in the action tend to become ideas in dialectical opposition. Narratives of action reveal the interdependence of the careers and destinies of men; narratives of inquiry and speculation bring men together in common ideas encountered and in the common efforts to interpret them. In the treatment of intellectual and spiritual problems the individual mind is in contact with universal relations, and the grasp of a basic problem or the comprehension of a true idea is not an individual possession to be explained

Reprinted from "Richard McKeon," in *Thirteen Americans: Their Spiritual Autobiographies,* ed. Louis Finkelstein (New York: Institute for Religious and Social Studies, Jewish Theological Seminary of America, 1953 [distributed by Harper & Brothers]), 77–114.
1. Thucydides, i. 22.

adequately by personal traits or prior history. On the other hand, the order of experience takes on a significance, usually unsuspected until a problem is resolved, when the stages of the experience are rearranged as steps in the discovery or proof of what is later conceived to be valuable or true. In spiritual biographies the protagonist properly tends to lose his personal identity and his actions tend to be separated from the local conditions and temporal circumstances, for, as Spinoza proved, "insofar as men live under the guidance of reason, thus far only they always necessarily agree in nature."[2]

Habits of philosophic analysis and historical research, consequently, although they might seem useful instruments adapted to the effort of interpreting the memory of past problems with which one has worked and the sequence of the stages by which one has become aware of their implications and the requirements of their solution, in fact inhibit interpretation and reconstruction by suggesting prior questions. The account of one man's difficulties in speculation about principles, in deliberation about means, and in inquiry about consequences, is significant only if, on the one hand, the statement of his arguments has a bearing on ideas and aspirations as they are at once shared by other men of the time or tradition and involved in timeless principles or implications, and if, on the other hand, the account of the sequence of his efforts to clarify notions and achieve ideals contributes to the clarification of universal thoughts and common actions. Conversely, a slight knowledge of philosophy and historical method is enough to suggest suspicions concerning much that purports to be narrative accounts of thought or action: history is often made by equipping developments in theory or practice with subjective motivations which might justify but did not cause them, or by stringing events on significances later discerned but unexpressed and unknown at the time of occurrence.

The power and significance of autobiography and confession have their sources in these paradoxes, however much they may distress those who seek simple meanings of what is said and simple separations of the facts of narrative from the ideas of argument. The interdependence of actions and the interrelation of theory and fact tempt men to seek in the absolutes of independent empirical facts or eternal truths the significance of occurrences on which a life has touched and the developments which bind occurrences in a line of action or a growing insight. The

2. Spinoza, *Ethics,* iv. 35.

actions of men are directed to satisfying like needs in like circumstances, and the thoughts of men encounter common matters and explore common patterns, yet the significance of the common and unchanged is rendered more intelligible by the circumstances and the changes that led to its expression in the particular manner of one person, one period, and one mingling of traditions. Doubtless motives may be manifest in any autobiographical account other than those recounted by the writer, and principles of selection operate in the determination of what occurrences should be chosen and emphasized, even in an account of speculation and inquiry other than the emergence of common problems and the clarification of universal ideas. The significance of the narrative can be sought in the delineation of a person and the circumstances of his times and culture, as well as in his approximations to ideas which influence many men and many times. Yet the reasons for writing about the circumstances which influenced one's thoughts and about the processes and events in which they were involved, can be only that the significance of thoughts, which is broader than the occurrences of one man's life, can be grasped concretely only in the particularities of expression and implication which are parts of biography, rather than of metaphysics or logic.

These considerations have determined the selection of autobiographical arguments which are presented in what follows. I have been concerned successively, for three rather long periods, with three problems which are problems of our times, or more nearly accurately, three approaches which our times have made to problems of universal scope and to truths of universal significance—problems of philosophic scholarship, of educational practice and administration, and of international and intercultural relations. Viewed in retrospect, these three problems seem so closely interrelated and interdependent that they may be described more nearly accurately as three approaches to the same problem. The same considerations, therefore, suggest that the narrative should run in the reverse of the chronological order, for the significances which I attach to events as I retell them were usually later additions, not recognized at the time. It is doubtless true that a man's characteristic attitudes are determined at an early age, long before the philosophic vocabulary which is later used to express them is available, but even if an autobiographer limited himself to such evidence as he could find concerning those first few years of his life and to the interpretations of his later life which his psychological or psychosomatic

vocabulary permitted, those principles by which he arranges his narrative are themselves late acquisitions, grounded in philosophic presuppositions, as well as in psychological facts. The adjustments of the human organism are doubtless explained by basic principles, but those
principles are discovered and tested by the human organism: the principles and attitudes that might be found in any such theory in what I
have said would serve to characterize me, but I have been impressed by
the recurrent conviction that the significant part of what I know in
relation to what I do, always has been acquired during the past year,
and my narrative is therefore of the process and not of the fixities by
which it may have been conditioned. The story would, moreover, be
better told backwards, if that were possible, for the beginning of an
argument is its principles, and the principles emerge later in the evolution, but as it is impossible to present the narrative as argument, I shall
try at least to distinguish the occurrences and later significances attached to them from the vantage point of some turning at which the
two may be put in perspective.

I. The First World War was such a vantage point. I returned to my
studies at Columbia University in 1919. The interruption of the war
had been slight, for I had been assigned in the Naval Reserves to the
Student Army Training Corps established at Columbia during the last
months of the war. But I had been a "preprofessional" student before
the war, engaged first on a program of studies designed to prepare for
the law and later on a pre-engineering program; my further training in
the Navy had been for engineering. Like many other returning students
I found that my interests had shifted to humanistic studies, and for the
next few years I read literature, history, philosophy, and the classics. In
1920, I wrote a thesis for the Master of Arts degree in which I studied
Tolstoi, Croce, and Santayana, as expressions of three modern approaches to art and literature, and explored the relations and possible
conciliation of esthetic phenomena conceived in terms of moral influences, esthetic experience, and scientific or psychological explanations.
In retrospect I think the center of my interest was in the relation of
esthetic values to science and to morality and in the methods appropriate to investigate in the art object the esthetic qualities of the object,
the scientific foundations of the esthetic experience, and the moral and
political implications of the creation of art and its influences. I was later
to be impressed both by the need of new interpretations in art and

morals because of developments in science and technology, and also by the danger of superficial and insubstantial analogies between the scientific method and the processes of moral deliberation and esthetic appreciation.

These purposes can be found in the thesis, but the recognition and statement of them is doubtless a later addition. The thesis also shows the marks of a more complete and systematic philosophy than I have been able to develop since 1920. The main outlines of the philosophy were determined (I thought), and it stood in need only of application to the varieties of problems of philosophy and related fields. The three chief ingredients of which it was composed were a scientific basis in behaviorism to account for how we think and how we act, a normative criterion in pragmatism to determine the meaningful problems of philosophy and the marks of truth and value by which to solve them, and a symbolic system by which to achieve precision in analysis and statement. It was a highly satisfactory philosophy, because it could be applied to a succession of subject matters and problems with little need of adjustment and with only a minimum of knowledge of the particular subject matter to which it was to be accommodated. I have never since been able to achieve comparable scope of system or convenience of method, but experience with later generations of students has kept me in contact with the later forms of that philosophy. In all its forms it combines a foundation borrowed from some science, a system of explanation couched in a technical vocabulary, and a ready applicability in the same form to all problems. Struggles with the simple distinctions of such philosophies usually raise doubts in their originators concerning the ideals to which they are directed. They led me by indirect ways to an interest in the vast diversity of problems which tends to be concealed in the simplifications, the unifications, and the analogies conceived in the name of philosophy and in the diversified adaptation of methods to materials and problems which tends to be forgotten in the hunt for formal precision and symbolic elegance.

The influence of science and of social and economic changes on philosophy and the determination of philosophic principles of scientific inquiry and social action seem in retrospect to have been the dominant interests during my graduate work in philosophy. The problems of scientific method and its metaphysical implications were prominent in the philosophic literature and in the philosophy courses of the early 1920s. These inquiries led me back to readings in the philosophers of the seventeenth century who had engaged in highly elaborated and diversified efforts to apply the scientific method to man and to human actions and to interpret what is entailed in the scientific approach. I was influenced in this exploration of present implications of science and past speculations concerning it chiefly by Frederick J. E. Woodbridge and John Dewey. Woodbridge helped and guided me in my study of Hobbes, Spinoza, and Locke, and was quizzically tolerant of the enthusiasms I discovered for Descartes, Leibnitz, and Boyle. I learned from Woodbridge to find philosophic problems, not in the massive oppositions of systems and in the rival propositions certified by technical analyses, but in the simple occurrences of everyday life from which the dilemmas of philosophic disputation are derived. The operations of the mind, so conceived, encounter the elements of order even in their most arbitrary decisions, and the intelligible structure of the universe is encountered in the exploration of ideas derived from experience. Most of all I learned from Woodbridge to respect the integrity of philosophic thought and to hold tenaciously to the assumption that what philosophers said made sense, even when I had difficulty grasping it, and that what philosophers meant might be comparable or even identical, despite differences in their modes of expression. Dewey had just returned from a long visit to the Far East and offered two courses in which he related the diversities of philosophic systems and methods to his own mode of philosophizing. From Dewey I learned to seek the significance of philosophic positions in the problems they were constructed to solve, to suspect distinctions and separations which remove the processes of thinking from the experience in which they originated, and to relate the formulation of problems and the discovery of solutions to the cultural influences which determined the manner of their occurrence.

My Ph. D. dissertation was a study of Spinoza which took its beginning in Spinoza's conception of scientific method in philosophy and of the use of reason in the resolution of moral problems. The arguments of Spinoza contained refutations of conceptions of the nature of science, and the application of scientific knowledge to moral and political problems which I had previously accepted without question. His analysis of scientific method is developed in a long correspondence in opposition to Boyle in which he argues against false empiricisms (as elsewhere he demolishes verbal scholasticisms) contending that experience alone can never refute a theory, because contrary evidence can lead either to the abandonment or the modification of the theory, and ex-

perimentation alone can never give knowledge of the fundamental nature of things or of basic scientific law. His use of method in moral
problems can be studied in the massive attempt of his *Ethics* to treat the
problems of action and passion *in more geometrico* and to provide precise mathematical proofs of moral theorems, but he argued that knowledge has no direct effect in the control of the passions and the motivations to knowledge. Irrationality can be controlled and the operations
of nature can be understood, precisely because the universe is by nature
intelligible.

Yet even when I had come to some understanding of this view of
scientific method and its applications to morals, I was puzzled by its
relation to the other parts of Spinoza's philosophic work. In his own
time Spinoza was criticized as an atheist; during the eighteenth century
Lessing, Jacobi, Herder, and Goethe found inspiration in his conception of God, nature, and human existence; in the nineteenth century,
the great physiologist and comparative anatomist, Johannes Peter
Mueller, thought it impossible to improve on Spinoza's analysis of the
passions, and reprinted in his *Elements of Physiology* the aphorisms on
the passions in the third book of the *Ethics*. It is an accurate rough
description of the influence of Spinoza that its focus moved with the
centuries down the sequence of the books of the *Ethics* centering "On
God" in the seventeenth century, "On the Nature and Origin of the
Mind" in the eighteenth century, and on "The Origin and Nature of
the Emotions" in the nineteenth century. In the twentieth century the
moral and political problems involved in "The Strength of the Emotions" came to new attention in interpretations which are not always
consistent with the conception of God developed in the first book or
the conception of "The Power of the Intellect" expounded in the fifth
book of the *Ethics*.[3] I realized only later that the problems I encountered
in Spinoza were twentieth century problems and that the Spinoza who
influenced my thinking was neither the Spinoza criticized by Leibnitz
nor the Spinoza admired by Goethe or Mueller. The application of
scientific method to moral problems seemed to me to involve him in
two difficulties, the first in relating the knowledge of man and his pas-

3. Cf. R. A. Duff, *Spinoza's Political and Ethical Philosophy*, Robert MacLehose & Co.,
Ltd., Glasgow, 1903, pp. 8–9 and C. D. Broad, *Five Types of Ethical Theory*, Harcourt,
Brace & Co., Inc., New York, 1930, p. 15: "Before I begin to expound Spinoza's ethical
theory I must state that I shall ignore everything in his system which depends on what
he calls *Scientia Intuitiva* or the *Third Kind of Knowledge; i.e.,* I shall ignore his doctrines
of the Intellectual Love of God, of Human Blessedness, and of the Eternity of the Human
Mind."

sions to nature and its processes by means of God and His attributes, and the second in separating the methods and controls of politics from those of ethics. My dissertation explored the unity of Spinoza's thought both in the natural bases which permitted the application of the geometric method to nature and to man, and in the differentiation of the purposes and methods of religion and politics from those of scientific analysis and morals.

From 1922 to 1925 I studied in Paris, spending the summers traveling in Europe and working in the libraries which determined in part the itinerary of the cities I visited. Much of what I have said about the direction of my earlier graduate studies should doubtless be dated during these three years, for they gave perspective to what I had done, both because I was able to place the traditions in thought of which I had become aware in the United States in the context of the European traditions from which they were derived, and because I was able to push further back my examination of the historical origins of the ideas and problems with which I had been concerned. Sensed differences in attitudes, purposes, and ideas encountered in different times, places, and formulations, are easily converted into myths, which have the kind of truth that is recognized in jokes about national characteristics. The student of philosophy can hardly avoid being impressed by tantalizing similarities of idea, expression, and purpose, even in philosophic discussions distantly removed, in space or time, from those with which he is familiar; but even in those which are close in origin and influence, the similar purposes are differently achieved, the similar expressions have different meanings, and the similar ideas appear in different uses and contexts.

My studies in French philosophy were inseparable from my discovery of America. I had learned that Francis Bacon was the first modern philosopher and that he had first inquired into the organization of the new sciences and formulated the methods by which they were acquired; I now learned that René Descartes was the first modern philosopher and that his inquiry into method and into the foundations of the sciences were the beginnings of modern philosophy. The philosophic movements which engaged the attention of students in the United States at that time were forms of realism and pragmatism constructed in revolt against idealism; philosophers like Henri Bergson and Léon Brunschvicg were engaged on like problems in revolt against absolute idealism but I found, to my amazement, that they were idealists notwithstanding their congenial approach to familiar problems. In that different climate of doctrines I became aware of characteristic American attitudes toward ideas—a tolerance of diversity of ideas, an absence of ideological marks of class differences, and an attachment to the method and application of the sciences. The tradition of liberalism in the United States was the expression not merely of a tolerance of differences of doctrines, but of a confidence that truth is tested in the commerce of ideas and that values are derived from diversity; and when tolerance had been lacking in the growth of America there had been the physical space in which to move away from intolerance. Doctrinal differences had consequently become too numerous and complex to be organized into parties or to be made the mark of classes. When philosophies were constructed, they tended to claim relevance to present and actual conditions and to borrow examples and authority from scientific method. These attitudes gave a concrete pertinence to American philosophic speculation from the first, but they also exposed it to the dangers of that variety of intellectual and practical provincialism which results from employing principles insufficiently examined in relation to what other men have thought and done. Indifference to ideas may then pass as tolerance of diversity, and relativity of values may be substituted for the disposition to refuse to accept standards without further test merely because they are traditional. The absence of classes and parties based on differences or professed differences of ideas and ideals may invite the development of classes based on oligarchal differences and of parties based on economic differences. The cultivation of scientific method and real problems may be the excuse for the neglect of truths that have been discovered and of errors that have been exposed, and for the affectation of that spritely freshness of insight in which every philosopher recapitulates in his own person the whole history of thought.

Study in Paris provided the perspective not only of the approach characteristic of another culture to common philosophic ideas and problems, but also of the historical insight into the development of those ideas and the formation of those problems. The study of moral problems in their relation to scientific method and to social and political influences, had led me back to the first efforts of modern philosophers to treat those problems in the seventeenth century, and I had found in the study of those philosophers both the insight into later problems which comes from knowledge of their earlier forms and the insight into methods of analysis and resolution which comes from the rediscovery of alternative forgotten methods. But I also found much in their writings which was unintelligible and opaque without further historical study. I therefore worked with Brunschvicg on Spinoza and on the intellectual movements of which he was part. Brunschvicg had already published his study of the stages of development of mathematical philosophy, and he had begun to apply the same methods to the study of physical causality, moral conscience, and like concepts. I learned from Brunschvicg to use the historical development of concepts as part of the analysis of current problems in their interrelations in large departments of philosophy. I studied Descartes, Malebranche, and medieval philosophy with Étienne Gilson. My explorations of the background of Spinoza's philosophy had already brought me into contact with currents of medieval thought. My three years in Paris gave me the opportunity to study medieval philosophers more systematically—and to become interested in particular in the twelfth century background of Abelard and the fourteenth century context of Ockham—and I learned from Gilson to trace the basic patterns and unity of philosophic thought through the diversity of philosophic systems and expressions. Even before my medieval studies it had become apparent that Western thought is unintelligible without its Greek foundations. I therefore worked with Léon Robin on Plato and Aristotle, and learned from him philological and philosophical methods of interpreting the text and the structure of philosophic arguments. My indebtedness to these great teachers and the many others whose lectures I attended can hardly be summed up in a few sentences, and I suspect that I am unable to disentangle what I learned from the uses to which I put it, or to separate the ideas I was conscious of from the subtle modifications which the whole changed context of life worked in them. The interrelations of cultures must affect increasingly the developments of thought and its effective application, but life in Paris in the early 1920s cannot be rendered adequately in purely practical or intellectual terms.

I returned to New York in 1925 and taught philosophy at Columbia University for the next ten years. After the normal apprenticeship of teaching numerous courses in logic and introduction to philosophy, my teaching was divided between the history of philosophy and philosophic analysis. My historical courses concentrated on the Philosophy of the Middle Ages and the Renaissance, and my analytic courses, which were offered under the titles, "Metaphysics and Science" and "Metaphysics and Method," were devoted to the examination of the basic presuppositions and philosophic principles of the natural sciences, of the moral and social sciences, and of art and criticism. As I discussed these problems with my students and as I wrote about those portions of them in which the pattern of relations was clearest, I was brought to the conclusion that the startingpoint of philosophic discussion in our times must be the consideration of the vast diversity of analyses that have been made, and that are still being made, of problems which have a recognizable continuity, despite changes, revolutions, and new discoveries. There is a tendency in American philosophy to seek basic principles in operations or in linguistic forms of expression rather than in the nature of things or in the categories of thought. But the analysis tends to be of operations abstractly conceived, rather than of actual operations which define ideas in the context of associated ideas in cultures or systems and in relation to the subject matter to which they apply; or alternately it is an analysis of the forms of hypothetical pure languages, rather than the actual languages developed by men associated in cultures and engaged in the solution of practical and theoretic problems. The treatment of ideas and systems as functions of cultures and of intellectual methods and the exploration of the patterns of their expression in a kind of historical intellectual semantics have, therefore, seemed to me an important propaedeutic to the treatment of philosophic problems as such, and a defense against the shallow construction of patterns of culture which dispense with ideas, except as illustrative of cultural relations and of formal semantics which dispense with problems, except as consequent on the theory of language.

I have found that I returned often in these studies to the works of three philosophers whose speculations are explicit about the unity which they sought and about the distinctions which are important in the discovery of that unity. Aristotle found the basis of philosophy in experience, and sought to avoid the idealism of Plato and the materialism of Democritus; to that end he distinguished theoretic, practical, and productive sciences. Spinoza found the unity of knowledge and of things in Substance, God, or Nature, and sought to avoid the verbal explanations of Scholasticism (which he traced back to the tradition of Socrates, Plato, and Aristotle, as opposed to the tradition of Democritus, Epicurus, and Lucretius) and the constructions of "empirics and recent philosophers"; to that end he distinguished ethics, religion, and politics. Dewey found the unity of inquiry in experience, not as an epistemological beginning, but as the common cultural source of philosophic problems, and fought to avoid those abstractions from experience and nature which are embalmed in ideas constructed to solve problems of other cultures and times; to that end he distinguished problems, cultures, and forms of association. The problems which are presented in reconciling the truths of these three denials and assertions might as easily be approached from other beginnings, for the traditions of philosophy come to life in the debate concerning basic principles to order the whole range of philosophic problems in which each position is based on the denial of previous distinctions. The discovery of truth and the establishment of meaning are both dependent historically on the doctrines which become false or meaningless in the orientation of the new doctrine, and despite the impatience of practical men and dogmatists, there is fortunately no way to halt the eternal philosophic dialogue about things, knowledge, and systems.

11. During the early 1930s I met Robert Maynard Hutchins and discussed education in America with him, touching on both the problems of general education in the colleges and of the higher learning in the graduate schools. Among other questions, we talked about the relation of history to philosophy—the applications of history to the development of knowledge in the history of ideas and the application of philosophy to historical processes in the philosophy of history. I went to The University of Chicago as Visiting Professor of History in 1934–1935, to give a course in the intellectual history of Western Europe and a seminar in the philosophy of history, and I stayed on as Dean of the Division of the Humanities and as Professor of Greek and Philosophy. During my twelve years as Dean, from 1935 to 1947, I was able to take part in the replanning of humanistic studies in general education in the College, as well as to cooperate with the departments in the reorganization of graduate work in the humanities.

The problem of the humanities in the present world is compounded of several dislocations which extend into many of the compartments of contemporary life—the readjustment of values to altered conditions and circumstances, the readjustment of methods of inquiry to the data and methods of science, and the readjustment of conceptions of the place of the humanities in education and life to changed philosophic presuppositions. During the period between the two World Wars there was widespread agreement concerning both the predicament of the humanities and the contribution which humanistic studies normally make to a well rounded education in a mature civilization; but there was little agreement concerning what the humanities are, or concerning what should be done to improve their condition and to put them to the uses of which they are capable. Yet it seemed probable that the predicament of the humanities could be traced to a circle of interrelated causes—the failure to recognize the contribution of the humanities to civilization and the consequent construction of a civilization in which the place of humanistic values is attenuated; when accomplishment is marked by accumulation and value by place, humanistic studies offer less obvious attractions to young students than the precisions and effects of scientific studies or the utilities and problems of social studies; and, as cause or consequence in such circumstances, methods of teaching and inquiry vacillate between the irrelevant technicalities of tested traditional methods and the irrelevant innovations borrowed from fashionable sciences and technologies.

At The University of Chicago, graduate studies are organized in four divisions under the Physical Sciences, the Biological Sciences, the Social Sciences, and the Humanities. This organization facilitates the assumption that the methods of the humanities are distinct from those of the natural and the social sciences in the treatment of subject matters and problems whose close interrelations are reflected in the affirmations and negations of philosophers concerning the separations and identities of the parts of our knowledge and behavior. During the early years of my work as Dean, members of the faculty of the Division of the Humanities met in committees, in small informal groups, and in divisional meetings to discuss the common disciplines which unite the various departments of languages, literatures, art, music, history, and philosophy in the Division. Out of those discussions there came an agreement that studies in the humanities should be conceived in relation to two bases—a material basis in the knowledge of a culture, a time, and a subject matter; and a disciplinary basis in the practice of methods of inquiry and criticism, and in the insights essential to their practice. The traditional separation of humanistic studies into departments such as English, Romance, Germanic, Oriental languages and literature, into Music, Art, History, Linguistics, and Philosophy, is token of the importance of command of the materials essential to humanistic studies in any given field of culture. The faculty decided that that organization was fundamentally sound, provided the methods and disciplinary approaches to the materials were broad and relevant to humanistic objectives. In order to maintain what is important in such specialized knowledge and yet prevent the fragmentation of the humanistic enterprise, they set up four interdepartmental committees—to operate in much the way departments operate in preparing programs of study and presenting students for higher degrees—in the four disciplines practiced in varying ways in all the departments: in language, history, criticism, and philosophy. These four disciplines cross the departmental lines, and the organization of the committees permits a student in Language and Communication, in History of Culture, in Comparative Studies in Art and Literature, and in the Analysis of Ideas and the Study of Methods to take work which involves several languages and symbolic systems, or a variety of cultures and times, or a variety of critical systems and literatures, or the bearing of philosophic analyses on a variety of subjects. Moreover, the interdepartmental work of the committees was calculated to bring greater breadth into the departmental work, while the cooperation of the departments in the work of the committees would serve the purpose of avoiding the vague and tenuous generalities which so frequently remain as the only mark that comparative studies in literature, history, and philosophy retain from the universal ambitions which motivate them.

The close relation of the humanities to the social sciences and to the natural sciences, as well as the characteristic differences of the methods employed in humanistic studies on materials which may fall also under the scrutiny of the sciences, become less difficult to discern when they are considered in respect to the disciplines of the humanities. Literature and the arts have their uses as data in the social sciences, and in those uses they are sources of information concerning cultures and peoples. Literature and art are also expressions of truths about nature, man, and the cosmos, and the continuity of human knowledge is marked in the inspiration Copernicus found in Cicero and Freud in Sophocles, no less than in the stimulation Lucretius derived from Epicurus, Hume from Newton, and Dewey from Darwin. But literature and the arts may be studied for the values which they embody, as well as for the light they may throw on the manners and ideas of men. Times and cultural circumstances facilitate the recovery of meanings expressed by men in other traditions and places, but the discovery and appreciation of values in the creations and expressions of men present problems other than solely the recovery of what they meant. The same times produce good and bad art and the same intentions are well and badly expressed. The study of the arts for the world-view they embody, or for information about the circumstances in which they were produced, and the study of art as embodiments of esthetic values, are supplementary inquiries into related aspects of human activities.

In like fashion, the study of language may be approached by inquiry into the physical and physiological bases of speech, or into the history of the development of languages and their uses in the communities and civilizations of men, or into the effectiveness of their employment for particular ends of expression. Anthropological linguistics has developed a technique for recording the modes of expression in different tribes and peoples and in different circumstances; humanistic linguistics adapts its techniques to the examination of the employment of language in rhetoric, literature, science, and other modes of expression. The diversity of linguistic patterns revealed in the one approach and the normative standards discovered in the other are not rival hypotheses between which the linguist must choose, but supplementary considerations to be brought to bear on the problems of languages. History, likewise, presents dimensions in the succession of geological ages, the evolution of animals, the marks which astronomical and meteorological phenomena have left on the planets and the surface of the earth and in the theoretic relations of time and space, which are properly treated in the natural sciences. The reconstruction and interpretation of social, political, economic, and cultural conditions and changes require techniques and theories which are devised in the social sciences. The history of art, music, literature, philosophy and the development of ideas, theories and values reflect the evolutions of nature and the circumstances of man, but the reconstruction and interpretation of the history of thought and expression depend on knowledge of those forms and ideas, and that history is the context in which theories about nature and man are developed. Philosophy, finally, is one form of knowledge, profoundly affected by the development of the sciences and by their methods; it reflects the interests of times, peoples, and cultures in which it develops; its proper domain is the principles and the systematic relations of explanations of things and their processes, men and their communities, and values and their expressions.

Concern with the predicament of the humanities in the world today is both part and consequence of reflection on the humanistic aspects of culture. The appreciation of art, literature, history, religion, and philosophy is one of the characteristic marks of a great civilization, and in the

West the humanists have in various ages contributed to that appreciation by study of the tradition of art and learning. The humanists in
Rome and in the Renaissance were able to adapt the knowledge of the
past creatively to the formation of new cultures relative to new circumstances and new needs. The success of humanism depends on that
double achievement—the perception of values as broad as humanity,
and the expression of values in the living idiom of a people. Conversely,
humanistic studies face two dangers in any period—the danger of de-
basement when the press of problems, the growth of tensions, and the
confusion of education obscure common values, and the danger of ob-
solescence when the cultivation of traditional values and learned disciplines is removed from relevance to present situations and problems.

The problems of the humanities in scholarship and in the higher
learning are closely related to the problems of the humanities in general
education in the colleges. The problem of general education is basically
the problem of establishing a common basis of understanding and communication which is the particular need of a democratic community.
The determination of the contents of courses in the humanities in collegiate education, is part of the problem of constructing—with a view
to the ideal that the opportunity will one day be open to all young
people to continue their studies beyond the high school—an education
for individual development, for citizenship, and for the utilities and
amenities of common life. The solution to that problem determines, in
turn, the preparation which students will have if they choose to go on
to further studies in the humanities, and consequently the form which
higher studies and research will take. At the College of The University
of Chicago, work was in progress to revise the content of education for
the new four year degree of Bachelor of Arts, which had been constructed on the basis of a division of education into six years of elemen-
tary education, four years of secondary education, and four years of
collegiate education, instead of the customary division into eight, four,
and four years. In the new scheme a student normally receives the A.B.
at the age of eighteen or nineteen, and the program of more specialized
work in one of the departments for the degree of Master of Arts becomes a three year program, instead of the nominal one year allotted to
such training under older schemes. Having participated in the Division
of the Humanities in the planning for that enlarged M.A. training, I
was glad to accept the invitation of the College to take an active part in

planning and teaching in the new program of the College. The program for the A.B. was conceived as a common program for all students in the College, divided into courses according to the major divisions of subject matters and disciplines, and tested by objective comprehensive examinations based on the field rather than the peculiarities of courses or instructors. My own work on the program was in two courses, the general Humanities course and the Integration course.

The committee which planned the course of studies in the humanities approached its problem by discussing the general question of the place which humanistic studies should occupy in contemporary education. The functions and uses of the humanities, in turn, involved the committee in searching considerations of the nature of the humanities and the methods proper to study and teaching of the humanities. A one year general course in the humanities was required of all students of the College, as part of the "New Plan" which had been put into effect in the early 1930s. This was a pioneering course, and it is widely influential in American education—and indeed it is still frequently the basis of what is said, in criticism and in praise, about the Chicago course in the humanities, in spite of the radical changes of the 1940s. It was a good course, but it raised many problems, among which one had a recurrent and fundamental character. The course followed the historical sequence of artistic, cultural, and intellectual developments in the Western world, and the humanistic disciplines required for the appreciation and interpretation of arts, letters, and philosophy, tended to be lost in the story, while the story tended to be accepted uncritically. It could be argued that education should provide a training in the humanistic disciplines, as well as in the disciplines required for the understanding of the historical developments by which values and their environing circumstances evolved. The committee therefore recommended that two courses be planned—one in history and one in the humanities—and that a close relation be maintained between the history course and the general courses in the humanities, as well as the social sciences, and the natural sciences, by referring the materials and methods treated in those courses to their historical contexts and to the conditioning influences of historical times and movements. The problem of constructing a humanities course, when it is separated from questions of "covering" the history of art, literature, and philosophy, is the problem of determining the contribution which the humanities might make to contemporary life, and, therefore, the problem of making available to students and to the times such benefits as might come from knowledge of men's great achievements.

It would be dubious history—even beyond the autobiographical license of reading theories later conceived into the development of earlier actions—to attribute to the group that discussed the plans for the humanities course any large consensus concerning the nature and the present purposes of the humanities. In the course of discussion I urged three objectives: the development in the student of taste and broad acquaintance with the arts, literature, history, and philosophy, sufficient to direct his interests and afford guidance into the rich satisfactions and improvements which exploration in these fields might afford; the formation of the abilities which are necessary to the recognition and appreciation of artistic, cultural, and intellectual values, as opposed to the random associated reflections which frequently accompany the attentive attitude and proper remarks that pass for appreciation; and, finally, the analytical abilities needed to integrate taste and interest, on the one hand, and critical judgment and discrimination, on the other hand, into the context of the principles—philosophic and social, theoretic and practical—which are particularized in the character and attitudes of a man, and universalized in the philosophies and cultural communities men share.

In my opinion those three purposes have served to signalize objectives that might be attributed to the parts of the three year course in the humanities which grew out of the planning started in that early committee. The first year of the course was devoted to bringing the student to a broad acquaintance with literature, music, and the visual arts, and with the basic problems involved in their interpretation. The second year concentrated on the problems of literature, in the broad sense in which it includes, not only *belles-lettres* but history, philosophy, rhetoric, and like forms of expression, and undertook to explore, not the historical sequences or the spirit of ages, peoples, or writers, but the questions which the critical reader should learn to ask concerning particular kinds of works or concerning particular aspects of all works: in respect to history, questions concerning the adequacy of the narrative, representation, or argument to particular facts; in respect to rhetoric, questions concerning the adjustment of forms of statement and argument to particular audiences, and their effectiveness, and value; in respect to philosophy, questions concerning the principles and the development of arguments; and in respect to appreciation and criticism, questions bearing on the forms of dramas, novels, lyric poems, the utilization and expression in them of the tensions and aspirations of men, and the communication they afford and effect to the spirit of men. These questions were raised in a succession of readings in works of history, rhetoric, philosophy, drama, novels, and lyric poetry, and the student was trained, not in reciting a dogmatic humanism or philosophy of culture, but in framing and considering the questions which are presented to a critical mind by the varieties of forms, contents, and proposed values. Once he had learned to consider historical questions relative to works of history, philosophic questions relative to works of philosophy, and esthetic questions relative to poetry, drama, and fiction, he was expected to venture also into the tangled intermingling of questions which constitutes much of the literature of criticism and appreciation, by treating philosophy as poetry or history, exploring poetry as metaphor, argument, or ritual, and transforming history into a metaphysics of cultures, an appendage to scientific theories borrowed from thermodynamics or evolution, or a dialectic with poetic, scientific, or religious overtones. During the third year the student returned to the study of musical and visual, as well as literary arts, to treat them in the light of critical principles as they apply to individual works, as they relate works to men and times, fashions and tastes, or enjoyments and uses, and as they integrate life, expression, and community in basic philosophic forms.

The program of general education in the College was developed in the various fields by planning and discussion similar to that which led to the formation of the three year course in the humanities, and the program consisted, therefore, of courses which the student would normally take in preparation for the comprehensive examinations, constructed to test whether he had the abilities and information which are the marks of the possession of a general education. The interrelations of the parts of such an education seemed to the faculty to deserve particular attention, and an "integration" course, to be taken in the last year of work, was therefore included in the plans of the program. I was a member of the committee which worked out the curriculum of this integration course. The objectives of the course are briefly adumbrated in the title "Observation, Interpretation, and Integration," which was attached to it in the early stages of faculty discussion. The committee began by considering the various ways in which the parts of knowledge might be integrated: they might be fitted together in an inclusive and neutral frame in an encyclopedic manner; their interrelations might be found in the fashion in which they could be put to applications in life in a practical manner; or their integration might take the form of the development of a systematic view of the organic unity of experience and the world in a philosophic manner. A general education, however, does not depend on encyclopedic knowledge, but on a framework of information and acquaintance with the uses and checks of available sources of information. The practical applications of general education, moreover, are not something separate from education, to be simulated in classroom reconstruction of cases or in field tours of regions, and the philosophy required for a general education should take the form of insight into relations among the parts of experience and knowledge, rather than of deductions from doctrines or dogmas. The committee concluded that integration in a general education must come from critical awareness applied to what had been acquired as knowledge and belief, and from the will and ability to explore the grounds and interrelations of what is known or thought to be known, to estimate intellectual and practical consequences, and to judge the criteria used in such inquiries. Such an integration would also provide the skills by which to accomplish and test encyclopedic, practical, and philosophic integrations.

The student comes to the end of his four years of collegiate education—even in the new programs of colleges in which "general" courses are constructed to facilitate his contact with large areas of experience and knowledge—with a number of large subject matters and the variety of methods related to them adjusted somewhat haphazardly in his habitual attitudes and modes of explanation. The adjustment of these parts of knowledge, habit, and attitude is the problem of "interpretation" in the large sense in which personal attitudes and knowledge are arranged, often unconsciously, according to fundamental preferences and basic sciences and ultimately referred for explanation to precepts of psychology, sociology, or economics, to theology, physics, folklore, or literary taste. The student is made aware of the problems of interpretation and their ramifications by studying the ways in which such adjustments have been made and have been justified in the "Organization of the Sciences" in the first term of the course. The unity of the sciences, the diversity of the sciences, the relations of theory and practice, the metaphysical examination of the principles of sciences, the reduction of sciences to their physical elements, to their logical, psychological, and epistemological forms, to their social and political conditions, the influence of the natural sciences on logic and ethics, of ethics on politics, and of politics on logic and science, form part of the patterns in which the sciences have fallen.

This formal interplay among the parts of knowledge and the varieties of unity which have been found in the sciences or imposed on them, is usually established or rejected by appeal to the facts. What is known and what is believed are tested by experience and by the consequences of action in accordance with the tenets of knowledge and belief. The problems of "observation," conceived in a large sense, turn on the relation of knowledge to facts, and on the variety of methods employed to relate what passes for knowledge to what passes for facts, and to achieve in statements of fact precision, generality, and relevance. The student is brought to the problems of the discovery of facts and their adjustments to theory, in the study of the "Methods of the Sciences" in the second term of the course. The methods and data of mathematics, physics, biology, the social sciences, and the humanities, are studied in the formulation and resolution of problems proper to their respective fields, as well as in the transfer of methods by which mathematics is made a physical science, or the subject matter of physics becomes organic and that of biology, some form of physical forces, or chemical processes, while the social sciences debate the validity of analogies to the physical and biological sciences, and the humanities accept or resist the methods of sociology, physiology, or linguistics. Finally, the constructions of our habits and knowledge, of their interrelations and their references to facts and experience, are organized according to principles, casual and unobserved in the processes of action, or precise and tested in the demonstrations of the sciences. Principles are often signalized in the inquiries and discoveries of individual men; they are often acknowledged in the common acceptance of an age or a people; their impact or alteration is often the mark of revolutions in science and society. The systematization of knowledge, values, and the relations of men, is the problem of "integration," in the broad sense in which principles are found underlying the interrelations of habits and emotions, of actions, knowledge, and communication, of individuals, groups, and nations, which are in turn referred to the regularities and laws of nature by principles which determine the interrelations and systems of the sciences. The student encounters the problems of integration in the study of "Principles in the Sciences" in the third term of the course, and he examines concepts like "pleasure," which many moralists reject as an ethical principle, but which hedonists and utilitarians make the principle of all human actions, and "cause," which was long the basis of all scientific explanation until philosophers and physicists questioned the meaning and the very existence of causes.

The exploration of the problems of the humanities in general education and in graduate studies was reflected in my program of teaching during these years. I taught sections in the Humanities and Observation, Interpretation and Integration courses in the college; I taught in the various interdepartmental committees and in the two departments in which I held my professorship, Greek and Philosophy. Departmental distinctions have led to the separation of the Plato and the Aristotle taught in Philosophy Departments from the Plato and the Aristotle taught in Departments of the Classics: the former frequently held doctrines which would be expressed with difficulty in Greek, while the latter wrote works full of philological problems but relatively free of philosophy. I adapted the methods I had learned from Robin to read Plato and Aristotle with mixed classes in which philosophers learned some Greek, and Greek students learned to discuss philosophy. I read Cicero and Aquinas with combined groups of philosophy and Latin students. I gave courses in which literary and art criticism was related to the discussion of philosophy and esthetics, courses in which scientific methods and the varieties of logical theories were related to their metaphysical assumptions, courses in which political and moral theories were examined in their bearing on the relations of cultures and on the political disputes of our times, courses in the philosophy of education, the philosophy of law, the philosophy of language, and the philosophy of history. I came into contact in this curriculum of teaching with a more diversified group of students than could have afforded the adventure into philosophy in the older schemes of study. A generation of students is only a few years, and I can look back at several generations at The University of Chicago who have been able to move more widely in their studies than could their predecessors, both in the range of related interests and in the application of knowledge to present problems and things; who have conceived from the humanities a love for things human, for arts, letters, and sciences; who have learned to use languages, to apply methods of analysis and criticism, and to judge principles; who have acquired some sense of the histories and interrelations of peoples and cultures; and who can resort to reason without the suspicion that its cold light is destructive of humanistic values or irreconcilable with democratic processes. The educational practices which we established and the philosophic meanings which we explored, are already involved in the processes of change and misinterpretation, but the contacts with languages, with arts, with history, and with philosophy afford the student points of reference and support by which to judge their education and philosophy amid the changes; and the students who have made those skills and disciplines their own are a better expression of the ideals we set in education than any statement of our new plans or of the philosophies which animate them.

III. Planning for new forms of general education is grounded in present problems and in the relevance and efficacy of training in the major fields of human knowledge—in scientific method and knowledge of the results of scientific advance, in the background and problems of democratic life and man's attachment to the guiding principles of freedom, and in appreciation of humanistic values and powers of communication and expression. Teaching and research in the humanities consists in the exploration of the great achievements of man in the study of their continuity in history and universality in values, at the point where tradition affects the present in the use of languages, the appreciation of art, the interpretation of history, and the construction of philosophies. In modern times general education and humanistic studies have both been influenced increasingly by the interrelations of cultures and the broadening of interest beyond the limits of the traditions of Western European and American culture. The coming of the Second World War accentuated that process and gave it a practical turn. During the early 1940s, planning for the effective use of educational institutions in contributing to the military success of the United States in the war took many forms, in respect both to research and to teaching. I participated in the planning of the Army Specialized Training Program, particularly the Area and Language Studies, and I became Director of the unit of that program established at The University of Chicago. The purpose of the Area and Language course was to give Army personnel a speaking ability in the language and a knowledge of the geography, and of the social, economic, political, and cultural conditions of the country in which they might serve liaison and similar functions. The University of Chicago unit undertook training in German, French, Italian, Russian, Chinese, and Japanese, and the planning of the course included the choice of methods of teaching language and the determination of what kind of knowledge of the region, the people, their ideas, values, and institutions would be most useful to enlisted men and officers in the discharge of their duties. There are impressive indications that the courses served a useful purpose in achieving the practical ends set for them during the war, and the influence of the experiences of the units set up at the various universities of the country, have continued in the postwar period, particularly in the methods of language teaching and in the planning of studies concerned with areas and peoples which had not been treated conspicuously in prewar education.

The teaching of languages in the Area and Language Courses profited by the intensive training which was possible and by the motivation which was supplied by the circumstances. The student was under Army discipline and his continuance in the course depended on his progress in acquiring fluency in the language he was studying. A large portion of his day was devoted to classroom training, guided study, and practice with language records and reproducing apparatus. Some of the schools made use of the methods of teaching language developed in the teaching of "non-literary" languages for which few "informants" or speakers, and no experienced teachers, could be found, and extended it also to languages with extensive literatures, well known grammars, and tested techniques of teaching. Publicity in popular magazines during the war was calculated to give the impression that it was a method used in all units sponsored by the Army, and that the techniques of language training had been revolutionized by a "scientific linguistics" which used the example of "informants" to induce proficiency in foreign languages as one had acquired one's native language without the formalities of grammar. The linguists and language teachers at The University of Chicago concluded that the argument was based on a fallacy, for the analogy between acquisition of language in youth and in maturity neglected the devices which the mature mind might employ to facilitate learning, and on a misconception of the fashion in which grammar was used in recent language teaching. They found the linguistic method of language teaching wasteful: it dispersed the student's efforts by requiring some acquaintance with the distinctions and terminology of a linguistic theory which was not particularly pertinent to his problems, as well as with the language he was learning, and the peculiar objectives to which the method was directed extended little beyond acquiring phonetic ac-

curacy in the production of sounds. In languages possessed of literatures and related to cultures for which information is available other
than that assembled by the question techniques of anthropology, richer
and more efficient teaching resources are available. The teachers at Chicago were convinced that they could achieve phonetic accuracy more
effectively by other devices perfected in recent experiments in language
teaching and that they could also give proper attention to other related
objectives, such as use of a larger vocabulary, fluency of idiomatic and
grammatical speech, and development of ease and ingenuity in solving
problems of expression in new subject matters. Tests were devised in
which these various objectives were distinguished and the student's
ability was examined with respect to each. Any generalization concerning the effectiveness of methods of language teaching would depend on
the systematic construction and administration of such tests, but more
important than the decision among the rival methods which were tried
during the war has been the continued development of methods and
teaching materials along the directions indicated by those experiments.
The importance of strong motivation and intensive training, however,
is one of the undisputed lessons of wartime language training.

The problem of what to teach concerning the "area" in the short
time available in the course, was more difficult than the problem of how
to teach the language of the area, and the nature of the difficulty is
indicated in the choice of the word, "area," to indicate what was at least
a geographical expanse in each case, and in addition, in varying degrees,
a social, economic, political, cultural, and intellectual region, as well.
The criteria of selection of what to teach were set in a general way by
the range of possible duties that might be assigned to a soldier in the
territory of a friendly or an occupied enemy country; but the possible
duties were too variegated to determine categories of facts that might
be useful, and area courses were constructed in the various units on the
basis of indispensable minima of geographic, economic, industrial, social, historical, and cultural information integrated by a variety of accidents and schemes. At The University of Chicago the emphasis tended
to be more cultural and humanistic than at some other units, on the
ground that the problems encountered in any assignment would be in
part problems of information and in part problems of contacts with
people; and whereas it would be difficult, if not impossible, to anticipate the details of information that might be required, familiarity with
the culture and the values of the people would facilitate cooperation,

and in most cases provide the means of securing the needed information as well. Some knowledge of the literature, the philosophy, and the institutional, cultural, and intellectual history of the area was therefore woven into the information concerning rainfall, industry, transportation, and ethnic groups.

The area and language courses doubtless served a useful and urgent purpose in attacking a practical problem of liaison and contact during the war. That problem was the simpler form of complex problems of cultural contacts which were to have increasing attention in education and in political negotiations after the war. The history of the relations of the peoples of the world has been written in the past largely in terms of political, military, dynastic, and commercial contacts. Conquerors have swept across Asia Minor, Europe, and the Far East, frequently proclaiming the motive of "world dominion" to unite all mankind; explorers have skirted Africa and crossed the Atlantic from Europe in the interests of trade and as the precursors of settlers and missionaries; and it would seem, at first glance, that instruments, arts, and ideas traveled the pilgrim roads, the trade routes, and the paths of crusade and conquest, frequently unobserved in their immediate effects, following in the wake of these movements of power, profit, and salvation. The contacts of cultures are, however, older and more intricate than the tales of foreign lands which soldiers might bring back from their campaigns or sailors from their voyages: they are part of a texture woven into the folksongs which continued a living tradition after entering the Homeric epics; into the successive translation of Aristotle and Galen from Greek into Syriac, Arabic, Hebrew, and Latin; into the influence of the Bible in Judaism, Christianity, and Islam; into the spread of Buddhism, the migration of symbols, and the development of tools and technology. Since the war the contact of cultures has forced itself into prominence in the discovery that the economic, political, and social problems of the world are inextricably interrelated, and that knowledge and common values are indispensable instruments in the construction of a world community within which political institutions can operate on a world-wide basis.

The educational aspects of the problem of the relations of cultures had become apparent even before the outbreak of the Second World War. Education in the United States had been based largely on the tradition of "Western Europe," or even on efforts to concentrate on the American experience and what was peculiar to it: large regions of the world—the Far East, India, Austronesia, the Near East, Russia, Africa, and even neighboring Latin America—were touched on only glancingly as they impinged on that local interest. Important advances had been made before the war in the improvement of Far Eastern and Russian studies on the graduate level, and it became increasingly clear as the war drew to a close that general education and the higher learning would have to reflect the broad scope of common problems revealed by the contacts of peoples which resulted from, and the common aspirations which were made practicable by, the advances of technology. The temptation to carry over the techniques of the area and language courses as a means to solve this problem was strong and widespread, and the regional "institutes" specializing in Russia, Latin America, the Far East, or Europe which have proliferated so rapidly since the war are often mere rearrangements of information and of traditional courses of study in new boxes, presented as novel results of the reexamination of problems and of the use of new methods for their solution.

The organization of knowledge and the planning of education are not simply questions of arranging collections of data and information in patterns of time, space, and culture; they depend on involved relations of the problems of times, the methods of sciences, and the aspirations of peoples. In our times they reflect common practical and material problems of war devastations, of food, disease, and security, and of the effects of technology on the lives and cultures of peoples on whom the impact of the advances of industry and science has been sudden and late; they are instruments in the attack on the political and social problems of vast numbers of people who have recently acquired the right to self-government, in the extension of fundamental education and human rights, and in the development of the interrelations of the nations of the world; and they are the structures which determine approaches to problems of comprehension and achievement of shared values and of understanding and advancement of common knowledge. In our discussions of these problems in their bearing on studies in the humanities at The University of Chicago it was decided to subordinate new regional arrangements of the program to new considerations of problems and methods for their treatment. In the Division of the Humanities the interdepartmental committees afford a frame for treating problems of cultural relations in terms of their reflection in problems of language and communication, of the cultural significances of art and literature, of the broadened frame of cultural history, and of the prominent intrusion of ideas and methods into modern discussions and ideological conflicts.

The political aspects of the relations of cultures and of educational devices became apparent in the preparations for the peace. As early as 1942, the Conference of Allied Ministers of Education (CAME) met to plan for the reconstruction of educational facilities and means of communication destroyed during the war. The Charter of the United Nations, signed in 1945, provides for the promotion of "international cultural and educational cooperation." From these beginnings plans for the United Nations Educational, Scientific and Cultural Organization (UNESCO) grew, in the conviction, stated in the Preamble to UNESCO's Constitution that a peace based exclusively upon the political and economic arrangements of governments could not secure the lasting and sincere support of the peoples of the world and that peace must therefore be founded upon the intellectual and moral solidarity of mankind. UNESCO is an experiment in the relations of peoples; it is an effort to use education, scientific, and cultural instruments for a political end, the achievement and safeguarding of peace. I participated in some of the early meetings called in the United States to discuss the form which UNESCO's program and operation might take, and I was Adviser to the United States Delegations at the first three sessions of the General Conference of UNESCO, in Paris in 1946, in Mexico City in 1947, and in Beirut in 1948. I returned to Paris in 1947, after the establishment of UNESCO, to serve as the first Acting Counsellor on UNESCO affairs attached to the United States Embassy in Paris, and on my return to the United States I served as a member of the United States National Commission on UNESCO.

In September, 1947, a Committee of Experts was assembled in Paris to advise the Director General concerning the program of UNESCO in philosophy and the humanities. I attended the meeting as one of the United States experts, and as Rapporteur I drew up the basic document prepared at the meeting. The Committee differentiated three levels of activities in the field of philosophy and the humanities: the continuing service activities, such as the exchange of persons, information, bibliographical compilations and the like, in which philosophy and the humanities should share with the other disciplines; the activities related to its program which UNESCO would stimulate and encourage international organizations in philosophy and the humanities to undertake; and, finally, projects bearing directly on the purposes of UNESCO to be carried out under UNESCO's direct supervision. The Committee recommended two such projects, one in philosophy and one in the humanities. Both projects were conceived, not as scholarly enterprises undertaken in their respective fields, but as efforts to formulate the direct and immediate contribution which philosophy and the humanities might make to the peace of the world. The Committee decided that, if one asked what place philosophy has in the search for means to avoid conflict and to establish that dynamic order among the nations of the world which is the definition of peace, the answer must be found in the fact that philosophic issues were involved in the so-called "ideological conflict" which affects the discussion of diplomats, the reports and editorials of newspapers, and the ideas and formulations of men everywhere. The ideological conflict is basically an extension of philosophic problems to the discussion of problems of ordinary life, of national policy, and international relations, and a project was therefore planned to examine certain fundamental terms, such as human rights, democracy, freedom, law, and equality, as they enter into contemporary practical problems and statements about them. In like manner, if one were to ask how the humanities might contribute to mitigating the confusions and reducing the conflicts of our time, and how they might give emphasis to the elements of understanding and community which are beginning to emerge, the answer must be found in the study of humanistic aspects of cultures, in the communication which arts and letters establish, not in doctrines, but in basic values underlying differences of expression, tradition, and times, and in the community of traditions in their mutual influences and their common values. The Committee recommended, therefore, that a second project be set up to treat the hierarchies of values characteristic of cultures and expressed in artistic and intellectual productions as they bear on the relations of peoples and the problems which peoples face in common.

I continued work on both projects. The first form which the examination of ideological conflicts took was the study of human rights undertaken by UNESCO early in 1947, in cooperation with the Commission on Human Rights of the Economic and Social Council which had just started on the task of drawing up the Universal Declaration of Human Rights. UNESCO was to examine the intellectual bases of the rights of man, first, in their historical development from the philosophic principles on which they were formulated in the classical statements of human rights in the eighteenth century to the principles invoked in their definition and defense today, and second, in the present day opposition of principles which leads to diverse interpretations of human rights and in particular to the opposition of traditional political and civil rights to more recently asserted social and economic rights. The UNESCO Committee on Human Rights issued its report in July, 1947, and the collection of essays made in the course of its inquiry was published under the title, *Human Rights: Comments and Interpretations,* in 1949. The project was continued in an inquiry into the ambiguities which surround the word, "democracy," in recent discussions and manifest themselves in opposed institutions and practices, as well as in propaganda maneuvers and accusations. A volume entitled, *Democracy in a World of Tensions,* appeared in 1951, published by The University of Chicago; the study of the diversities and shades of meaning attached to the term, "democracy," is addressed both to clarifying differences of meaning and to exploring means of reducing differences of action.

The study of the humanistic aspects of cultures has meanwhile been directed to two related aspects of the relations of cultures—the study of the effects of new technologies on the customs and values of peoples who have been little affected by technological and scientific advances, and the structures of values in cultures that have adjusted themselves or are in process of adjustment to industrialization and political independence. The pattern of basic philosophic attitudes and values embodied in the institutions and in the ways of life of people or assumed in their statements about their institutions and actions, cannot be abstracted from the conditions or the relations of peoples; and with proper cautions against ambiguity and conscious deception, the relations of peoples can be better understood by reference to that pattern of ideas and values. Even the political and economic relations of the various parts of the world are affected by what men believe and by what their beliefs mean, and the promulgation of a universal declaration of human rights will be translated by the peoples of the world into comparable actions in recognition of those rights only after the different meanings of "rights" and the different hierarchies of values which give effect to rights in different cultures have been transformed into motivations to comparable common ends.

• • •

The three problems which I have presented in the guise of an autobiographical account of my activities during the past thirty years—the philosophic, the educational, and the political problems of our times— have close interconnections both in the logical interrelations they would assume in any philosophy and in the historical interdependences they would reveal in any time. They have only an accidental relation in the career of any one man, and the irrationalities and paradoxes which he encounters are frequently the marks by which to reconstruct a version of the relations which they have in logic or in culture. The form according to which I have arranged this account makes the events it treats fall into the sequence of a consecutive search for a truth which is unified, and the sequence of the narrative is easily restated in an argument which proceeds in sorites from basic premises. It could as easily be recounted as a sequence in which I backed at each stage into the interests and basic convictions of the next, and it could then be restated in an argument that proceeds by paradoxes in which the contraries of each stage are reconciled into one of the contraries in the paradox of the next.

I backed into philosophy as a means of securing insight into the conflicts of theory and practice, of values and actions, which became increasingly prominent at the time of the First World War. I moved down the history of philosophy in my study of the antecedents of contemporary intellectual and moral attitudes, and I have backed into the broadening of my philosophic position in an effort to understand what would be implied in the positions denied by a series of philosophers. Dewey denied the distinction between art and science, practice and theory, and I found that the significance and power of what he taught depended on understanding the differences which separated the pairs of terms he collapsed. Spinoza denied the separation of the order and sequence of things from the order and sequence of ideas by scholastics engaged with words and by empirics engaged with manipulations of things, and I first appreciated the value and validity of his denials when I understood that proof might be distinguished wholly from process or be reduced to operations which can be controlled and repeated. Aristotle denied the idealism of Plato and the materialism of Democritus, and I began to have some insight into the peculiarities of his scientific and philosophic method and into his influence on the later history of thought, when I learned the opposed contributions of the ideas of Plato and the atoms of Democritus to the inquiry of men into the nature of things and of change. The denials seemed to me at first encounter so plausible that I found it difficult to understand how any one could ever have held the positions so readily and so persuasively refuted, but in each case a return in history or a reconstruction in theory made the refutation one more example of how men turn easily away from the theories they criticize but seldom because they have discovered error and destroyed its grounds. The importance and use of denying the distinction between art and science and between theory and practice are indeed directly proportional to the force and validity of the distinction and the length of time during which a tradition and a culture have acquiesced in it.

The relation of scholarship to teaching and of both to the social and political relations of our time, may be stated in terms of the same dialectical processes which are forced unobtrusively or reluctantly on scholarly inquiry. It is not merely that the pursuit of philosophy is itself both a process of education and a consequence of problems encountered in or induced by the educational process, but the education of a time and a people is a philosophy stated in genetic form and it serves to organize available knowledge and cogent beliefs in a kind of metaphysics of habitually accepted principles of action. When knowledge has been vastly increased, when the actions, productions, and relations of people have in consequence been altered, and when communications among men have been facilitated but obscured, then values that have been recognized to be common to all men are increasingly difficult of access to any man and the problem of reviewing and reorganizing education becomes in a fundamental sense philosophic. Yet philosophy, in our times, has become an academic pursuit and the philosopher backs from speculation to teaching as a career which permits leisure for scholarship and thought. Moreover, teaching has become a middle term, in our times as it has frequently before, to connect knowledge and scholarship to the status and operations of citizenship. Propaganda, communication, and education were seen to be powerful political instrumentalities during the war, and the political relevance of education and philosophy, which were doubtless apparent long before Plato constructed a perfect state by educating philosopher-kings, must continue to be recognized increasingly during the peace because of the dangers, as well as the opportunities, presented by new media of communication, new subjects of knowledge, and new recipients of education.

The logical relations among these three problems must be inferred from the accidental relations in which they fall in the life of a man or the intercourse of a group. I have talked about myself, therefore, by recalling the ideas I have encountered in a manner which would be justified by Aristotle's argument that the mind which is actively thinking is the objects which it thinks, or by Spinoza's conclusion that men agree in nature and are united by the common possession of the true ideas which they share. Either account of their interrelations—the metaphysical account of their essential interdependences or the autobiographical account of the accidental sequence in which their intermingling is discovered—is an index to the nature of our times. We face a *philosophic* problem of formulating the organization and interrelations of our knowledge and our values, the interplay of our ideas and our ideals, the influence of our new sciences in providing means for the solution of old problems and in laying the beginnings of new problems, and the distortions and misapplications of what is called scientific method and of what is claimed as democratic practice. That philosophic problem is inseparable from the *educational* problem of equipping men with abilities and insights to face the new problems of our times and to use the new instrumentalities with wisdom and freedom. The philosophic and educational problems are both implicated in the *political* problem of achieving common understanding among the peoples of the world who might, if ideas continue to become opaque in the oppositions of interests, be divided into parties determined by classes, the wealthy and the dispossessed, rather than by ideas and purposes. Understanding of common ideas and common ideals is the one means to combat and discredit the assumption that values and ideas are simple reflections of class interests and ideologies, that philosophy, art, and education are simple badges of privilege or instruments of revolution, and that the differences which threaten to divide the world are impervious to methods devised for the peaceful resolution of differences and for agreement and cooperation on common courses of action, but can be resolved only by subterfuge, violence, and suppression.

The philosophic problem is not one for the speculation of the isolated scholar engaged in the construction of a personal doctrine. It depends for its statement and examination on participation by a broadly educated public and on testing of basic doctrines and values against the fundamental presuppositions of other philosophies, religions, systems of values, and modes of life. Philosophic universality is easy to achieve by reducing all other views to the requirements and limits of one preferred creed and system, but it distorts the doctrines it refutes; and a similar easy and violent victory in imposing uniformity in political practices, with its consequences in suppression and hostility, is the only alternative to a political universality based on common understanding and on common values. True universality in intellectual, as well as in practical relations, depends on insight into the diversities of cultures, philosophies, and religions, and on acquaintance with the methods and consequences of science. The educational problem is not a simple choice between preserving the old and denominating anything new as good, but requires an integration of a new kind to be achieved both by applying new knowledge to values and by according new recognition to the claims of peoples and the values of cultures. International understanding, finally, will not be achieved either by programs of propaganda and information, or by setting forth the patterns of cultures and laboriously trying to think and feel as other people do. Values are based on the peculiarities of cultures, but they are understood and appreciated, even by those who share the culture in which they originated, because of their universality, and international understanding is based on the recognition of common values in the vast diversity of their forms and idioms. Understanding has a practical bearing both on action (because education and knowledge can build a foundation for international cooperation and world institutions) and on theory (because understanding and the preservation of peace are indispensable conditions for the progress of science, the construction of values, and the cultivation of the good life). These three—the understanding of order in nature, in the relations of men, and in knowledge, the education of men sensitive to the marks and uses of that order, and the appreciation of differences in the modes in which peoples express that order and seek their fulfilment in accordance with it—are the three related aspects of a problem which we all face in our individual lives, our communities, and in the world relations in which all communities have been placed.

2

Philosophy and History in the Development of Human Rights

Human rights are natural, inborn, inalienable; yet they have a history, they are acquired, and they are increased and developed. Human rights have a universal common basis in human thought and community; yet they are differently interpreted, and their recognition and practice depend on the development of a common understanding of rights and freedoms. For this reason the Preamble to the Universal Declaration of Human Rights, adopted twenty years ago, proclaims "recognition of the inherent dignity and of the equal and inalienable rights of all members of the human family"; it recognizes that in the Charter of the United Nations "Member States have pledged themselves to achieve, in cooperation with the United Nations, the promotion of universal respect for and observance of human rights and fundamental freedoms"; and it declares that "a common understanding of these rights and freedoms is of the greatest importance for the realization of this pledge."

Human rights have a philosophy as well as a history; and the acquisition, extension, increase, and exercise of human rights depend on the historical situation in which they are asserted and achieved, and on the views and convictions which make statement of them, and actions in accordance with them, possible. The historical situation conditions the conception of human rights developed in those times and circumstances; and in turn, the conception of human rights and of human nature and society conditions the statement of the history of human rights and the varieties of historical accounts in which knowledge of the past and of the present is set forth. Philosophy and history are in-

Reprinted from *Ethics and Social Justice,* ed. Howard E. Kiefer and Milton K. Munitz. Contemporary Philosophic Thought—The International Philosophy Year Conferences [at campuses of the State University of New York], vol. 4 (Albany: State University of New York Press, 1970), 300–322.

separable in the development of human rights. Ideas and values are ingredients in recognized or *known facts;* what is the case, and true statements about conditions and needs, are both determinants and consequences of accepted or *sought values.* The history of human rights must be rewritten, at each stage of its progress, from the point of view of the ideas and values, the philosophy, of that period. The philosophy of human rights must be reformulated from the point of view of the problems and opportunities presented by the facts and desires of the historical situation in which oppositions and agreements constitute the community of a people and of a time, and form their philosophy in action.

The investigation of the philosophy and history of human rights has been an integral part of the formulation and promulgation of a declaration of human rights, and of conventions to advance human rights, in the United Nations. An inquiry into the theoretical problems raised by the preparation of a universal declaration of human rights was part of the program of UNESCO in the first year of its operation. A Committee on the Theoretical Bases of Human Rights (it was also referred to as the "Committee on the Philosophic Principles of the Rights of Man" in UNESCO documents) was established in 1947, a month after the ratification of the Constitution of UNESCO. The Committee was convinced that the perspectives open to men, both on the planes of history and of philosophy, are wider and richer today than ever before, and that the hopes that emerge as possible become greater the deeper the reexamination of the bases of human rights that is made. A series of questions was prepared in March 1947 "concerning the changes of intellectual and historical circumstances between the classical declarations of human rights which stem from the eighteenth century and the bill of rights made possible by the state of ideas and the economic potentials of the present,"[1] and was circulated to a select list of scholars of the world. The Committee met from June 26 to July 2, 1947, to study the replies to the questionnaire that had been received and to draw up a history of human rights and a theoretical schematism of rights based on that history.

Replies to the questions concerning the theoretical bases of the rights of man had been received from scholars and statesmen in many

---

1. *Human Rights: Comments and Interpretations,* A Symposium edited by UNESCO with an Introduction by Jacques Maritain (London, A. Wingate, 1949), p. 262.

of the major parts of the world in the few months between March and June 1947. The selection of replies later published by the Committee included letters or essays by Mahatma Gandhi, Benedetto Croce, Teilhard de Chardin, Aldous Huxley, Salvador de Madariaga, Jacques Maritain, E. H. Carr, Harold J. Laski, F. S. C. Northrop, and Humayun Kabir. The Committee made use of these replies in drawing up its Report on "The Grounds of an International Declaration of Human Rights," but presented its report as conclusions concerning the history and nature of human rights which did not represent the opinions of all the scholars who had contributed to the Symposium.

It is the conviction of the UNESCO Committee that these inquiries into the intellectual bases of human rights may contribute to the work of the Commission on Human Rights in two fashions: first, by a brief indication of the places at which the discovery of common principles might remove difficulties in the way of agreement and the places at which philosophic divergence might anticipate difficulties in interpretation and, second, a more precise and detailed examination of the common principles that may be formulated and the philosophic differences that have divided men in the interpretation of those principles. The document which is here presented is an attempt to perform the first and preliminary task. The Committee is convinced that UNESCO will be able to muster the scholarly resources necessary for the accomplishment of the second task.[2]

The celebration of the twentieth anniversary of the adoption of the Universal Declaration of Human Rights can take no more fitting form, it seems to me, than a review and extension of the history of human rights and a reexamination and restatement of the philosophy of human rights sketched by the UNESCO Committee twenty-one years ago. In what follows I shall divide that review and reexamination into two parts: first, a statement of the ideas and the situation twenty years ago, and second, what has happened in thought and practice in the twenty years since the Declaration was made, including changes of ideas, attitudes, and relations which have resulted from the Declaration.

The United Nations and Human Rights, 1948

"An international declaration of human rights must be the expression of a faith to be maintained no less than a programme of actions to be carried out."[3] These are the opening words of the Committee's Report,

2. *Ibid.*
3. *Ibid.*, p. 258.

"The Grounds of an International Declaration of Human Rights." The Committee argued, therefore, that the preparation of a Declaration of Human Rights faces fundamental problems concerning principles and interpretations as well as political problems concerning agreement and drafting. The task which scholars might undertake to assist the Commission on Human Rights of the Economic and Social Council of the United Nations was the examination of the intellectual bases of a modern bill of rights to uncover common grounds for agreement and to explain possible sources of differences. Members of the United Nations share common convictions on which human rights are based, but the committee was also convinced that those common convictions are stated in terms of different philosophic principles and on the background of divergent political and economic systems. Examination of the grounds of a bill of rights should reveal common principles and anticipate differences of interpretation. The common faith of the United Nations in freedom and democracy and its determination to safeguard their power to expand is recorded in the Charter of the United Nations. That faith in freedom and democracy is founded on the faith in the inherent dignity of men and women.

It is this faith, in the opinion of the UNESCO Committee, which underlies the solemn obligation of the United Nations to declare, not only to all governments, but also to their peoples, the rights which have now become the vital ends of human effort everywhere. These rights must no longer be confined to a few. They are claims which all men and women may legitimately make, in their search, not only to fulfil themselves at their best, but to be so placed in life that they are capable, at their best, of becoming in the highest sense citizens of the various communities to which they belong and of the world community, and in those communities of seeking to respect the rights of others, just as they are resolute to protect their own.[4]

In the United Nations the nations of the world combined in their expression of a philosophy of human rights and in their efforts to contribute to the history of the advancement of human rights. The history of the philosophic discussion of human rights, of the dignity and brotherhood of man, and of his common citizenship in the great society is long, but, the Committee pointed out, the history of declarations of human rights and of institutions established to protect them is short, going back no further than the British Bill of Rights and the American

4. *Ibid.*, pp. 259–260.

and French Declarations of Rights of the seventeenth and eighteenth centuries.

The first question considered by the Committee was the philosophy of human rights. Does the fact that human rights depend on ideas and on a philosophy mean that men must come to agreement on a common philosophy before they can make a Declaration of Rights, or does the philosophy of human rights take a more flexible form congruent with the freedom to philosophize which is a basic human right? After long and detailed discussion the Committee agreed that the recognition of common grounds of human rights, the enumeration of particular rights, and agreement on the actions required to achieve and protect them, do not require a doctrinal consensus or agreement concerning the philosophic definition of basic terms. There was no "natural law" philosophy in the seventeenth and eighteenth century: Philosophers as different as Hobbes, Spinoza, Locke, Puffendorf, Bellarmine, and Grotius made use of the term "natural law" without sharing a philosophy or ideology; and the statesmen who borrowed the term when they drew up Declarations of Rights or interpreted them did not define natural law more rigorously than had the philosophers.

The Committee is convinced that the philosophic problem involved in a declaration of human rights is not to achieve a doctrinal consensus but rather to achieve agreement concerning rights, and also concerning actions in the realization and defense of rights, which may be justified on highly divergent doctrinal grounds. The Committee's discussion, therefore, of both the evolution of human rights and of the theoretic differences concerning their nature and interrelations, was intended, not to set up an intellectual structure to reduce them to a single formulation, but rather to discover the intellectual means to secure agreement concerning fundamental rights and to remove difficulties in their implementation such as might stem from intellectual differences.[5]

The Committee therefore agreed on working definitions of "right," "liberty," and "democracy," susceptible of divergent particularizations. They were definitions which contained a deliberate, pragmatic, and productive ambiguity.

For the purposes of the present inquiry, the Committee did not explore the subtleties of interpretation of right, liberty, and democracy. The members of the Committee found it possible to agree on working definitions of these terms, reserving for later examination the fashion in which their differences of interpretation will diversify their further definition. By a right they mean a

5. *Ibid.*, p. 263.

condition of living, without which, in any given historical stage of a society, men cannot give the best of themselves as active members of the community because they are deprived of the means to fulfil themselves as human beings. By liberty they mean more than only the absence of restraint. They mean also the positive organization of the social and economic conditions within which men can participate to a maximum as active members of the community and contribute to the welfare of the community at the highest level permitted by the material development of the society. This liberty can have meaning only under democratic conditions, for only in democracy is liberty set in that context of equality which makes it an opportunity for all men and not for some men only. Democratic liberty is a liberty which does not distinguish by age or sex, by race or language or creed, between the rights of one man and the rights of another.[6]

In terms of the living and developing philosophy of human rights and liberties in which these working definitions were formed and used, the Committee examined the broad lines of the history and evolution of particular rights.

The History of Human Rights

CIVIL AND POLITICAL RIGHTS. The rights of man have moral and social foundations which were discussed in all cultures and societies, Eastern and Western, ancient and modern, in literature, religion, and philosophy. In the West the growth of universities and the diversification of higher education, the proliferation of popular religious movements, and the development of national states, focused attention on action needed to free man from unwarranted interference with his thought and expression, and a series of freedoms were formulated more and more precisely and insistently from the late Middle Ages to the eighteenth century: freedom of thought and expression, of conscience, worship, speech, assembly, association, and the press, gradually took definite form. Legal implementations for their protection, by the institution of courts or the extension of the jurisdiction of existing courts, associated these rights and other personal rights with the right to justice by appeal to law and in that appeal to be protected from summary arrest, cruel treatment, and unjust punishment. As civil rights these rights were closely related to political action by which the function of citizens in states is defined. *Political* rights were written into instruments and institutions of government. *Civil* rights, protected from interference by governments by recourse to courts, were written into bills

6. *Ibid.*, pp. 262–263.

of rights. Political rights were discussed in the eighteenth century in close connection with the right to rebellion or revolution and with the right to citizenship, and in the nineteenth century the dependence of political rights on the right to information became increasingly clear.

ECONOMIC AND SOCIAL RIGHTS. The development of industry and technology in the nineteenth century, by making the means of livelihood potentially accessible to all men, led to increased recognition that to live well and freely man must have at least the means requisite for living. Economic and social rights were sometimes treated, as in the Anglo-American constitutional tradition, as extensions of civil and political rights. They were sometimes treated, as in the French and Continental political tradition, as distinct rights, and since the achievement of political rights had required political revolutions, their achievement seemed to depend on further economic and social revolutions carried out by planned violent action or gradual reform, or by unplanned chance or necessity, or by rhetorical persuasion or manipulation, incitation or deception. In the Anglo-American tradition, the right to property was closely associated, in statement and conception, with the right to the pursuit of happiness. The evolution of economic and social rights depended on the discussion of the ownership and use of property, of private and common ownership, and of private rights and public responsibility. Recognition of the right to education led to the institution of public systems of education; the right to work was a freedom consequent on the right to property and led to legal provision for bargaining and arbitration; the right to the protection of health was first given institutional form in pure food and drugs legislation under the provisions of police power, was extended to minimum medical and dietetic services, and finally in the twentieth century to provisions for social security.

CULTURAL RIGHTS. With increasing technological advances, the right of all to share in the advancing gains of civilization and to have full access to the enjoyment of cultural opportunities and material improvements came to be recognized and to be extended. Since the ideals and accomplishment of an age find their expression in art and literature, a new emphasis has been placed on the rights of the mind, on the right to inquiry, expression, and communication. Whether the purpose of communication be the expression of an idea or an emotion, the furthering of an individual or social purpose, or the formulation of an objective and scientific truth, the right is grounded both in the purpose of developing to the full the potentialities of men and in the social consequences of such communications. Moreover, much as the development of economic and social rights transformed and enlarged the interpretation of civil and political rights and the number of men and women who exercised them, so the development of cultural rights has transformed civil, political, economic, and social rights by an increase of mutual understanding and cooperation and an appreciation and development of the values which are accessible to men associated in the community of mankind and humanity.

The Fundamental Human Rights

The evolution of men's conception of human rights clarifies not only the problems which man and society faced at each stage of the formation of the idea of human rights, but also the means that have been found in the institution of human rights for the solution of those problems.

Human rights have become, and must remain, universal. All rights which we have come slowly and laboriously to recognize belong to all men everywhere without discrimination of race, sex, language or religion. They are universal, moreover, not only because there are no fundamental differences among men, but also because the great society and the community of all men has become a real and effective power, and the interdependent nature of that community is beginning at last to be recognized. This universality of the rights of man, finally, has led to the translation into political instrumentalities of that close interdependence of rights and duties which has long been apparent in moral analysis.[7]

All the rights which men have acquired through the centuries are important in the life of man and in the development of human communities and a world community. New rights, made possible by advances in knowledge and technology and by the institution of the agencies of the United Nations, have assumed priority in the development of rights and in the extension of rights—those long recognized and those newly conceived—to more and more people, for the new rights have not only added to the list of rights, but they have also made clear the full sense of the older rights and have made them universally practicable. The UNESCO Committee was therefore convinced that it is

7. *Ibid.*, p. 267.

possible to draw up a list of fundamental rights on which all men are agreed. They may be viewed as rights implicit in man's nature as an individual and as a member of society, and therefore they all follow from the fundamental right to live. The Committee therefore organized a list of fifteen rights under three headings.

(1)The right to live is the condition and foundation of all other rights. The first group of rights are specifications of the right to live as they bear on man's provision of means for subsistence, through his own efforts or, where they are insufficient, through the resources of society: (2) the right to the protection of health, (3) the right to work, (4) the right to maintenance in involuntary unemployment, infancy, old age, sickness and other forms of incapacity, and (5) the right to property. The right to live is more than the right to bare living, and the first group of rights designed to safeguard bare living is supplemented by a second group of rights "providing intellectual foundations for living well, training for the proper use of human abilities, as well as the opportunities for self-development and the advancement of the common good:"[8] (6) the right to education, (7) the right to information, (8) freedom of thought and the right to free inquiry, and (9) the right to self-expression. A third group of rights bear on man's participation in society and his protection from social and political injustice: (10) the right to justice, (11) the right to political action, (12) freedom of speech, assembly, association, worship, and the press, (13) the right to citizenship, (14) the right to rebellion or revolution, and (15) the right to share in progress. These rights are of fundamental importance not only to the enrichment of the human spirit but to the development of all forms of human association, including the development of national cultures and inter-national cooperation. The Committee laid particular emphasis on "the dynamic character of the interrelations of human rights and the need, therefore, to explore and control the basic ideas which are in the process of being fitted to new industrial and technological means for the achievement of the human good."[9]

The Philosophy and History of Human Rights, 1948–1968

The *Preamble of the Universal Declaration of Human Rights* recognizes that the *Charter of the United Nations* established institutional arrange-

8. *Ibid.*, p. 269.
9. *Ibid.*, pp. 271–272.

ments to promote fundamental human rights, and the *Declaration* itself states in specific detail the rights which are referred to in the *Charter.* The Declaration is a statement of principles. As such it has been influential in the last twenty years, but it has also been the basis for international conventions and covenants, for national declarations of rights in new constitutions of new states, for new laws and radical changes in social and economic conditions and relations, and, finally, for increased opportunities and increases in the number of people who can make use of those opportunities as well as in the scope and variety of aspirations which color and guide the lives of men. The Universal Declaration of Human Rights has had an educational effect on the lives of individual men and of societies and associations of men, on nations, and on the community of mankind. It has also had a direct effect on the Conventions and Protocols instituted by the United Nations and its Specialized Agencies. The history of human rights during the last twenty years, as well as the philosophic problems encountered in that history, may be seen in institutionalized form in the development of conventions which have restated the principles of the Declaration as law, much as the Declaration had restated the objectives of the Charter as principles.

The Universal Declaration of Human Rights was adopted by the General Assembly of the United Nations on December 10, 1948, by a vote of 48 to 0 with eight abstentions and two absences. The Commission on Human Rights started at once to work on the draft international conventions. They were divided into two conventions based on the distinction of kinds of rights suggested by the philosophic principles that had emerged in their discussion. In 1954 the preliminary texts of a draft covenant on civil and political rights and a draft covenant on economic, social, and cultural rights were completed and sent through the Economic and Social Council to the General Assembly where they were considered article by article from 1955 to 1966. The two Covenants and an Optional Protocol were adopted by the Assembly on December 16, 1966—the Covenant on Economic, Social, and Cultural Rights by a vote of 105 to 0, the Covenant on Civil and Political Rights by a vote of 106 to 0, and the Optional Protocol to the Covenant on Civil and Political Rights by a vote of 66 to 2 with 38 abstentions.

Although it took eighteen years to come to agreement on the overall covenants which give a legal or treaty status to arrangements by which the principles stated in the Declaration might be made operative, a whole series of conventions had been formulated, adopted, and ratified during that period. A convention or covenant differs from a declaration because it requires not only approval by the General Assembly but also ratification by the member states which decide to become parties to the covenant. The declarations are statements of position on which *member states* take a stand and vote; the conventions or covenants are international treaties which *states parties* to the convention ratify and undertake to follow. There have been declarations and conventions on many of the varieties of rights stated in the Universal Declaration: a recognition of self-determination as a human right, a declaration on the granting of independence to colonial countries and peoples, campaigns to promote freedom from hunger and the right to health by the Food and Agriculture Organization and the World Health Organization, and programs to promote education and reduce discrimination in education by UNESCO as well as a Convention and a Recommendation against Discrimination in Education and a Protocol instituting a Conciliation and Good Offices Commission. There have been conventions on Genocide, on the Status of Refugees, on the Political Rights of Women, on Slavery, and on Statelessness.

Part of the philosophical and practical problems of human rights and their implementation and advancement may be seen in the problems encountered in securing ratification of conventions. It is, for example, proper and fitting to note, at this celebration in the United States of the twentieth anniversary of the Universal Declaration of Human Rights, that the United States has not ratified any of the Conventions or Covenants—not even the Convention on the Prevention and Punishment of the Crime of Genocide adopted in 1948 and ratified by 71 states by the end of 1967, or the Convention on the Political Rights of Women adopted in 1952 and ratified by 55 states by the end of 1967, or the Convention against Discrimination in Education adopted by UNESCO in 1960 and ratified by 41 states by the end of 1967. The two Covenants and the Optional Protocol on Human Rights adopted in 1966 are not yet in force because each of the Covenants must be ratified by 27 states, and the Optional Protocol by 18 states, before it goes into force. The United States has ratified none of them.

Why is it easier to vote for a declaration than to ratify a convention? It is customary to find reasons in considerations of power. Responsible Bar Associations have published committee reports which support the position that ratification of a United Nations Convention would diminish or endanger national sovereignty. This is a dubious argument since ratification of the conventions does not grant rights of inspection or policing, or agree to submission to judgments pronounced by an international body, and even the protocols require only answers to complaints and charges. The conventions provide means to implement the rights set forth in the Universal Declaration as well as some few which are not explicitly contained in the Declaration. They are implemented by a system of reporting. Thus in the two Covenants on Human Rights, the States Parties undertake to submit reports every three years on the measures they have adopted and the progress they have made in achieving observance of the rights recognized in the Covenant. In the Covenant on Civil and Political Rights there is also a system of state-to-state communication and conciliation. The Optional Protocol to the Convention on Civil and Political Rights adds a third method of implementation. A State Party recognizes the competence of the Human Rights Committee to receive and consider communications from individuals subject to its jurisdiction who claim to be victims of a violation by the State Party of any of the rights set forth in the Covenant. The Committee is required to bring the communication to the attention of the State Party, which in turn undertakes to submit to the Committee written explanations or statements clarifying the matter and the remedy undertaken. The question is considered at a closed meeting. The implementation of the covenants is by report; the implementation of the protocol is by replies to charges. It would be desirable and wise for member states to undertake such stock-taking as regards progress in human rights even if they decided not to ratify the covenants and the protocol. The question of power and sovereignty is less meaningful—both in the sense of corresponding to objective reality and in the sense of adapting to the situations and processes of change—than the question of discovering and achieving realizable values and effective rights. In a period of social and cultural revolution violent change can be avoided only by institutionalized revolution; and the only stable society is a self-renewing society.

Philosophy in the Development of Human Rights

The history of the development of human rights is more than an account of "facts." Facts are contingent and particular. Human rights have a history, but it is neither necessary nor fortuitous. The evolution of human rights is not a "necessary" process, but the rights which evolve are "unconditioned" and they are claimed "unconditionally." The rights which are achieved are "particular" rights of particular men, but they are inborn, "universal" to all men, and they are attributed "universally" and fully to each man. The structure of the history of human rights is a structure of particular events and ideas which give concrete application to a "universal declaration of human rights." As a history of rights, it is a history of unconditional universality; its necessity and essentiality are linked to the nature of man; and like other powers and functions of man, the rights of man are used and developed in the midst of contingencies and discriminations. The unconditional universal structure is manifested in the universalization of existing rights to all men, of new rights essential to existing rights, of transformation of existing rights in the light of new rights "which have made clear the full sense of older rights and have made them universally practicable,"[10] and of action in a context of increased material resources which bear on the life of man and the development of human communities and the world community. The history of human rights may easily be reduced to a game of random chance or a mystery of divinely imposed destiny when it is recounted as a report of what has happened or as a myth of what men have done, without recognizing that it is also a history of ideas and that the structure of a continuing argument and inquiry enters into the structure of the empirical narration and of the impassioned myth. The history of human rights is paradoxical, because it embodies concretely all the great antitheses and paralogisms explored by philosophers—the problems of the whole and the part, the universal and the particular, the internal and the external, the apparent and the real.

When the UNESCO Committee examined the history and philosophy of human rights in 1947, the members of the Committee recognized that their task involved both the discovery of common principles which might remove difficulties in the way of agreement, and the places at which it might be anticipated that philosophic divergences might lead to differences and difficulties in interpretation. They also anticipated a second step in which a more precise analysis of the common principles and philosophic differences would be made. The Committee recognized that the ambiguity of the terms in which human rights and policies for their achievement are stated is the source both of agreement and differences at each stage of discussion and action. They therefore

10. *Ibid.*, p. 267.

laid down working definitions of "right," "liberty," and "democracy."
They interpreted the ambiguity ideologically in the fashion of the
1940s, and classified rights as civil and political, economic and social,
and cultural, and worked out questions of priority and interrelations
among the kinds of rights and liberties in a democracy. These are still
ambiguous terms today, twenty years later, but the discussion of human
rights now centers on a different set of basic terms which uncover new
meanings and applications for right, liberty, and democracy which continue and enrich their ambiguity.

The relation between rights, liberty, and democracy depend on the
relation between "right" and "law," and problems of right and law have
moved to the center of debate and agitation as questions of particular
rights have taken more concrete form in the context of universal rights
during the last twenty years. Right and law provided the basic distinction in the brief history of rights and conventions sketched in the preceding pages, as well as in the antithesis between power (sovereignty is
the power to make binding laws) and justice (the just is the right, and
justice protects rights from impositions of power, including the power
of the state), and within states the opposition between rights and interests, public good and private advantage. The determination of the hierarchies of rights and their limitations and negations reflects a continuing structure of philosophic interpretations in which a succession of
basic terms is taken as fundamental in stating, understanding, and
acquiring rights. Changes in the vocabulary, brought about both by
adding new words and by changing the meanings of retained words,
complicate the recognition of common principles and of differing philosophic interpretations, and the ambiguity opens the way to the use of
interested misrepresentation as an instrument of power and the distrac-
tion of irrelevant quibbling advanced in lieu of rational analysis. John
Stuart Mill makes a suggestive distinction in tracing the history of liberty between the problems presented when rulers and the ruled are
thought to be distinct, and the problems presented in a democracy in
which the ruled rule. The characteristics of recent discussions of liberty
may be understood by adding a third relation, since the statement of
the claims of many of the new freedoms are made in terms of situations
in which the ruled oppose the rulers. The different forms of the statements of right may be given systematic form by considering them in
terms of schemata of rights in which civil and political, economic and
social, and finally cultural rights are in turn taken as fundamental.

When ruler and ruled are conceived to be different in nature in the analysis of liberty and rights, their differences are found in the character of those who rule or should rule, and of those who are ruled or should be ruled, and those differences are institutionalized in constitutions, monarchical, aristocratic, and democratic. Natural law takes its significance from these conceptions; the true forms of government are directed to the good; and the chief danger to liberty and rights is in the tyranny of the ruler. When the ruled are conceived to be the rulers in the analysis of liberty and rights, the basic problems of liberty and rights are not found in nature or in the nature of men, but in the relations between the individual and society. Responsibility takes its significance from the difference between actions for which the individual is accountable only to himself and those for which he is accountable to others and to society; and the chief danger to liberty and rights is in the tyranny of the majority or of common opinion. When the ruled are conceived to be the antagonists of the establishment, the basic problems of liberty and rights are not found in generalizations like nature or convention but in the inequities of current situations and in the lack of recognition, by themselves as well as others, of the victims of injustice. Assertion and initiation take their importance from the need to bring the situation to awareness and to do something about it; and the chief danger to liberty and equality is in the tyranny of the unrepresented minority.

We have not yet taken seriously or examined rationally the grounds or the consequences of the third way of formulating rights. We tend to translate it into the first vocabulary and to argue about right and wrong in terms taken from the vocabulary of civil and political rights, or to translate it into the second vocabulary and to argue about the ideologies of the cold war or the class war or some like confrontation in terms taken from the vocabulary of economic and social rights. We have not yet listened to the statements of action which translate civil and political, economic and social rights into a vocabulary based on terms taken from cultural rights. Instead of listening, we react with perplexity or indignation to "resistance" (nonviolent and violent), to "demonstration" (manifestation and disalienation), and to "imperialism" (military, political, economic, colonial, social, and cultural). We continue to talk in terms of old conceptions of nature and the good, or of power and sovereignty instead of adapting our vocabulary to new conceptions of revolution and relevant change.

The hierarchy of human rights formulated by the UNESCO Committee had made use of the new cultural rights to transform and order the older civil and political, economic and social rights. Cultural rights were treated as the last historical development and as the apex of the hierarchy which ranged from needs and wants to aspirations and wishes, from external undergoing to internal impulsion, from rights dependent on protection from external restriction of liberty to rights whose attainment would depend on the attitudes and actions of all people. Therefore, in sequence and in hierarchy, human rights were rights of living (the satisfaction of needs), of living well (self-development and advancement of the common good), and of living in society (justice and protection from the varieties of injustice). The recent emergence of rights which depend on the action of other men and eventually all men is symbolized in the prepositions of the four freedoms of the Atlantic Charter: freedom *of* thought and expression, which requires institutions to protect men from interference, and freedom *from* want and fear, which depends on a society of men who produce the requisites of life and do not resort to violence in the solution of problems. But cultural rights—the conception but not the fact—were new in 1947. The UNESCO Committee described cultural rights briefly in the traditional terms of the arts and sciences: the emerging cultural rights, their problems and their potentialities, were not investigated and the nature of their effect on the other rights was not elaborated.

The twenty years since 1947 suggest the need of a restatement of the philosophy of human rights and therefore, since the facts of history are affected by the philosophy of the time of the historian, a retracing of their history. Conceived in terms of cultural rights, neither men nor the rights of man can be ranged significantly or usefully in hierarchies: all rights are cultural rights, and cultural rights contribute to the satisfaction of needs, aspirations, and justice as well as (or more correctly, as instances of) the creation and appreciation of values; and in the history of mankind, justice and the enjoyment of truth and beauty were sought as early as the satisfaction of any other needs and wants. In the same fashion, freedoms *of* and freedoms *from* have been transformed by new developments of freedoms *to*—freedoms to participate in the values of culture and the fruits of progress. Cultural freedoms contribute to relating rights to the right and to the good, and to relating desires to what is desirable and what is possible. Their nature and effects are in part philosophic problems and in part empirical and practical problems, which are profoundly affected, like all empirical and practical facts, by the philosophical perspectives and conceptions in which they are encountered and experienced.

Philosophy in Conception and Action in Human Rights

Problems arise from difficulties in action and ambiguities in thought and statement. The ambiguities of philosophic problems are frequently stated as paradoxes. One of the most persistent paradoxes which men have faced has been the paradox of right and law. It has found profound and suggestive formulation in myth, religion, poetry, law, and philosophy. If the historical and current statements and manifestations of the paradox of right and law are examined formally (to clarify the meanings and applications of rights and laws) it is apparent that four relations are possible between them as between any pair of terms. All four sets of meanings have been advocated by men in all periods of the discussion of rights and laws, and all four are still advocated in discussions and arguments today. Two of the possible relations may be called *ontic,* since they imply and depend on something real grounding the diversity of forms of rights in actual situations or institutions: either *transcendent,* inborn, or inalienable rights which provide the grounds for *laws* and constitutions, or *underlying* laws of the universe and of the nature of man which provide grounds for the assertion and pursuit of rights. Two of the possible relations may be called *phenomenal,* since they deny transcendental and underlying groundings and make rights and laws dependent on what men do and what they institute, and they place rights and laws in two possible relations as a result of the actions of men: *mutually exclusive* actions by which *rights* are freedoms and *laws* obligations, and rights are consequently found in actions concerning which laws are silent; or *mutually implicative* or dependent actions in which *rights* acquired in society and associations carry with them obligations, and *obligations* undertaken in law and custom carry with them rights. The "common principle" of human rights is stated in all four of these formulations of the relation of right and law, and all four conceptions have entered into the institution of human rights at all stages of their development. The divergent philosophic interpretations of the common principle have been the source of differences and oppositions; they have also been the source of ongoing progress in understanding and acquiring human rights.

Two dimensions of rights have been made apparent from the oppositions of the two fundamental pairs of relations between right and law: in phenomenal conceptions, freedom is the right to do as one pleases whether or not it is thought for any reason that one should do what one chooses to do; in ontic conceptions, freedom is the right to do as one should whether or not one wishes to do what is right. Justice has a place in each of these conceptions of right (as is apparent in the etymologies of right and justice in the ancient languages from which Western discussion of philosophy and politics derived its vocabulary: *dikaiosune* and *dike, justitia* and *jus*), since justice is a formulation of the relations of rights to the right and of the desired to the desirable in each of the philosophic conceptions of right; rights are conceived and sought in a context of power of action and of judgment or jurisdiction, and judgment takes the form of expressing what men think to be honorable or good and useful or effective; the inclusive context of practical thought and action is power and justice.

The evolution of human rights in the history sketched by the UNESCO Committee in 1947 is a history of rights stated in bills of rights since the seventeenth and eighteenth centuries. It was carefully separated from the history of philosophic conceptions of rights developed prior to the seventeenth century or expressed in parts of the world which drew up bills of rights only on the model of Western institutions. When the importance of cultural rights is recognized, that history must be reconsidered because the very conception of law and of constitution is changed in the context of cultural rights, and the possibility of the development of the rule of law, and of human rights and international obligations, must not be limited to the legislative powers of an international assembly, or the police powers of an international force, or the compulsory jurisdiction of an international court. As in the case of other transformations of human rights in the light of cultural rights, the main lines of the history of rights may be made the basis for the restatement of the institutional history of rights in the broader framework of the philosophy of rights and laws.

The first human rights to emerge in law were civil and political rights. The conception of justice in terms of which their formulation was made, "rendering to every man his due," was borrowed from Roman law. When the pattern of the evolution of this conception of justice is sought, it is worthy of note that it was given expression earlier by a philosopher who undertook to show its insufficiency as a definition of justice. Plato puts this definiton in the mouth of Polemarchus in the first book of his *Republic*. It is refuted by Socrates, and in its place Socrates established, in the fourth book, a definition in which justice consists in each man performing his appropriate function in the state. The passive conception of *rendering* to men gives way to the active conception of each man *doing*, and the division of men into friends and enemies, or classes based on considerations of benefit and harm, yields to the division of men according to functions and work, or classes based on contribution to the common good. The definition of justice as rendering to every man his due was refuted by Socrates, but it was installed in Roman law and in the legal systems of the West and it was declared in the Universal Declaration of Human Rights.

The second group of human rights to emerge in law were economic and social rights. The conceptions of the division of labor and reward and of the status and relations of men, which were used in the development of economic and social rights after the industrial and technological revolutions, had earlier philosophic beginnings. When Socrates constructs a series of states in which to find and define justice in Book II of the *Republic*, the division of labor is the principle which guides the formation of the successive states, and his definition of justice in Book IV reflects that principle. Similarly, Aristotle, having defined justice as the virtue which renders men apt to do just things, and having differentiated between legal justice, which is exercise of virtue as a whole relative to others, and equal justice, which is a particular virtue relative to the state, and between distributive and rectificatory justice as kinds of equal justice, treats the distribution of honor, wealth, and other divisible assets of the community, which may be allotted among its members in equal or unequal shares, argues that there are as many kinds of justice as there are kinds of constitutions of states, and relates legal to equal justice by arguing that the different kinds of justice proper to each state reflect natural justice which is the same in Athens and in Persia. Even in Greece, the consideration of economic and social rights transformed the meaning of civil and political rights. It is frequently said that Aristotle was no lover of democracy, yet he defines the state in terms of citizens, and he defines citizens as those who share in the administration of justice and political functions—that is, as the ruled who rule—remarking that his definition might seem best adapted to the citizen of a democracy; and when he distinguishes between good constitutions, which are directed to the common good, and bad constitutions, designed to further private interests, the name which he uses for the good form of democracy, is "polity," *politeia,* the word which means "constitution."

The final human rights to emerge in law are cultural rights. The objects cultivated by man, which give content to the conception of "culture" and "cult," include fields and herds, God and man's own mind and capacities. We are once more brought today, as were the Greeks and the Romans, to a recognition of the pluralism of justice, the pluralism of legal justice and also of equal justice, to borrow and adapt Aristotle's terms. It is a pluralism which has been in effect in economic and social rights, and it reflects a pluralism of philosophic interpretations in any policy proposed to extend and broaden the equality of equal justice. Before we draw up, or in the process of drawing up, a new legal formulation of the justice of equality we must reexamine, rethink, and restate the philosophic conception of man's function or his task in human societies and in the community of mankind. The philosophic problem of the paradox of rights and laws is at the bottom of the puzzling paradoxes encountered in efforts to define and advance human rights. It is at the bottom of the paradoxes of our hesitations over conventions, which are laws to implement and enforce rights we have already approved in a universal bill of human rights. It turns up again—in a particular form in the United States—in the need for a "civil *rights law*" to put into effect rights already guaranteed in an amendment to the Constitution. It is the paradox of the need of obligations to be free, of heteronomous laws to enforce autonomous rights and freedoms, of passionate attachment to principles warranted by cognitive analysis, of using legal equality to state equal rights. It is a paradox which appears in the terms we have been using to restate the philosophy and history of human rights: We have seen that all rights— civil, political, economic, and social—have become "cultural" rights, yet we watch new movements to advance rights, which state their objectives, and indicate the means that must be used to achieve them, by reducing all rights to "civil" rights.

The paradoxes are not ambiguities resulting from confusion or contradiction; they are productive ambiguities which embody the knowledge and experience men have acquired in the long history of rights, and which provide the beginning points for further advances. They encapsulate the history of the language of human rights as well as the history of the rights themselves, and they are restated in the language of the cultural revolution which is the present stage of the advancement of rights. Bills of rights are universal; conventions and laws are particular to circumstances and to specific rights. The distinction between rights and laws bearing on rights can be made in terms of natural law and the good; it can be made in terms of sovereignty and power. It is also made forcefully and pertinently in terms of revolution, for the statement of common principles and ideals is indicative of injustices and wrongs. The importance of conventions or laws is that they are ratifications or enactions of means by which to remove particular injustices and establish conditions for the acquisition and exercise of particular rights, of "freedoms to do." Revolutions are violent or peaceful changes of those in power under a constitution, or of the interpretation of the constitution, or of the constitution itself; and the vocabulary and methods of revolution extend far beyond the devices of political or military revolution, to include industrial and technological revolutions, social and cultural revolutions. Colonialism has likewise been analogized, in statement and program, to more relations between peoples than merely political affiliation or dependence, or even economic interdependence or exploitation, or social development or stratification, and has been further extended to include relations of groups or classes within a single nation or society. The ideas and the histories of revolutions and constitutions are closely intertwined: appeals to innovation and progress are made in the name of both, as are appeals to tradition and renaissance. The constitutions of the United States and of France, which were the basis of the constitutionalism and the economic and social reforms of the nineteenth century, were based on revolutions. Political, economic, and social changes that affected the lives of hundreds of millions of people and the whole structure of their relations with the other people of the world, and the modes of life of those other peoples, were initiated in the twentieth century by the revolutions of Sun Yat-sen, Gandhi, and Lenin. Considerations of natural law and oppositions of power were modified in revolutionary consideration of means of removing inequities revealed by a common principle.

Revolutions, from the beginning of the use of that term and concept, could be violent or nonviolent. They could be brought about by direct action or by circuitous manipulation; they could result in changes in the organization of society and the state, or changes in the government and the officials of government. They could be exercised by overt changes, real or apparent, or by occult changes, real or apparent—as Augustus preserved the forms of the Constitution of the Ro-

man Republic when he set up an Empire, or Napoleon continued the
innovations of the French Revolution when he set up an Empire which
used forms and structures borrowed from the Roman model. They
could be achieved by practical action directed purposively and causally
to a ladder of values; they could be achieved by indicative action
pointed demonstratively and manifestively to a list of injustices. "Demonstration" is used in many arts—in logic, rhetoric, poetry, geometry,
politics. The semantic changes are not a play of games in which stakes
are not for keeps or a use of words in which meanings are not for sense:
"Demonstration" may be used for human rights, to prove that a given
mode of action is an exercise or an instance of a right; to persuade that
a given end is good or to be accepted as good, or that a given means is
useful or to be accepted as practicable; to manifest or expose a given
action or relation or institution or establishment as wrong; to impede
or delay or prevent activities of a given kind or of any kind whatever
until actions or policies are changed.

As part of the range of meanings of "demonstration," civil disobe-
dience and nonviolent resistance may be interpreted, and may therefore
be, consequences or contributions to maintaining the constitution or
to furthering the revolution. The transition from acting as a good citizen in accordance with the law and the constitution and acting as a
good citizen to change the law and to amend the constitution; or the
transition from nonviolent demonstrations to performing or undergoing violent actions, is gradual and subtle. It is not treated adequately
by appeal to established and rigid conceptions of natural law or of
structures of social or political powers and functions, although adequate analysis and interpretation of the transition could be made if
those conceptions of civil and political, economic and social rights were
given the flexibility they acquire in a context of cultural rights. The
revolution is no longer basically a political, economic, or social revolution; it is a cultural revolution. It is not a revolution to establish the
rights of a people, or of the inhabitants of a region, or of a "class" in
any of the many senses in which men may be grouped in genera or
species; it is a revolution to establish the group and the consciousness
of the group as a step to acting to secure the rights which the group,
once constituted by action, seeks or claims, not wholly unlike the revolution by which the Jews became a people chosen by God and withdrawn from the esteem of other peoples, or the United States avoided
the entangling alliances and enmities of Europe and offered mankind a

model of democratic government for imitation. Gandhi's program of nonviolent action and resistance was a revolution which went through several stages: a first step to give the Indian people a sense of self-identity, a second step to lead them to act as Indians in ways not approved by society or common opinion and even to risk disapproval by imprisonment, a third step to risk economic disadvantage and loss of social status, a fourth step to secure political independence. With political independence, the Indian people had the opportunity to determine what ends to pursue and what to do to secure those ends, and even to discover that the political use of nonviolent resistance may lead to large scale violence. The adoption of the policy of nonviolent resistance by black people in the United States required adaptations: the group was marked for constitution as a group by the skin color of its potential members in a white society, and the rights they sought were stated in the Constitution of the nation. A hundred years of inaction modulated by minuscule and partial changes, however, provided a situation in which demonstrations and manifestations of injustices prepared for the broad recognition of a principle and for the formation of opposed and supplementary policies of what to do or not to do in order that black men might achieve opportunity and motivation for self-realization. Students in the United States and in many other countries, dissatisfied with educational and with political and international policy, sought in demonstration means by which to realize their identity as students, as young people, as members of universities or of the republic of science and letters, and to determine what ought to be done or what ought not to be done by those constituted groups in a world of change and revolution.

It is to neglect the semantic change of language and of situation to criticize such movements for lack of clarity in statements of purpose, if what is sought is the clarity of a preamble to a political constitution or to an economic or social manifesto. The relevant clarity will be found by examining what the movements are against, and what can be done to repair the indicated injustices and the felt wrongs. Action and statement are employed to bring unclearly defined but clearly sensed wrongs to attention. The revolution is not contrary to reason or to nature or against the constitution and the rule of law, for in the process of semantic change traditional values are preserved in changed formulation as part of the revolutionary innovation: For all our distress concerning the ambiguity of natural law we find ways of asserting inborn rights;

for all our suspicion concerning the implications of consensus and sovereignty we find ways of seeking and asserting power; for all our emotive ambivalence concerning revolution we seek ways to institutionalize revolution in progress. The Constitution is based on and is an expression of the law of nature, the operation of sovereignty, and the institutionalization of revolution. Progress and revolution have become the basic terms from which nature and power derive their meanings as a result of our growing recognition of the importance and the priority of cultural rights.

Rights and the right are independent. In the light of cultural rights, freedom of thought and expression are rights of the wise and the foolish, and the right of the wise to be wise in fact and reality, in statement and action, depends on recognition of the right of the foolish to be foolish. There is no criterion antecedent to consideration and interpretation of their action and statement by which to determine which is wise and which is foolish, because the best attested and the most widely accepted criteria would impede the activities and forestall the statements which contribute to wisdom and knowledge and the realization of values. Freedom to philosophize, as a cultural right, is freedom of thought and expression, and the exercise of the right broadens philosophizing to include philosophies of life as well as the treatises which express the philosophizing of professed or recognized philosophers. A new mode of philosophy emerges as an instance of cultural rights and as a common principle of rights and the right, and of the organization of knowledge and wisdom and of values. A pluralism of philosophies parallels the pluralisms of societies devoted to and dependent on cultural rights.

The philosophic differences in the interpretation of the common principles by which men live, yield programs of action relative to selected aspects of common experience directed to selected values of common ends. If common problems are considered from a variety of basic philosophic orientations, common policies may be agreed on and common actions may be undertaken for a variety of reasons under the guidance of a variety of professed philosophies. Differences of philosophies and confrontations of groups lead to controversies of opposition. When action and policy are discussed in the vocabulary of the structure and oppositions of power, the differences are sought in differences of intention or differences of consequences, that is, in terms of imputation (as Kant and his continental predecessors analyzed problems of moral action) or in terms of accountability (as Mill and his English predecessors presented moral problems). The concept of responsibility which emerged from the reflexive joining of considerations of antecedent purposes and posterior consequences has moved the center of the application of responsibility from the responsibility of an agent who carries out the directions of his principal, to the responsibility of a representative who makes decisions for the people he represents, to the responsibility of an activist who acts to change the structure within which decisions are made.

Semantic controversies are concerning the proper, or the preferable, or the "relevant" formulation of the common principle. Discussion of the common problem might take the place of controversy concerning the formulation of, or orientation to, the common principles of the parties brought together to consider the common problem, and might shift the issue from oppositions of parties to applications of reasons for the actions formulated to resolve the problem, and might open the possibility of coming to agreement on common action or policy for the different reasons of the opposed formulations. Criteria in such a discussion would be sought in the actions proposed to resolve a concrete problem, rather than in the principles, or methods, or interpretations used in statements of the problem. Once the focus of the discussion is on concrete problems and concrete consequences of proposed actions, rather than on the intentions, ideologies, and beliefs of the parties to the discussion and to the proposed action, the movement of the exercise of liberty and rights might be an ongoing confrontation of new problems and new opportunities. Within the peace and security of the common institutions of the pluralistic society built on the exercise of cultural rights, men would have the circumstances and incentives conducive to developing the implications and the consequences of the varieties of philosophies and of self-realizing activities, and in moments of leisure from creative inquiry and expression they would be free to undertake the task of refuting and converting each other. In such a society a new mode of philosophizing would take form by the addition of discussion of common problems to the continuing opposition of preferred positions and interpretations; and under the influence of such a philosophy, a peaceful and progressive society would take form by use of the diversity of philosophies to uncover and verify common principles and to test them by the falsification of proposed formulations and systems.

3

The Development and the Significance
of the Concept of Responsibility

The diversity of approaches to a practical problem is one of the problems of cooperation, and the diversity of vocabularies in a discussion is one of the problems of communication. When the International Institute of Philosophy was founded in 1937 the problems of cooperation among philosophers in different parts of the world were conceived wholly as problems of philosophical information and communication—the preparation of bibliographies and abstracts of books and articles, the establishment of a clearing house of information concerning research and speculation in progress, and the organization of meetings, discussions and symposia. The second World War added a further dimension to this felt need for communication among philosophers. The war itself was an extension in armed conflict of differences concerning the nature of human communities and concerning the use of power, which had been based ideologically on what purported to be philosophical principles. The uneasy peace which has followed the close of the war has reflected a more complex conflict of ideologies set in oppositions, which, despite ambiguities in their statement, have become rigid, because differences of policy and action are seen or anticipated as consequences to opposed doctrines acknowledged or imputed.

On the one hand, the scope of philosophic problems has broadened and the differences which in the past have separated philosophical schools have become part of the political negotiations of nations and the cultural communications of peoples. Everyone has become involved in philosophical problems to the extent that he is concerned with human rights, freedom, justice, independence and self-determination, se-

Reprinted from the *Revue internationale de philosophie* 34 (1957, fasc. 1): 3–32.

curity, cultural continuity and renovation, welfare and wellbeing. On the other hand, the methods proposed by philosophers for the discussion and solution of problems have narrowed into opposed sectarianisms among which there is no agreement or even communication. Free discussion of philosophic problems is difficult when the state is established on an official interpretation of a single philosophy and a single conception of history. Even when the lines of opposition are not determined by direct political or doctrinal pressure, however, discussion is impeded by disagreements concerning the questions at issue, concerning the character of satisfactory statements or acceptable solutions of questions, and even concerning the meanings of the words employed in formulating these initial problems. Philosophic discussion within a single tradition is less frequently the discussion of common problems than the characterization of positions opposed—the enumeration of meaningless questions raised by one's opponents or the exposure of abstract and formal methods employed, and the demonstration that any such approach neglects problems of philosophic importance, ignores tested methods of scientific analysis, or yields dubious or dangerous practical applications and consequences. These devices are easily extended to characterize the philosophic doctrines and attitudes developed in other national and linguistic traditions.

Since the establishment of UNESCO in 1946, the Institute has cooperated closely with it in these two tasks of communication and understanding—the analysis of the relations of peoples, cultures, and traditions and the examination of basic ideas underlying the practical problems of conflict and cooperation. More recently the subjects which have been chosen for discussion at the plenary sessions of the Institute have not only brought out the relations between problems of action and cooperation and problems of philosophic analysis and communication but have also begun to sketch an interrelated sequence of such subjects. In 1955 at Athens, the subject of discussion, *Dialogue and Dialectic,* included both the problem of reestablishing and continuing the dialogue among philosophers which constitutes the history of philosophy and the problem of making the contacts of cultures and traditions a dialogue to advance the exchange of ideas and the appreciation of values. In 1957 at Warsaw we shall treat the relations of *Thought and Action* under three aspects: (1) philosophic analyses of the relation of theory and practice, (2) practical uses and applications of philosophy and the humanities, and (3) practical responsibilities of philosophers.

It is appropriate that the intervening meeting, in Paris in 1956, should be devoted to the discussion of the conception of *Responsibility,* since the accountability of an agent for his act serves as transition between the intelligibility of ideas and values in communication and the efficacy of theory in practice.

These considerations were in the back of my mind when I began to organize the lines of consideration of the concept of responsibility which might be sketched for the Entretiens of Paris. Responsibility has three related dimensions. It has an external dimension in legal and political analysis in which the state imposes penalties on individual actions and in which officials and governments are held accountable for policy and action. It has an internal dimension in moral and ethical analysis in which the individual takes into account the consequences of his actions and the criteria which bear on his choices. It has a comprehensive or reciprocal dimension in social and cultural analysis in which values are ordered in the autonomy of an individual character and the structure of a civilization. These distinctions stirred a distant memory. I had come upon L. Lévy-Bruhl's *L'Idée de Responsabilité* while exploring the works of my professors at the University of Paris, motivated by a curiosity which apparently has since disappeared from the customs of students. Returning to that book some thirty years later and with a new interest in responsibility, I found that my distinctions had doubtless been based on half-conscious memory of Lévy-Bruhl's differentiation of the objective and the subjective analysis of responsibility and their interplay. Lévy-Bruhl assumes that responsibility is an idea basic to morality as well as to ethical theory[1]; he is able therefore to sketch its

---

1. L. Lévy-Bruhl, *L'Idée de Responsabilité* (Paris, 1884), pp. 5–6: "La notion de responsabilité est évidemment une pièce nécessaire de notre édifice moral. Qu'on la retire, il s'écroule. La moralité disparaît, les sentiments essentiels à la conscience perdent leur sens. Il ne se peut, semble-t-il, qu'une notion de cette importance ne soit parfaitement claire, et chacun pense, en effet, concevoir la responsabilité avec une netteté très suffisante. Cette clarté pourtant n'est qu'apparente, comme nous aurons bientôt l'occasion de le voir; mais l'illusion est presque inévitable, à cause de l'étroite connexion qui enchaîne à l'idée de responsabilité nos autres idées morales. Il y a là tout un système de notions associées qui se renvoient pour ainsi dire l'une à l'autre leur clarté propre. Clarté peut-être factice: mais chacune ne s'en impose pas moins à notre esprit avec une autorité dont les autres sont garantes. Par exemple, si l'on fixe son attention sur l'idée de responsabilité, aussitôt les notions voisines de liberté, de justice, de mérite, de remords, de moralité, une foule d'autres encore, surgissent dans la conscience, et empêchent que l'on ne remarque la moindre obscurité dans une idée si riche d'associations."

history from antiquity to the present; yet he finds that the idea has never been studied or analyzed.[2]

In the perspective of an additional seventy years of development the evidence assembled by Lévy-Bruhl suggests somewhat different conclusions. His investigation of responsibility is one of the first analyses of the concept of responsibility. In 1876, eight years earlier, F. H. Bradley had published as the opening essay of his *Ethical Studies* an analysis of "The Vulgar Notion of Responsibility in Connexion with the Theories of Free-Will and Necessity." The statement of John Stuart Mill, "Responsibility means punishment," which is quoted by both Bradley and Lévy-Bruhl with reservations, because, according to Bradley, it is the vulgar idea but incorrectly expressed, and because, according to Lévy-Bruhl, it is not the fundamental idea of responsibility, was made in 1865. Alexander Bain, in 1859, substituted the literal term "punishability" for the figurative term "responsibility" in the interests of clarity.[3] Prior to 1859, however, I was able to find no philosophic treatment of responsibility. Moreover, these analyses of responsibility had their beginnings in controversies, in which the word "responsibility" was not used. Bain's references to Lord Brougham and Wardlaw bear on the controversy concerning "accountability" for one's beliefs. Mill's dictum is part of his refutation of the argument attributed to Sir William Hamilton, that freedom of the will is implied in our consciousness of moral responsibility; but neither Hamilton nor Reid, from whom

2. *Ibid.*, p. 21: "Si la philosophie n'eût pas été d'abord toute au mystère du libre arbitre, on aurait vu sans doute que les deux idées, quoique connexes, sont distinctes, et qu'il vaut la peine d'étudier pour elle-même la notion de responsabilité. Elément nécessaire des conceptions morales et de la vie sociale de l'homme, elle a dû avoir son histoire, comme ces conceptions morales, comme cette vie sociale elle-même. Peut-être la notion mal assise qui subsiste aujourd'hui dans les esprits doit-elle son incohérence et ses contradictions en apparence inexplicables à la juxtaposition successive d'éléments d'âge et de provenance différents, qui se sont mêlés en elle sans pouvoir s'amalgamer."

3. Alexander Bain, *The Emotions and the Will* (London, 1859), p. 564: "The term 'Responsibility' is a figurative expression, of the kind called by writers on Rhetoric 'Metonymy,' where a thing is named by some of its causes, effects, or adjuncts, as when the crown is put for royalty, the mitre for the episcopacy, etc. Seeing that in every country, where forms of justice have been established, a criminal is allowed to answer the charge made against him before he is punished; this circumstance has been taken up and used to designate punishment. We shall find it conduce to clearness to put aside the figure, and employ the literal term. Instead, therefore, of responsibility, I shall substitute punishability; for a man can never be said to be responsible, if you are not prepared to punish him when he cannot satisfactorily answer the charges made against him."

Hamilton borrowed the argument, uses the word "responsibility"—
Mill substitutes it for their word "accountability."[4] Bradley explains responsibility or accountability in terms of imputability; Lévy-Bruhl substitutes imputability for accountability.[5] This abrupt beginning of the
discussion of a concept, which is none the less assumed to be fundamental to moral action and theory, suggests that the word was of recent
origin and that in philosophic discussion it was identified with existing
controversial terms rather than examined to determine whether its occurrence indicated a need to define a new concept which alters the significance of the old.

Available evidence indicates that the origin of the word "responsibility" preceded the philosophic analysis of the concept by about seventy years. The first occurrence of "responsibility" recorded in Murray's
Oxford English Dictionary is from the *Federalist*, paper 64, by Alexander
Hamilton, published in 1787. According to Bloch and von Wartburg's
Dictionnaire Etymologique de la Langue Française, the noun "responsabilité" also is used for the first time in 1787, the privative adjective

4. Sir William Hamilton, *Lectures on Metaphysics*, "Lecture XL, The Regulative Faculty—Law of the Conditioned in its Applications—Causality" (Boston, 1860), p. 558:
"And in favor of our moral nature, the fact that we are free, is given us in the consciousness of an uncompromising law of Duty, in the consciousness of our moral accountability
. . ." Cf. *Discussions on Philosophy and Literature* (New York, 1853), "Conditions of the
Thinkable Systematized; Alphabet of Human Thought," p. 586: "*How*, therefore, I repeat, moral liberty is possible in man or God, we are utterly unable speculatively to
understand. But practically, in *fact*, that we are free, is given to us in the consciousness of
an uncompromising law of duty, in the consciousness of our moral accountability." Hamilton edited the works of Thomas Reid. In the fourth essay of Reid's *Essays on the Active
Powers of the Mind* (1788) three arguments for moral liberty are presented: (1) man's
natural conviction or belief that he acts freely in many cases, (2) man's consciousness of
his accountability, and (3) his ability to prosecute an end by a long series of means
adapted to it. Mill refutes the first two arguments, but he substitutes "responsibility" as
a synonym for "accountability" in the second.

5. Bradley, *Ethical Studies*, p. 5: "So far we have seen that subjection to a moral tri-
bunal lies at the bottom of our answering for our deeds. The vulgar understanding that
we answer; that we answer not for everything, but only for what is ours; or in other
words for what can be imputed to us. If now we can say what is commonly presupposed
by *imputability*, we shall have accomplished the first part of our undertaking, by the discovery of what responsibility means for the people." Lévy-Bruhl translates "accountability" by "imputabilité." He renders Mill's statement, "And it is worth consideration,
whether the practical expectation of being thus called to account, has not a great deal to
do with the internal feeling of being accountable; a feeling assuredly, which is seldom
found existing in any strength in the absence of that practical expectation," (*op. cit.*, p.
289) by "Il faudrait bien rechercher si l'expectative réelle de cette imputabilité n'est pas
pour beaucoup dans le sentiment interne de la responsabilité, sentiment qu'on trouve
rarement bien vif là où manque la menace de l'imputabilité."

"irresponsable" making its appearance in the same year and the noun "irresponsabilité" in 1791. Heinrich Heine was the first author to use "Verantwortlichkeit" according to the Grimms' *Deutsches Wörterbuch*, but whereas in English "responsibility" moves into the place of "accountability" and is then related to the broader term "imputation," in German the discussion of "Verantwortlichkeit" is superimposed on a preceding discussion of "Zurechnung" or imputation. In each language the adjective was used earlier: as early as the 13th century in French, in the last year of the 16th century in English, and in the middle of the 17th century in German.[6] Neither the noun nor the adjective occurs in classical Latin, and the adjective "responsabilis" is not found in medieval Latin until the 14th century, after the formation of the French word.[7] There were, however, Latin terms which expressed the concepts which entered into the later definition of "responsibility"—*causa* or *actio* and *peccatum* or *error*. These were respectively translations of the Greek αἰτία (cause or imputation of praise or blame) and ἁμαρτία (missing the mark or guilt or sin).[8]

6. "Responsible" was used by Ben Jonson in 1599 in the sense of "correspondent" or answering to something; it was used in the sense of accountable or liable to be called to account (i.e., responsible to kingdom or Parliament) in 1643, in the sense of answerable to a charge in 1650, in the sense of "trustworthy" or capable of fulfilling an obligation in 1691 by John Locke, in the sense of morally accountable in 1836. Bloch and von Wartburg report the occurrence of "responsable" in the sense of "se porter garant" in 1284. French philosophers, theologians, and moralists of the 17th and 18th centuries—Pascal, Bourdaloue, La Bruyère, Fénelon, Rousseau—use it in senses which bring out the paradoxes of the relations of individual to group and of character to action (Pascal, *Les Provinciales* (1656): "Tout notre corps [des Jésuites] est responsable des livres de nos pères; cela est particulier à notre compagnie;" Rousseau, *La Nouvelle Héloïse* (1761): "Croyczmoi, je ne suis pas responsable de moi-même"). In its first occurrence, the German adjective "verantwortlich" is applied in 1644 to ministerial responsibility. J. G. Walch's *Philosophisches Lexicon* (1740) does not contain an article on "Verantwortlichkeit" but it does expound "Zurechnung," (imputation, ascription) as treated by the Natural Law philosophers. W. T. Krug's *Allgemeines Handwörterbuch der philosophischen Wissenschaften* (1827) contains a brief article on "Verantwortlich" emphasizing the dependence of the concept on the existence of a judge, and in particular of a supreme judge, God, as well as an article on "Zurechnung." There is no article on "Verantwortlich" in R. Eisler's *Wörterbuch der philosophischen Begriffe und Ausdrücke* (1899) but an entry is added in the second edition (1904) and expanded in later editions, referring the reader to the article "Zurechnung," where the treatment of "Verantwortlichkeit" is based on philosophers and sociologists of the late nineteenth and the twentieth centuries.

7. Charles du Fresne Ducange, *Glossarium Mediae et Infimae Latinitatis* (Niort, 1833–1887), s.v., "Responsabilis."

8. Cf. L. Gernet, *Recherches sur le développement de la Pensée Juridique et Morale en Grèce* (Etude Sémantique) (Paris, 1917), Troisième Partie, Chapitre Premier "Comment la no-

In the history of philosophic discussions the appearance of the new term "responsibility" passed almost unnoticed; at best it was a new instrument for use in current and ancient controversies, and philosophers divided between those who presented it as the essential foundation of all moral distinctions and those who disposed of it as vacuous and useless. Far from clarifying the concept, the philosophical analysis of responsibility became a dispute among philosophers for and against the concept itself, and the importance attributed (or denied) to responsibility as a fundamental term in morals made explicit an opposition which had grown up in the analysis of the imputation of actions to agents and of the accountability of acts and agents in applying penalty or punishment.

Greek philosophers analyzed both causality (or imputation) and punishment (or accountability) as applied to actions. The two problems are closely related, but in the various statements of their interrelations, the meanings of the related terms and the scope of their applications vary. At one extreme, human "actions" include whatever a man does, and they are distinguished into voluntary, involuntary and nonvoluntary; at the other extreme, "actions" are limited to the voluntary. The problem of imputation turns on the question whether or not the causality of human actions is essentially the same as the causality of physical motions. Whereas the modern formulation of the problem begins with a conception of cause derived from the natural sciences and raises questions concerning the causality of moral agents, the Greek word for cause, αἰτία (like the Latin word *causa*), began as a legal term and was then extended to include natural motions. Socrates' definition of virtue as knowledge and his constant analogy of the virtues and the arts provided Plato with the criteria for identifying and evaluating hu-

---

tion de responsabilité se transforme. Etude du mot ἁμαρτάνειν," pp. 305–348. In this *Platon: Lois, Livre IX* (Paris, 1917), M. Gernet sets forth Plato's treatment of the relation between penal law and moral philosophy. Contrasting the system of religion to the system of law, he finds tabu the dominant concept of the former and responsibility at the center of the latter. See p. 11: "La notion de droit, c'est ici celle d'organisation de justice; et l'idée qui est au centre du droit pénal, c'est celle de responsabilité. Toute proche du 'peuple' qu'elle s'associe du plus près qu'il se peut, la juridiction criminelle n'en est pas moins spécialement instituée. Et elle a son esprit à elle: ce n'est plus un bouc émissaire qu'elle atteint, c'est un délinquant qu'elle examine. Il y a des fautes qui pour elle ne requièrent pas expiation; il y a des délits qui pour elle entraînent des pénalités variables, selon la gravité objective d'un acte et selon la part de causalité attribuable à un agent."

man actions. Aristotle set up literal distinctions between four varieties
of causation: nature and intelligence are contrasted as essential causes
to chance and fortune, which are accidental causes.[9] In either analysis,
moral causation or imputation delimits voluntary actions, which are
susceptible of deliberation and choice: they are subject to praise and
blame, reward and punishment, but these external recognitions and instituted consequences are not therefore moral criteria. The opposed
theories hold that opinion or might makes right, and therefore that the
causality operative in the formation of opinions or in the advancement
of private interests provides the only available moral criteria.

The problem of accountability turns on the interpretation of the operation of the punishments, penalties, and indemnities imposed by a
community to rectify or prevent injuries arising from crime, misde-
meanor, breach of contract, or negligence. Plato and Aristotle treat it
as part of the problem of justice: the concept of justice provides Plato
with grounds on which to argue that it is better to suffer than to do
injustice and that it is better to undergo than to escape punishment for
injustice; Aristotle's conviction that justice varies under different constitutions leads him to investigate institutions by which injustice is rec-
tified. In both analyses justice has a moral application, in which justice
and injustice are imputable to actions and men, as well as a social and
political application, in which men are held accountable for injustices.
These differences are made clearly in the distinctions of Aristotle. In
political applications there are as many varieties of justice as there are
constitutions. In moral applications to actions, "justice" is an ambiguous term: it means the "lawful," and then it is complete virtue in relation to our neighbor, and it means the "fair," and then it is a particular
virtue which takes two forms: distributive justice, which operates by
imputation through honors, money, and other rewards, and rectificatory or commutative justice, which judges accountability for voluntary
and involuntary damages and injuries. There is therefore a scale of
wrong-doing in accountability for injuries: (1) when the injury occurs
contrary to reasonable expectation, it is a misadventure; (2) when it is
not contrary to reasonable expectation, but results from external accident rather than a vice of the agent, it is a mistake; (3) when the agent
acts with knowledge, but not after deliberation, as when he acts in
anger, it is an act of injustice; (4) when he acts from choice he is an

9. Aristotle, *Physics, ii*, 6, 197a36–198a13.

unjust and a vicious man. But these distinctions depend on recognizing natural as well as legal justice. The opposed theories hold that the state is a contract or a power structure and therefore that justice is an agreement designed to secure the interests of all or an imposition employed to secure the interests of the stronger. Moral criteria are based on the application of these sanctions to the actions of men.

For the ancient Greek philosophers, "justice" was the fundamental term which related ethics to politics. If there are independent marks of justice, which can be recognized by wisdom or which are universal and natural, imputation and accountability function as subordinate terms applied according to the criteria of justice: imputation (or cause) delimits the scope of actions subject to moral and political approval or disapproval, and accountability (or guilt) delimits the scope of actions subject to legal penalty. If, on the other hand, justice is conventional rather than natural, it must be defined variously and arbitrarily by opinion, contract, and power: the external marks of imputation (praise and blame, honor and disgrace) and the negative controls of accountability (punishments and sanctions) supply the place of positive criteria and internal motives.

The statement of these distinctions and oppositions is profoundly altered when it is made in terms of "duty" rather than "justice." If justice is conceived as a virtue in the individual and an order in the state, what one "ought" to do, and therefore the relation of morals and politics, is determined by the interplay of virtues and institutions. Zeno the Stoic was the first to reverse this analysis and to use duty, τὸ καθῆκον, instead of justice, to explain both virtues and laws and their interrelations. The concept of "duty" was easily read back into the distinctions of earlier philosophers, since they did use verbs meaning "ought" and participles meaning "fitting" and "due" (including τὰ καθήκοντα), much as "responsibility" is found in the theories of philosophers who did not use the term because they did employ the concepts of causality of actions and blame for actions. Duty, as it was first conceived by the Stoics, was a universal term applicable to plants, to animals, and to the cosmos (since it too is a living creature) as well as to human conduct. Zeno defined it in terms of accountability and causal imputation: duty signifies "that for which, when done, a reasonable defence can be adduced,"[10] and the causal basis of duty is found in the harmony discern-

10. Diogenes Laertius VII, 107.

ible in all living creatures. In the course of subsequent discussion, however, duty is sometimes limited to human actions, and then accountability is made to depend on the operation of political institutions rather than on the rationality of nature and imputation to depend on choice and deliberation rather than the harmony of natural processes. At one extreme, the Stoics established a hierarchy of duties, differentiating the useful from the good-in-itself, the *utilia* from the *honesta*, while at the other extreme the Epicureans reduced good to pleasure and justice to expediency.[11] Cicero was convinced that the language of duties and natural law could be used to express truths on which the various schools of philosophy were in accord (except those, who, like the Epicureans, were demonstrably in error), and it entered into the formulation of the principles of Roman Law. The formula that justice is rendering every man his due, which Polemarchus was unable to defend against the criticisms of Socrates in Plato's *Republic*, reappears in the definition of justice in Justinian's *Institutes*.

The language of duties and natural law was adapted to Christian doctrine by Ambrose and Augustine. Accountability found a universal basis in divine law, old and new, and imputation a natural basis in original sin. But within the Christian framework the old distinctions reappeared, not only in theological problems of the relation of free will to foreknowledge and of human virtue to supernatural grace, but also in the problems of the relation of divine law to civil and moral law and of good and evil to praise and blame. The term *imputation* came into use in treating the latter problems. Cicero had used the verb *imputare*, but the adjective *imputativus* and the noun *imputatio* made their first appearance in Christian apologetics and Roman Law. "Imputation" is sometimes used in a strict sense limited to the ascription of an act to an agent; it is sometimes used in a broad sense to include questions of accountability or punishment as well as questions of causality. Thomas Aquinas, after analysing goodness and badness in actions, turns to their "consequences," laudability and blameability, merit and demerit. Good actions are laudable and bad actions are blameable because of imputation: "evil" is a more inclusive term than "sin," and "sin" is more inclusive than "blameable": "an act is said to be blameable because it is imputed to its agent, since praise or blame is nothing else than imputation

---

11. Epicurus, in Diogenes Laertius, X, 150: "Natural justice is a symbol of expediency, to prevent one man from harming or being harmed by another."

to some one of the goodness or badness of his act."[12] On the other hand, good or evil acts have merit or demerit only in relation to the retribution imposed according to justice on acts helpful or harmful to others.[13] Duns Scotus likewise makes laudability and blameability, merit and demerit, depend on a prior analysis of goodness and badness of acts, but he extends the term "imputation" to include both pairs of terms. Imputation has two respects: one relative to the power and dominion of the agent, according to which a good act is laudable and a bad act is blameable; the other relative to something corresponding to the act according to justice, by which a good act is rewardable and a bad act is punishable.[14]

Political and social changes and the advancement of science led, in the seventeenth century, to a widespread and diversified effort to establish a science of morals and of law, or a science of human nature and the state, on the analogy of the natural sciences. The language of natural law and of duties provided a common vocabulary but not a common philosophy in these moral and political inquiries. The major alternatives turned on a choice between accountability and imputation. If, on the one hand, the science of human nature and morals is based on the assumption that human actions are determined by a causality or necessity similar to that which determines physical change, no special moral cause or imputation is needed, and moral good and evil are defined by reward and punishment and identified by praise and blame. If, on the other hand, the science of law and practical reason is based on the assumption that the causality of human actions is free (as distinguished from physical necessity), since action depends on will and intellect, the basis of law and duty is found in human action, and the external accountability imposed by power or judged by pragmatic utility must be judged by an internal law recognized by conscience and reason.

Hobbes, Locke, and Hume, among others, worked out variants of the first hypothesis. For all three, liberty means only the power of acting or not acting according to the determinations of the will, and morality is based on necessity. According to Hobbes, every man calls what pleases him good and what displeases him evil; since men differ in constitution they differ also concerning the distinction of good and evil, and therefore justice and injustice, mine and thine, right and wrong,

12. *Summa Theologica,* Ia, IIae, quaest. xxi, art. 2 resp.
13. *Ibid.,* art. 3 resp.
14. *Quodlibeta,* quaest. 18, nn. 9–11.

good and evil are all consequent on the establishment of the state and the enforcement of law. According to Locke, things are called good which are apt to cause or to increase pleasure, and evil, which are apt to cause or increase pain; but Locke does not reduce all law to civil law: men judge whether their actions are sins or duties according to divine law, whether they are criminal or innocent according to civil law, and whether they are virtues or vices according to the law of opinion or reputation; virtue is everywhere that which is thought praiseworthy and the enforcement of the law of virtue and vice is commendation and discredit. Morality is the relation of actions to the rules established by the three laws, and we are frequently misled when the same word is applied to the action and to the rule. Hume's arguments to show that morality depends on necessity are based on accountability and imputation: (1) A person is not answerable or the proper object of punishment even for actions which are blameworthy and contrary to all the rules of morality and religion, unless they proceed from some cause in his character and disposition,[15] and (2) human actions which are not free, in the sense defined, are not susceptible of any moral qualities nor can they be objects of either approbation or dislike. The problem of morals is to analyze "merit", and the experimental method Hume employs is based on language and the existence in all languages of words signifying praise and blame; the function of reason is to discover what is common in the estimable qualities and what is common in the blameable. All three moralists account for human actions by causes that require no separation of necessity from imputation, and they all derive their normative distinctions from external devices of accountability— from the enforcement of civil and criminal law; from the penalties of the law of God, the law of politic societies, and the law of fashion or private censure; or from the universal agreement among men discovered in their language of praise and blame.

Pufendorf, Wolff, and Kant, among others, elaborated variants of the second hypothesis. For all three, morality is based on free action, and a universal science of the practical depends on distinguishing freedom from necessity, and persons from things, by examining the nature of reason and will. Pufendorf's ambition was to establish a demonstra-

15. Hume, *An Enquiry concerning Human Understanding,* Sect. VIII, Part II, 76. This argument is repeated with little change from the *Treatise of Human Nature* (Bk. II, Part III, Sect. 2), but in the earlier form the word "responsible" is used instead of the word "answerable."

tive science of law, despite common opinion and the authority of Aristotle that such a science is impossible. He argued that moral or human action can be treated as a positive entity (*ens positivum*) distinct from physical entities, consisting of a material element (physical motion), a fundamental element (deliberative reason, *ratio proaeretica,* by which that physical motion is understood as produced by a decision of the will), and a formal element (imputation). "The formal element of a moral action consists in the imputation, or rather in the imputativity, by which the effect of a voluntary action can be imputed to the agent, whether the agent himself has produced the effect physically or has had it produced by other."[16] The first of the two books of the *Elements of Universal Jurisprudence* is devoted to the exposition of twenty-one definitions bearing on properties of moral action, the second book to two axioms (based on reason alone) and five observations (which take account of experience as well). Axiom I lays down the conditions of imputation, Axiom II the operation of authority on obligations.[17]

Pufendorf had begun with a distinction of three sources of the knowledge of duty: reason (or natural law), civil law, and divine law; his science of law made use of the method of reason, and provided arguments for concluding that the three are in harmony. Christian Wolff sought rather to establish by use of the scientific method a universal practical philosophy. His analysis of action led him to differentiate between natural and necessary actions of body and soul and free actions which are not determined by the essence and nature of the body and the soul, but depend on the freedom of the soul. The differentiation of goodness and badness of free actions is by means of their ends: if free actions are determined by the same final causes as natural actions they are good, if by different final causes they are bad;[18] actions which are essentially good are directed to the happiness or perfection of man. Virtue is the habit of directing one's actions in conformity to natural law; vice is the habit of acting contrary to the prescriptions of natural

16. S. Pufendorf, *Elementorum Jurisprudentiae Universalis Libri Duo,* Bk. I, Def. I, par. 4 (Cantabrigiae, 1672), p. 3.

17. Cf. Pufendorf, *De Officio Hominis et Civis, juxta Legem Naturalem,* Bk. I, Ch. I, par. 17–27 (Cantabrigiae, 1682), pp. 8–12; and *De Jure Naturae et Gentium* (Amstelodami, 1688), Bk. I, Ch. V, "De Actionibus moralibus in Genere, deque earumdem ad Agentem Pertinentia, seu ad Imputationem Aptitudine," pp. 45–59, and Ch. 9 "De Actionum Moralium Imputatione," pp. 93–98.

18. C. Wolfius, *Philosophia Practica Universalis, Methodo Scientifica Pertracta* Pt. I, Ch. I, par. 12 and 55 (2nd ed. Halae Magdeburgicae, 1744), Vol. I, pp. 8 and 48.

law; and sin is action contrary to natural and divine law. The causes of free actions are free causes and the imputation of action is "the judgment, by which the agent is declared the free cause of that which follows from his action, good and evil, for himself and others."[19] Imputation may be in accordance with natural law, or positive law and may apply to vice, fault (*culpa*), or crime (*dolus*).[20] Kant, finally, sought to establish a metaphysics of morals, by an analysis of will as practical reason, in which he distinguished the moral laws of freedom from the necessary laws of nature. Moral laws are juridical when they refer only to external actions; they are ethical when they are themselves the determining principles of action. Imputation distinguishes a person from a thing, since a person is a subject who is capable of having his actions imputed to him, while a thing is incapable of being the subject of imputation.[21] "Imputation (*Zurechnung, imputatio*), in the moral sense, is the judgment by which any one is said to be the free cause (*Urheber, causa libera*) of an action which is then regarded as his moral deed (*Tat, factum,*) and is subject to law."[22] Duty is the constraint of the free elective will by law. Since man is free, the notion of duty is self-constraint, and the autonomy of the will is the supreme principle of morality. All three moralists account for human action by imputation to a free cause, and their normative distinctions depend on the nature of free action rather than on external devices of accountability or punishment—on the nature of the action itself, on the natural end to which it is directed, or on the nature of will or practical reason.

From the beginning, these efforts to establish a science of morals were involved in a controversy concerning freedom and necessity. Since

19. *Ibid.*, Ch. VI, par. 527, p. 394.

20. *Ibid.*, Ch. VI, "De Imputatione morali, Dolo et Culpa," pp. 394–592.

21. Kant, *Die Metaphysik der Sitten*, "Einleitung der Metaphysik der Sitten." IV. Vorbegriffe zur Metaphysik der Sitten (*Philosophia practica universalis*) (*Immanuel Kants Werke*, ed. E. Cassirer [Berlin, 1922]), vol. VII, p. 25.

22. *Ibid.*, p. 28. The basic problem of *Die Religion innerhalb der Grenzen der bloßen Vernunft*, whether man is by nature morally good or morally evil, depends on a preliminary distinction between nature and freedom, that is, on imputation; cf. *Werke*, Vol. VI, p. 159 and *passim*. For Kant's reaction to imputation as conceived by Wolff and Baumgarten, cf. *Eine Vorlesung Kants über Ethik*, ed. Paul Menzer (Berlin, 1924), in the first part, "Philosophia Practica Universalis una cum Ethica," the section "De Imputatione" and the following sections, pp. 69–85. Throughout Kant uses the term imputation, "Zurechnung," not responsibility, "Verantwortlichkeit," although he occasionally uses the verb "verantworten" as well as the verb "zuschreiben"; cf. *Grundlegung zur Metaphysik der Sitten*, *Werke*, vol. IV, p. 318.

the fundamental conception of law—natural, moral, and civil—was applied to human action, they became involved also in a controversy concerning whether the basis of moral distinctions was found in judgments or sentiments. At the end of the eighteenth century, the fundamental question had shifted from the nature and operation of law to the analysis of human nature and understanding. Hume remarked that the discussion of "the general foundaton of morals, whether they be derived from Reason or from Sentiment," was "a controversy started of late," but worth examination.[23] Reid elaborated the remark: "Mr. Hume observes very justly, that this is a controversy *started of late*. Before the modern system of Ideas and Impressions was introduced, nothing would have been more absurd than to say, that when I condemn a man for what he has done, I pass no judgment at all about the man, but only express some uneasy feeling in myself."[24]

The paradoxes to which Reid calls attention follow as consequences from one of the interpretations of accountability and imputation: if men's actions are necessary, it follows that we do not desire a thing because it is good, but we call it good because we desire it; moral criteria must then be found either in accountability established by negative prescriptions and punishments of civil law, as Hobbes argued, or in the grounds of imputation of praise and blame. Negative or external marks are criticized as relativistic even when they are transformed into universal and internal criteria in a moral science which is made certain or experimental by the analysis of ideas. But the opposed alternative is involved in like paradoxes: if men's actions are free, it follows that the restrictions of law must enter into the definition of free actions, human perfection, or free will. Kant pointed out, from the vantage point of the Copernican Revolution instituted in his critical examination of reason, understanding, and imagination, that external principles or the heteronomy of the will cannot provide moral principles. Not only does this mean that empirical principles—happiness or moral feeling—provide no principles for good conduct, but also that rational principles based on heteronomy, such as Wolff's ontological concept of perfection, are empty, indefinite, and consequently useless for finding in the immeasurable field of possible reality the greatest possible sum which is suitable to us.[25] The autonomy of the will and the categorical imper-

23. *An Enquiry concerning the Principles of Morals,* Section I, 134.
24. *Essays on the Active Powers of Man,* Essay V, Ch. VII, p. 670.
25. Kant, *Foundations of the Metaphysics of Morals,* Sect. II "Classification of All Pos-

ative have unfortunately to be subjected to the same criticism of vacuity and indeterminateness.

The concept of "responsibility" was first used in this situation of philosophic controversy with a pertinence and significance which are lost if the situation is ignored. Mill used the concept in an effort to break away from both controversies, the endless metaphysical disputes concerning freedom and necessity, concerning intentions, motives, and consequences, and the endless efforts to find the criteria of morals and politics in sentiment or reason, approbation or duty. He argued in his notes to his father's *Analysis of the Phenomena of the Human Mind,* that the sentiments of moral approbation and disapprobation are not a sufficient basis for morality, precisely because they cannot account for the feeling of duty or obligation, which is a very different state of mind from the mere liking for the action and the good will to the agent accounted for by the association theory.

"I have examined this question in the concluding chapter of a short treatise entitled 'Utilitarianism.' The subject of the chapter is 'the connexion between Justice and Utility.' I have there endeavoured to shew what the association is, which exists in the case of what we regard as duty, but does not exist in the case of what we merely regard as useful, and which gives to the feeling in the former case the strength, the gravity, and pungency, which in the other case it has not.

"I believe that the element in the association which gives this distinguishing character to the feeling and which constitutes the difference in the antecedents in the two cases, is the idea of Punishment. I mean the association with punishment, not the expectation of it."[26]

He uses the same argument against the position of Reid, Mansel, and Hamilton that accountability is evidence of moral liberty. Responsibility means punishment—not the expectation of actual punishment to be inflicted upon us by our fellow-creatures or by a Supreme Power, but a consciousness that we shall deserve that infliction.

"In discussing it, there is no need to postulate any theory respecting the nature or criterion of moral distinctions. It matters not, for this purpose, whether the right and wrong of actions depends on the consequences they tend to produce, or on an inherent quality of the actions

---

sible Principles of Morality following from the Assumed Principle of Heteronomy," and *Critique of Practical Reason* Pt. I, Bk. I, Ch. I, par. 8, Theorem IV, Remark II.

26. James Mill, *Analysis of the Phenomena of the Human Mind,* ed. by A. Bain, A. Findlater, and G. Grote (London, 1869), vol. II, p. 325.

themselves. It is indifferent whether we are utilitarians or anti-utilitarians; whether our ethics rest on intuition or experience. It is sufficient if we believe that there is a difference between right and wrong, and a natural reason for preferring the former; that people in general, unless they expect personal benefit from a wrong, naturally and usually prefer what they think to be right: whether because we are all dependent for what makes existence tolerable, upon the right conduct of other people, while their wrong conduct is a standing menace to our security, or for some more mystical and transcendental reason. Whatever be the cause, we are entitled to assume the fact; and its consequence is, that whoever cultivates a disposition to wrong, places his mind out of sympathy with the rest of his fellow-creatures, and if they are aware of his disposition, becomes a natural object of their active dislike. He not only forfeits the pleasure of their good will, but the benefit of their good offices, except when compassion for the human being is stronger than distaste towards the wrong-doer; but he also renders himself liable to whatever they may think it necessary to do in order to protect themselves against him; which may probably include punishment, as such, and will certainly involve much that is equivalent in its operation on himself. In this way he is certain to be made accountable, at least to his fellow-creatures, through the normal action of their natural sentiments. And it is well worth consideration, whether the practical expectation of being thus called to account, has not a great deal to do with the internal feeling of being accountable; a feeling assuredly, which is seldom found existing in any strength in the absence of that practical expectation."[27]

Lévy-Bruhl used the concept of responsibility to differentiate two notions that seemed to him to have been confused previously: the notion of legal responsibility which is purely objective and adapted to concrete reality (which was Mill's exclusive concern) and the notion of moral responsibility which is purely subjective and empty of concrete content. The idea of justice will, as a result of this distinction, be clarified without weakening either the energy of social repression or the sentiment of moral obligation.

The philosophic controversies did not cease with the introduction of the term "responsibility." Mill gave it a meaning based on the tradition of accountability—responsibility is punishment—but generalized

27. John Stuart Mill, *An Examination of Sir William Hamilton's Philosophy*, Ch. XXVI (New York, 1884), vol. II, pp. 288–289.

beyond the expectation of actual punishment. Lévy-Bruhl gave it a meaning based on the tradition of imputability—responsibility is implied in the conception of a reasonable free being—but generalized beyond reference to a kingdom of ends or a noumenal world. Each of these theories can be criticized and refuted on grounds supplied by the other, and philosophers have continued the controversies about motive and intention and the relation of freedom and necessity, about cognitive and emotive grounds of ethics and the relation of right and good. Yet both Mill and Lévy-Bruhl indicated a region of practical problems opened up by the concept of responsibility and unaffected by doctrinaire philosophic differences: Mill by suggesting that the operation of responsibility as punishment uncovers, but does not create, the distinction between right and wrong; Lévy-Bruhl by showing that responsibility as subjective sense of freedom and rationality originated in society and developed with the evolution of society. If philosophers began with the fact of responsibility in its social context, they might explore and guide its extensions and applications without either deserting basic principles or negating the practical significance of principles by making the choice of principles the center of controversy. Bradley summarized the problems of philosophic speculation concerning the practical in the three sardonic morals with which his essay on the vulgar notion of responsibility closes: the first two have been amply illustrated, both the vulgar moral, that since philosophy looks away from the facts of our unenlightened beliefs and vulgar moralities, we should leave these philosophers to themselves, and the philosophic moral, that since the vulgar are after all vulgar, philosophers should esteem themselves according as their creed is different and higher; but the third, which depends on a philosophy which *thinks* what the vulgar *believe,* is no more fashionable among philosophers today than it was eighty years ago, in spite of the development, in the sphere of practical action, of implications associated with the idea of responsibility.

If the term "responsibility" and the concepts by which it was defined did little to alter the lines of philosophic discussion and controversy, the appearance of the term and the circumstances in which its meanings were elaborated raise philosophic problems which not only present a theoretic interest but also force themselves on the attention of practical men even when they are neglected by professional philosophers. The formation and use of an abstract noun marks an effort to define forces which have become operative for the first time or whose operation has, in recent situations or theories, been advanced or thwarted. The word "responsibility" appeared in English and French in the year 1787. It was not only used first to apply to the operation of political institutions in the context of the American and French revolutions, but it continued in use during the nineteenth century when constitutional government was vastly extended, in scope of operation and in spread among nations, as a result of contacts of cultures and peoples. Since 1787 the idea of responsible government has developed and its practice has enlarged; the ten years since the close of the second World War have provided conditions for the practical realization of self-determination and self-government for an enormous number of the peoples of the world who had not previously enjoyed those rights. The period since 1787 has witnessed a vast increase in our knowledge of the values of divergent patterns of cultures and of the history of divergent cultural traditions; the last ten years have brought the peoples of the world into contacts in which the claims of divergent value systems must be respected. The moral significance of responsibility can be clarified only be examining its elaboration and operation in the content of these political and social changes.

In a significant sense, the idea of *political* responsibility takes precedence in the evolution of the idea of responsibility. The idea of responsible government as developed in the British constitution or of a republic as embodied in the constitutions of France and the United States had originally two ingredients: a government or a republic is responsible (1) if it operates within a framework of law in which official action and control are reasonably predictable, and (2) if its government reflects the attitude of its people through institutions which provide for the regular election of personnel and regular review of policy. These two aspects of the idea of responsibility are recognizable extensions of the older conceptions of accountability under the rule of law and the imputability of the actions of elected officials with limited terms of office. The full extension of the second notion was not achieved in Great Britain, France, and the United States until limitations on suffrage were removed in the twentieth century. The resistance to universal suffrage was always on the ground of some form of the argument that citizenship should be limited to those who could exhibit some sign of responsibility, such as property qualification or education. The extension of suffrage was not merely the result of political pressure made possible by changed economic conditions; it also reflected a change in the idea of political responsibility.

The original elements of the idea of responsibility depended on a reciprocal relation of individual and state, but they were negative and external: a man is responsible under law if he is accountable for the consequences of his action, and he can be responsible only if the law is not subject to arbitrary change or enforcement; officials are responsible to rulers or to citizens, and a citizen is responsible if he possesses the political means of influencing the policies of government. However, since laws may be unjust and the demands of a constituency may be perverse, these negative and external determinations would have been incomplete if they had not been supplemented by two positive and normative elements in the development of the concept of responsibility. The first was a reformulation of the conviction that in matters of the common good the people are better judges than an uncontrolled ruler or élite. The earlier formulation of this convicton tended to be restrictive: representative government or democracy will work only if the people is ready for it, that is, responsible. The reformulation inverts the relation: responsible government depends on a responsible people but a people acquires responsibility only by exercising it. The second normative element has emerged, with the development of responsibility as freedom, as a concept and as a possibility in a political community: the justice and moral sense of community is better advanced by free choice of moral criteria rather than by imposition and prescriptions, precisely because the decision is more likely to be rational and truth is more likely to be advanced by free competition among ideas than by authoritative prior decision concerning the true. These positive and normative functions—by which values are advanced by the free pursuit of values and truth is advanced by the free exploration of ideas—supplement and complete the original negative and external operations of punishment and approval, and the conception of responsibility which has slowly emerged from the process embodies four aspects—accountability, imputability, freedom, and rationality.

The idea of political responsibility, however, influenced and was influenced by the development of the concept of *cultural* responsibility. Political responsibility is a relation of citizen and political community; but the citizen is a member of many cultural communities—determined by religion, education, taste, ethnical derivation, economic situation, occupation, and many other factors—and the political responsibilities of nations reflect and protect the cultural values of societies. Cultural or social responsibility provides the connection by which political and moral responsibility influence each other. The modern development of new self-governing nations has been in part a result of cultural demands and sensitivity to those demands. A community is responsible to other communities as well as to its members. Both forms of responsibility are advanced by political institutions. A community is responsible to other communities when it recognizes that it is accountable (that is, when it fulfills engagements it has undertaken and makes reparations for injuries it has caused) and when it acknowledges imputability for actions (that is, when questions of accountability can be treated in negotiation and discussion leading to agreement). Responsibility in these two senses functions in a framework of institutions, legal and political, national and international. But the viability of these institutions depends on two additional senses of responsibility which transcend institutions. A responsible community reflects a tradition of responsibility based on the character of the community or nation and responsive to the requirements of common values and of the common good. Negotiations among nations, when it departs from the calculation of balances of power, depends on the possibility of confident expectation of action determined by an enduring attitude and character and on respect for such attitudes and for the values that form such characters. Responsibility, finally, reflects and depends on a common rationality and on common values revealed in discussion and sought in action.

The concept of responsibility relates actions to agents by a causal tie and applies a judgment of value to both. It involves assumptions, therefore, about the agent and about the social context in which he acts. The agent may be an individual or a group acting in the context of a society or a political state, or an individual, group, or community acting in the looser association of free individuals or independent communities or states whose actions affect each other. In either situation, responsibility is a reflexive relation: the responsibility of the individual and the responsibility of the community of which he is a member are interdependent, and independent communities assume responsibilities with respect to each other which constitute a kind of inclusive community. A society or a nation develops responsibility externally in its relations to other corporate bodies and internally in the structure of its institutions and of the actions of the individuals who compose it.

The evolution of the concept of responsibility depends on a like evolution of the concepts of freedom and understanding. The elements from which the concept of responsibility developed, accountability and imputation, are both external limits put on the freedom of action. Accountability is an external and negative restraint on action imposed by law and punishment; imputation is an external constraint, positive as well as negative, imposed by public opinion in approbations constraining to performance of action of a given kind and in disapprobations constraining to abstention from action. Accountability becomes internal when it depends on the moral judgment of the individual rather than on the prohibition of law, and it becomes a manifestation rather than a restraint of freedom in the pursuit of recognized values. This transition is doubtless implicit in the answer Xenocrates is said to have made when asked what his disciples learned: "To do of their own free will what they would be compelled to do by the laws."[28] Imputability becomes an internal rather than an external judgment of causes when the agent understands the consequences of his own actions and when his choices and actions are determined by that understanding rather than by social approbations or disapprobations.

"Understanding" and the other words by which rational choice is expressed undergo like shifts of meaning. "Understanding" has a negative and external meaning limited to the recognition of prescriptions and conventions entailing penalties and sanctions when it is applied to "understanding the law" or to "coming to an understanding" in a contract or an agreement. It means simply that the citizen or the party to the contract or treaty may be presumed to know what penalties will be imposed on certain actions and on failure to perform other actions. "Understanding" has an external meaning, positive as well as negative, when it is applied to "understanding what is to one's own interest" and "what is to the interest of others." It means recognition of the mores of a community, including the honors and rewards accorded actions socially esteemed and the disgrace and disadvantages attached to actions socially disapproved. It may also mean sympathetic "understanding" of the problems, needs, and aspirations of others. But the understanding of interests may be transformed into an understanding of the common good and of common values. Understanding in this sense may operate

---

28. Cicero, *De re publica,* i. 2. 3: "ut id sua sponte facere, quod cogerentur facere legibus."

to transform the civil and criminal laws which determine accountability and to shift the emphasis in conventions and agreements from the calculation of interests to mutual understanding of values, including those which also have artistic, cultural, religious, and philosophical expressions. The understanding of social pressures and preferences, finally, may be transformed into an understanding which undercuts what is at the time preferred and what is thought to endanger one's interests by examining arguments, data, assumptions, and conclusions. Understanding in this sense is the comprehension of beliefs and of the reasons for holding them. The external operations of coming to an understanding and of understanding each other find internally acceptable criteria in the operations of understanding common values and of understanding common problems.

The idea of *moral* responsibility originated and developed in the context of the evolution of political and cultural responsibility. There was no moral responsibility until there were communities in which men were held accountable for their actions and in which actions were imputed to individual men. There were no moral individuals prior to the development and recognition of moral responsibility. Moral ideas were first formed within religious and political institutions. The great systems of moral theory reflect this origin in the variety of frameworks they constructed in the morals of prescription, maxim, and law, in the morals of consequence, utility, and power, and in the morals of virtue, habit, and rational choice. Accountability and imputation provide the mark by which the individual agent is identified in ethical systems. Men could be accountable under civil or divine law, as they had not been in primitive communities, for error, injury, and sin. Good as well as evil actions might be imputed to them in a community in which they were held accountable.

With the development of responsible representative governments and with increasing awareness of other cultures and value systems, "accountability" and "imputation" took on enlarged meanings. The concept of "responsibility" could be used, in the absence of despotic government or authoritative prescriptions, to provide criteria of value as well as to determine the incidence of punishment and of approval and disapproval. The exercise of responsibility in the sense of accountability and imputability in this enlarged political and cultural context constitutes a means of developing the moral character which is imputed to the individual and which is at once a sensitivity to moral issues in the agent and an explanation of his decisions and choices in the minds of others. This interplay between the operation of political and cultural institutions and the establishment of criteria and norms of decision should work a profound change in the structure of moral assumptions and theories. In the light of that interplay and of that history the analysis of moral action can proceed both in terms of the consequences of the free exercise of choice and deliberation and in terms of the universal imperatives of reason and will without commitment to either theory or to dogmatic fixities of prescription, ends, or customs. The responsibility exercised in such choices relative to values, finally, profoundly alters the relation of reason and knowledge to responsibility. Responsibility has assumed a reflexive relation to truth as well as to values; the ideal of a science of morals conceived in the seventeenth and pursued in the eighteenth century must now be sought in a science of responsibility which can be adapted to different views of morality and provide the basis for the continued testing of ideas in the further advancement of knowledge. The basic elements of responsibility are accountability and imputation, but the moral problem of responsibility is to find the means so to use them in discussion and common action as to increase the probability that responsible action will develop moral character and rational perceptiveness.

Responsibility, as accountability and imputation, marks off two inescapable problems in a world in which all peoples aspire effectively to independence and self-government and in which the needs and aspirations, the judgments and values of any people affect the situation, the attitudes, and the actions of others and eventually of all. The basic problem of accountability in the development by a world community is the transformation and extension of the institutions by which accountability operates in small communities and in national states to adapt them to the world community and the interrelations of nations. The basic problem of imputation is to insure that the external and material changes in the communities and nations of the world operate to enrich the lives of men and to render newly accessible values secure rather than to erect new threats to freedoms and impediments to the use of new opportunities for the satisfaction of needs and the cultivation of values. The enlarged concept of responsibility provides an essential means for the treatment of these problems in theory and in practice. It provides, so far as theory is concerned, a way to discuss moral problems of individual action, political problems of common action, and cultural problems of mutual understanding, without commitment to a single philosophy or to the expression of values traditional in a single culture, and thereby to diversify and deepen the values of men by exploring possible common bases and interrelation of philosophical assumptions and cultural traditions. It provides, so far as practice is concerned, a way to appreciate the history of the development and the present circumstances of responsibility as it emerges from application to material needs and individual interests to applications which advance the common good and build on understanding.

These problems of accountability and imputation, moreover, even in the negative and external forms in which they are forced on our attention, entail the larger and more fundamental problems of responsibility operating positively and internally as freedom and rationality in choice and decision. They are problems which enter into the determination of the policies of nations and the attitudes of men so directly that a clear statement of them might contribute to transforming oppositions and tensions into understandable and reconcilable formulations of more fundamental issues. They are problems which have their origin in the development of the concept of responsibility, since the resolution of problems which were faced at one stage of social development has created new problems whose complexities exceed the expectations and the analyses which seemed to be justified in the earlier stage. Accountability and imputation, in their external forms, operate through penalties and rewards in property and honors. One of the consequences of the development of responsibility as an internal source of criteria has been an inversion of these instrumentalities of wealth and reputation in an increased responsiveness to the needs and to the opinions of men. On the other hand, the warnings of ancient moralists concerning the dangers of making wealth, pleasure, and honors the ends of life find their echoes today in criticisms of the materialism and the conformism of our ways of life. It was a reasonable expectation that if man's material problems were solved, and if his uncertainties and laborious occupations were reduced, music, poetry, and contemplation (in Hume's words) might form his sole business, and conversation, mirth, and friendship his sole amusement. We have improved the instrumentalities for solving material problems without making corresponding advances in increasing sensibilities or lessening tensions: can the analysis of responsibility provide a new basis for a hierarchy of values based on material goods but not dominated by them? It was a reasonable expectation, similarly, that responsibility and respect for the beliefs and opinions of others would provide a basis for freedom and the development of the individual. Our progress in extending the participation of all men in political and social decisions, and in developing social and institutional structures in which the individual might express himself, has had the contrary effect of binding him by still more intrusive restrictions on thought and action: can the analysis of responsibility provide a means by which the moral character of the individual may be strengthened to withstand the influence of approval and disapproval and in so doing give meaning and significance to that influence?

The modern forms of the problems of accountability and imputation are reflexive: we could go far to free man from the pressure of material needs, but we have succeeded in binding him to the pursuit of material ends; we could go far to free men to realize themselves as individuals, but we have succeeded in building new despotisms of political suppression and submission to public opinion. These problems are closely related to two further problems of criteria implicit in the uses of responsibility. Both are treated as dilemmas. The dilemma of tradition and innovation, of conservation and revolution, grows out of the need for a hierarchy of values, which is expressed in antagonistic terms derived from the foundations to be preserved and from the ends to be achieved: can the analysis of responsibility increase the responsiveness to values that would substitute a dynamic process for this stultifying choice between alternatives set in artificial opposition? The dilemma of right and good, of custom and duty, grows out of the need for criteria of values, which is expressed in antagonistic terms borrowed from the authority which they should possess and the rationality which they should embody: can the analysis of responsibility increase the reliance on reason that would re-establish the relation between actual preferences and ideal values? The concept of responsibility leads away from the ancient logomachies of freedom versus necessity and of consequences and utilities versus intentions and intuitions to such problems as these found in the circumstances and history in which the concept itself was formed.

4

Communication, Truth, and Society

Communication

The task of diagnosing the problems of one's own time involves the same difficulties as characterizing past ages. The historian, however, can hardly escape the realization that the perspective of the observer has influenced the qualities ascribed to times, at least in the case of other historians. The characteristics of ages tend to change in conformity with the conditions and values of successive historians. During the twentieth century the darkness of the "Dark Ages" has grown shorter and less obscure, and the distinction between sleep and waking during the "Renaissance" has grown more subtle. Recent changes in aesthetic and dialectical taste have altered the historically recorded characteristics of Hellenistic and fourteenth-century art and logic. The vast increase of available information concerning primitive thought and expression is a result of preoccupation with mores and values today, but it has had the effect, in turn, of altering the "primitive mind."

The analyst of contemporary problems encounters these differences of perspective as opposed views and solutions, which he shows to be inadequate or false in the development of his own analysis. His statement is based on "facts" which have no alternative interpretation and which therefore preclude alternative antecedent histories. There is no direct or simple way of altering or supplementing the facts on which an analysis is based; and, as a consequence, efforts to initiate a "discussion" of problems usually produce "disputation" or, even worse, "controversy." The experience of historians with past ages, however, suggests

Reprinted from *Ethics: An International Journal of Social, Political, and Legal Philosophy* 67, no. 2 (January 1957): 89–99. © 1957 by The University of Chicago. All rights reserved.

an indirect means by which contemporary problems might be treated in the broader and more tolerant modes of "discussion," at least as preparation for disputation, and possibly as prevention of controversy. An age usually characterizes itself effectively by the manner in which it poses basic problems and by the means which it employs in seeking solutions to them. These characteristics of attitude and method do not share the ambiguity of the more disputable characteristics with which the historian elaborates his construction, and they reappear in the varieties of historical interpretation. The analyst of contemporary problems, likewise, does not question these basic approaches but accepts them as unanalyzed and probably unavoidable ingredients in the fashions of his times. Future historians who record what is being said and done today will find it difficult to avoid giving a prominent place to our preoccupation with "communication." It is a wise precaution, by the same token, to begin the statement of any broadly inclusive contemporary problems with an examination of how those problems are formulated in terms of "communication" and what the implications of such a formulation are.

"Communication" does not signify a problem newly discovered in our times, but a fashion of thinking and a method of analyzing which we apply in the statement of all fundamental problems. It is a term which has spread in use and implications during the past two or three decades from the problems of mass media, public relations, and promotion, to include all practical and social problems. Together with its companion term "behavior," it has modified the technical vocabulary of the social sciences, and the social sciences, in response, tend to become, in name and in fact, "behavioral sciences" and communication arts, for communication has become verbal behavior, and behavior has become an extension of communication to non-verbal symbols. Moreover, the change is reflected in the statement of basic problems in other fields. Natural scientists are concerned about the conditions of communication—difficulties of digesting their massive literature, dangers of restrictions on publication, consequences of limiting access to data—and they tend to express criteria for the acceptability of theories or interpretations of experiments in terms of consensus of experts rather than in terms of the structure of nature or phenomena. Artists are concerned with the influence of conditions of communication—economic, social, and political—on the work of creative artists and thinkers and on its reception. Philosophers have learned to talk about ordinary language and formal language, about symbols and sentences, semantics, syntactics, and pragmatics.

Other ages have found their characteristic vocabularies for the statement of theoretic and practical problems by recourse to things or to thoughts rather than to words. There have been ages which have returned from all questions to principles found in being and existence, in permanence and change, and which have adjusted thought and expression to cosmological frames and to metaphysical distinctions. There have been ages which have hesitated to pronounce on the nature of things before examining the forms of thought, the limits of knowledge, and the foundations of certainty. There have been ages, finally, which have abandoned the quest for certainty and the search for reality except as they are involved in problems of symbols, signs, and actions, and in so far as they are determined by the structure, limits, and efficacy of communication. The speculative innovators who herald these changes —as Kant used the expression "Copernican Revolution" to celebrate the transition from problems based on the nature of reality to problems based on the forms of thought—justify them in the hope that they will simplify inquiry by separating real from meaningless questions. Yet fundamental questions reappear in translated form in the new vocabularies as discoveries made possible by the new methods. The language of reality is an inclusive one: a metaphysics of being carries implications concerning how beings can be investigated and known, and concerning how knowledge and values are adequately and appropriately expressed. The language of criteria and forms of knowledge implies a conception of the nature of things and of the requirements of statement, proof, and construction but the specter of an unknown *ding an sich* usually rises in the background of phenomenal and known things. Some philosophers have hoped to avoid problems of reality and of mind by recourse to the language of semantics and communication, for sentences about being and non-being are unlike sentences about particular things and therefore may be dismissed as meaningless, and meanings expressed by sentences need no "mentalistic" interpretations. Yet unstated dimensions of things and thoughts spread out from the interpretation of language: discourse denotes objects and embodies values, and communication is used by men to express themselves and to establish communication with other men.

All problems can be stated as problems of communication. The nature of a problem may be explored by examining what we are talking about or the warrant for asserting anything we propose to say about it; it may also be explored by considering the conditions of stating the problem or saying anything whatsoever about it. A problem is determined not merely by what is the case, or by what is understood to be the case, but also by what is stated and by communication elucidating what is said. The problems of an age arise in what is said—in the communications of the age—and they cannot be formulated accurately, intelligibly, or effectively without taking into account how they arise and in what context they are stated. The vogue of "communication" today is no accident, but rather a response to the problems we face. When problems are broad and complexly interrelated, the initial distinctions must be found in communication itself. The consequences of beginning with communications, however, run contrary to the sense, which we carry over from times when society and knowledge were more orderly, that communications should be adapted in form and structure to the subject matter they set forth or to the thoughts they express. Yet recognition that the discovery of truth and the formation of thought are evidenced and tested only in communication need not lead to skepticism or relativism. On the contrary, the means to avoid sophism and dogmatism are provided by communication, and criteria of truth and value are translated into means of improving the content and efficacy of communication and of forestalling its use as an arbitrary and authoritarian instrument of control.

Some insight into the uses of communication can be derived from the experience of previous ages which shared our propensity to state fundamental problems in terms of discourse and expression. The Romans and the men of the Renaissance speculated concerning the nature of statement and communication in their bearing on political, aesthetic, historical, moral, and philosophical problems. Their analyses yielded insights into the relations of freedom and society and of expression and values, which continue to influence communication and theories of communication. We have come to a similar interest in communication but for different reasons, and our problems are similar in general statement but not in means available for resolution. The problem of communication became central during the Roman Republic and Empire as a result of the growth of the state and the assimilation into it of peoples of diverse cultural values, social structure, and political institutions. The problem of communication was a problem of establishing contacts among peoples within a political structure. That structure was provided

by the development of Roman law—*jus gentium* as well as *jus civile*—
and the instrumentality by which it was advanced was the elaboration
of rhetoric as a forensic art of pleading, in spite of the decay of the
deliberative rhetoric of debate as a result of the concentration of impe-
rial power, and in spite of the proliferation of the display rhetoric of
entertainment. The problem of communication became central during
the Renaissance as a result of growth of interest in art and literature
under the influence of classical models. The problem of communication
was a problem of expressive forms and of values expressed rather than
of contacts of peoples and agreements arrived at. It led to the development of humanism as a way of life and as a theory of values and to
the elaboration of rhetoric as an art of criticism which embraced problems of deliberation and adjudication as well as problems of appreciation.

We have returned to the problems of communication today as a result of the invention of instruments of communication and the massive
extension of their use. The contacts of peoples and the forms and contents of communication are not primary motivating causes but consequences of the availability and use of media of mass communication.
The distinctions we use in treating the resultant problems are similar to
those developed in Roman and Renaissance theories of communication, but the context of their application has altered. There is no universal frame of law within which to order the communications of the
peoples of the world as they bear on practical questions. Opposed legal
and political conceptions contend in communication today, and fear is
expressed that they might be extended by force—as the Romans extended their empire—in military, economic, cultural, or political im-
perialisms. There are no commonly esteemed models or forms to guide
the expression of traditional or new values, and the problems of basic
education for all men have taken precedence over the problems of increasing the efficiency, refining the taste, or elevating the morals, of
princes and merchants. Societies have themselves become systems of
communication uniting men, and the problems of communication in
one society reflect the larger problems of communication concerned
with all the peoples of the world and with the plurality of cultures in
which they have been formed. Individuals and nations are alike engaged in an effort to preserve and to create values, while resolving their
respective and common problems, modifying traditions to adjust them
to changed conditions which include the influence of other traditions
of action and culture.

When we take communication as our beginning point for the statement of problems, without common frame to determine how means of communication should be utilized or common content of values to determine what they should express, we tend to consider the means rather than the communication and to be put off by the mechanical analogy. We impute motives to speakers, analyze structures of content, and study opinions, in order to account for communication as effect or as cause; and we study the powers, habits, and virtues of machines in cybernetics, to construct a model for negotiations, societies, inquiries, and the creation of values. The prospect that the problems of communication might yield to a mechanical solution derived from the instrumentalities which caused them is attractive, but the result of these analyses of how, why, and to what effect statements are made is that communication is ignored or transformed into the oppositions and cautions of disputation and controversy. The alternative to treating communication as causal or discursive sequence on the model of the machine is to consider what is said and how what is meant might be influenced by communication.

One of the striking characteristics of communication in all fields is the uniformity of verbal statements concerning basic attitudes, purposes, and principles. In international communication, where common influences are few and slight, all major nations profess to be "democratic," and to be concerned with the advancement of "freedom," the cultivation and extension of "values," and the pursuit and recognition of "truth." At worst these statements indicate nothing more than a prudential use of means of communication to placate the people; at best they are ambiguous and often lead to opposed courses of action. Ambiguities are faults in proof and statement, but they have their uses in providing latitude for continuing discussion and inquiry. The only alternative to profiting by ambiguity to continue discussion until ambiguity is removed by communication is to control, restrict, or prohibit forms of communication thought to be injurious or dangerous. Much communication—or at least the communication with which we disagree—is ambiguous, disingenuous, deceptive, false, immoral, and, fortunately, ineffective. Verbal agreement, however, provides a minimum basis for the continuation of communication, and if men say often enough and explicitly enough that they are democratic, and that they promote freedom, seek values, and pursue truth, the possibility is left open that they may approximate a common meaning, and that their practice may come to approximate their profession. Communication depends on common principles—assumptions and meanings, purposes and values—but common meanings can be established only by communication and agreement. Only our tenuous agreements in communication can provide a frame today comparable to the frame of law of the Romans or the frame of values of the Renaissance—which were not without their working ambiguities—but we shall also need to elaborate an accompanying art of deliberative rhetoric or speculative grammar to reduce ambiguities for the discussion of differences and to provide common significances for values. The character of that art can be made apparent by examining what is involved in a radical reduction of basic problems to problems of communication. Its purpose must be to use communication to make men of one mind in truth, and to accomplish that purpose its devices must extend beyond consideration only of opinions, emotions, and interests.

Truth in a Pluralistic Society

The primary function of communication is to establish relations between men. It provides a bond of association and of community. A democratic society may be defined as a community based on communication: it is a framework of institutions and customs which are an expression of common acceptance and agreement and which provide means to discuss further differences and to come to agreement concerning them. To translate problems into terms of communication, therefore, is to place them in a social dimension of interchange. Moreover, the interchanges of communication provide both the initial definition of problems and the dynamism of their evolution: agreements begin with the conceptions men have of situations, interests, and dangers, and the consequences of agreements can be worked out only by communication, even when the result is a reluctant acquiescence under the influence or fear of force. Exercise of the primary function of communication depends on the exercise of three related functions of discourse: the communication which relates men to men also provides conditions essential to self-expression and freedom; it provides a medium for the embodiment of common values; and it provides an instrument for the discovery of truth. Viable communication moves in four dimensions: it relates man to man, and that relation determines and is determined by what man can become, by the ideals which inspire him, and by his conception of the objective circumstances which environ him.

These four functions are inseparable parts of the problem of communication. Their interrelations provide the only means of solving problems of communication. In spite of the vogue of "communication," we are reluctant to submit all problems to this process, for we would prefer to reserve some assumption, some fear, some preference—or when we express the reservation abstractly, some truth, some freedom, some value—from the uncertainties of discussion. Even the statement of this limit, however, must survive the processes of communication if we are to make it generally effective by securing agreement concerning it. The consequences of treating all basic problems as problems of communication can be discovered only by examining the nature of communication in its broadest scope, in which the strand of verbal agreement is most tenuous and ambiguous. The ambiguities of the "cold war" and of the numerous less inclusive controversies which color all the problems of our times depend on their ambiguities for the continuation of communication such as it is; and the threats of force and violence which would follow a rupture of communication can be understood best by analyzing opposed theories of communication as they operate in reducing ambiguities. Since communication functions as a bond binding people together in society, the ways in which communication operates can be stated as opposed conceptions of how truth functions in a society and how it influences the workings of society, or—what is the same thing—how men are made of one mind in truth. The differences which separate opposed theories of communication are differences concerning how the four dimensions of communication are interrelated.

The theory of truth in a unitary society is a simple equation of the four functions of communication established by control of communication. Society should be ruled by truth, and therefore a single philosophy should be imposed on all men. The values of art, science, philosophy, and religion should be cultivated in the service of that truth and according to its prescriptions. Freedom is advanced not by permitting men to act as they please but by inducing them to act as they should to advance that truth. The agreements or institutions which are the basis of society must be established by a dictatorship of the men who possess the truth, at least until such time as contrary errors have been extirpated and force is no longer necessary. The ambiguities of discussions to which this project of communication leads can be traced to the perverse meanings which are attached to all the basic terms. A truth which is not subject to discussion is an impediment to the discovery of truth; an

ideal which is used as an instrument is an impediment to the enrichment of values; a freedom of conformity is an impediment to the freedom of self-realization; an authoritarian society is an impediment to all
processes of discussion and government by agreement.

We deceive ourselves, however, if we translate these statements about
conditions of communication into statements of fact. We cannot assume that the effort to make men of one mind in a unitary society is
doomed necessarily to be ineffective. The facts of history and contemporary observation are evidence contrary to the assumption that truths,
values, freedom, and agreement are not achieved in an authoritarian
society or that a unitary conception of truth is without attractions to
uncommitted minds. Science has flourished under despotisms in the
Hellenistic kingdoms, in the Roman Empire of the second century
A.D., and in the Prussian Empire: the Soviet Union has made vast
progress in technology, and evidence concerning progress in science
there is not clear. The arts have flourished and have waned under highly
diverse conditions. Freedom has developed slowly and in parts, and it
has nowhere reached the ideal point at which it applies to all men and
to all human rights: a sense of freedom is a sense of liberation, and men
in various parts of the world value freedoms to which other men are
insensitive and they see threats to freedom where other men see none.
Men support agreements which they had no part in establishing, finally,
through interest, fear, and inertia; and unexpressed dissent, like the
aversion which "good Germans" discovered to naziism after its fall, is
tacit agreement. The processes by which men are made of one mind by
the processes of unitary communication will not be stopped by mechanical or inevitable impediments; they will be stopped only by the
clarity and efficacy of communication which provides and employs alternative ways of making men of one mind.

To state the opposed conception of truth in a pluralistic society as a
problem of communication is not to abandon truth to a relativism of
opinions, formative influences, and force, or to the prudential calculations of skepticism. Such a statement should, on the contrary, be an
exploration of means by which opposed errors can be combated. A
truth which we do not succeed in expressing and communicating is
ineffective, and we shall not be able to communicate it to others if we
do not understand the communication by which we achieve it, put it
into operation, and safeguard it. A pluralistic society is one in which
the four dimensions of communication function independently, and the

basis of truth in a pluralistic society is communication which facilitates the statement and discussion of differences, and the clarification and utilization of agreements. Men are unified in the institutional agreements of society, and their lives are enriched by the diversity of the interpretations and developments of these agreements. The basic problem of a pluralistic society is to use unity to promote diversity and diversity to strengthen unity. A society which is based on agreement through communication must provide conditions in which truth will emerge from the oppositions of opinions in communication. If the frame of discussion and agreement predetermines what shall be accepted as truth or gives undue weight to what one party to the discussion says, communication takes on the characteristics of communication in a unitary society.

If we knew the *truth* and if the truth could be stated once and for all, it would be reasonable to argue that deviations from that truth should be prohibited since they would, by its standard, be unclear, indistinct, inadequate, or false. But the truths with which we deal are humanly stated truths, and they are neither certain nor final. We have a natural disposition to view doctrines to which we are attached as if they possessed that certainty and finality. But the problem of truth in society is not limited to the use of truths already established; it is also a problem of inquiry to discover new truths and their applications, in the course of which old truths must be restated in new contexts, and truths, old or new, must he distinguished from falsities, fictions, and errors. If truths emerge in the oppositions of opinions, no marks antecedent to discussion suffice to distinguish truth and error; nor are there reasons to suppose that truth might be advanced by restricting communication or access to information.

If we possessed a unique and satisfactory expression of the *values* which inspire and motivate mankind, it would be reasonable to argue that deviations from its form or content should be prohibited, since they would, by its standard, be trivial, improper, obscene, or dangerous. But the expression of values has its basis in the circumstances and forms of expression of a time; and the potentialities of circumstances are expressed in ideal realizations. The function of creative artists and thinkers is to discover the unexpressed values of the society in which they live and to express them creatively in forms which other members of society may experience. The common values which unite men of different times and places are given different expressions appropriate to, and determined by, their respective periods and cultures. Values are brought to attention and operation by communication, and they exist only as expressed.

If we possessed a unique pattern for human behavior, it might be proclaimed as the model and rule for *free* action. But even those philosophers who hold that the wise man or the good man alone is free do not suppose that freedom is therefore reduced to a single pattern of action. Wisdom and virtue depend on conditions of choice; and men achieve their destinies and are free on different patterns, which are determined by their individual powers and circumstances. Freedom is individualism; it is absence of external constraint; it is the condition of advance in the moral and intellectual virtues. There is no freedom except the freedoms men feel and employ. Truths and values may enter as conditions influencing choice if men are free, but restrictions and prohibitions are external constraints poorly suited to make men either free and responsible or wise and good.

If we knew unquestionably what the form of the perfect *society* is—whether a utopia ruled by philosophers or scientists, or a classless society of free men who need no coercion—it might be argued that we would be justified in using every means for its realization. But societies are communities of individuals and, short of liquidation or the use of stratagem, individuals can be formed into a community only by communication. Societies may be established or destroyed by force; but they are continued and improved only by means of communication. Since communication depends on discovery of truths, cultivation of values, and extension of freedoms, a society must, if it is to endure and grow, permit the plurality and promote the communication by which those ends are realized.

The basis of truth in a pluralistic society is the independent functioning of communication in the four dimensions which bear on truth, values, freedom, and community. The simple statement of that independence, however, is nothing more than the construction of an ideal which has at best the virtue of indicating the requirements for preserving communication from the errors and distortions imposed by a unitary society. The problems of how to achieve and preserve that independence are difficult and paradoxical, for if all problems are problems of communication the independence of the four dimensions of communication can be preserved only by interrelations established among them by communication. The pattern of communication in a pluralistic society is diversity and unity, pluralism and agreement, freedom and control. To maintain that pattern, diversity must be prevented from disrupting unity and agreement from suppressing differences. Communication is an art, and it must develop powers as well as achieve effects: communication will contribute to truth, values, freedom, and community if the processes of communication are such as to foster responsiveness to truth, sensitivity to values, recognition of the implications of freedom, and concern to preserve the institutions by which men resolve their differences from perversion by force, fraud, or neglect. General considerations concerning communication will not solve the subtle and difficult problems of control and freedom, but they will suggest distinctions for their analysis and criteria to guide their discussion. The dimensions of communication range between the agreements of society and the requirements of truth, value, and freedom. The basic problems which occupy communication in all fields range likewise between the extreme of demands for limitation, restriction, control, prohibition, isolation, censorship, segregation, and preservation; and the extreme of demands for rights and freedoms for all kinds and classes of people, in all phases of life, for all varieties of purposes. Some of them are problems which have become pressing because the increase in communication makes their solution practicable for the first time; some of them are problems which have arisen from the development of communication. Both kinds are firmly grounded in communication, and their treatment depends on the limits and nature of communication.

If society is an agreement based on communication, it would seem that some limitations must be put on communication in the interest of preserving that agreement and the institutions by which agreement is advanced. Pressure for censorship and for other limitations on many sorts of communication has recently been advanced by such arguments. Arguments for and against censorship are arguments in a tradition of communication; and examination of its implications provides, not the solution of the problems treated in it, but criteria to clarify the complex issues it treats. The arguments for censorship, restriction, labeling, and control rest on the consequences of the communication to be censored, not on its characteristics as communication. Obscenity and the depiction of violence may affect the character and actions of the immature, the uneducated, and the defective; disloyal, dishonest, and unscrupulous men may conspire to mislead, confuse, and subvert; bigots may misrepresent and libel groups, peoples, races, and beliefs. The form of the argument is not an accident. Error, obscenity, conspiracy, and libel are the recurrent grounds advanced for censorship, and they have often been used in conjunction or even interchangeably. The provisions for freedom of the press in the first and the fourteenth amendments of the United State Constitution have been interpreted as precluding censorship in the strict sense of prepublication supression, and secondary forms of suppressing or of restricting distribution and accessibility have concentrated on the effects attributed to communication, and their defenders have argued that they do not interfere with truth, value, or freedom. The distinction is itself an achievement of the tradition of communication established in political discussion and law. It provides a minimum element of agreement, a basis of communication, and criteria for arriving at further agreements.

Defenders of censorship, while seeking to control consequences in action, acknowledge the distinction between communication and action and the guarantee of freedom of speech and expression. Opponents of censorship, while urging the dangers of any restriction on communication, acknowledge the existence of official communications—some of them in the statute books of the states, postal regulations, and customs procedures—which do restrict communication. The problem of freedom or restriction of communication is in the middle range in which statement is distinguished from action. All the terms of the discussion are so vague as to be indefinitely extensible: "obscenity" was applied, in France in the seventeenth and eighteenth centuries, to censor scientific and philosophic writings; "libel" was employed, in eighteenth- and nineteenth-century England, to eliminate political opposition; "conspiracy" and "treason" have been extended, in the United States in the twentieth century, from their strict senses to apply to any position one opposes—to a point where the two major parties can play with the terms as means of describing and criticizing each other. The statutes are poorly written and difficult to enforce, and there is a growing tendency to have recourse to extra-legal action and influence—to arbitrary action by chiefs of police, to economic boycott, or to social pressure. The dangers of these tendencies to truth in a pluralistic society are obvious, and the criteria of communication concerning those dangers is no less obvious: objective examination of whether the consequences alleged could plausibly follow from the communication; clearly formulated statutes and explicit regulations to control consequences; legal procedures of enforcement and easily available legal procedures of

review; communication and discussion based on probable consequences rather than on alleged intentions imputed to the author or on
distaste aroused in the critic by the communication; effective discour-
agement and control of extra-legal procedures.

Criteria of control based on consideration of the limitations of communication, however, must be supplemented by criteria of use based
on consideration of the nature of communication. Communication can
be controlled only when communication in any true sense has failed.
Communication can embody values, realize freedom, promote the ends
of society, only by advancing truth and using truth. To do that it must
form in those who participate in communication an attitude and ability
to judge truth, to be sensitive to values, to develop in the use of freedom, and to build confidence in the institutions of society on truth,
values, and freedom. To strengthen these attitudes and abilities is to
make men of one mind in truth; and the art of communication—which
has been referred to earlier as deliberative rhetoric—is the art by which
that can be done.

We have tended in our analysis of communication to reduce the
minds of men to opinions and to neglect active attitude and ability by
concentrating on what is passively received. Communication is education, and education should train men to judge all communication, not
in its technical details but as it bears on common problems, to appreciate the statement of ideals, and to be inspired by them, to use freedom
to regulate passions by reason and interests by right, and to temper
caution and fear by tolerance and love in social and political activities.
It is in this development that the four dimensions of communication
find their proper and effective interplay: a just society is advanced as its
citizens advance in truth, values, and freedom. The art of deliberative
rhetoric is not a technical or abstruse discipline. On the contrary, it is
the instrument of democracy in so far as democracy is based on a conviction that the people are better qualified than any limited or select
group to make decisions concerning truth as it affects them, concerning
the values presented for contemplation and guidance, concerning their
individual destinies, and concerning their common good. Men of one
mind can build a society, a nation, and a world community. But to be
of one mind is not to be of one opinion. Men are of one mind when
they possess reason to judge statements of truth, understanding to appreciate statements of their own values and those of others, desires or-

dered under freedom, and love of the common good for which men are associated. When men are of one mind in these abilities, they can be of different opinions without danger to society or to each other.

Communication can make men of one mind, and understanding the nature of communication can guide its use. Moreover, the order in which our problems must be treated becomes apparent from the analysis of communication. There is no simple means to bridge the gap between the communication of a pluralistic society and the communication of a unitary society: the frame within which communication between those two modes of communication takes place is a tenuous, temporary, and ambiguous agreement. We must begin by understanding better the implication of communication as it is committed to the truths of a pluralistic society and by bringing our actions more and more into accordance with the requirements of that communication. To the extent that we succeed in understanding and promoting communication in our own society, we advance in our communication with other peoples who are engaged, like us, in an effort to come to one mind by communication, and who suspect what we say and the nature and purpose of the communication we employ in saying it. If the scope and effectiveness of communication is extended, the ambiguities of the communication between the extremes are likely to be lessened. The danger to communication in a pluralistic society is that it may be transformed by imperceptible degrees and unsuspected devices into forms of communication which make for a unitary society; but by the same token the hope for communication in a unitary society is that it may be transformed by circumstances, if not by reason, into forms of communication which prepare for a pluralistic society. The primary problem is not an external threat beyond the limits of communication but an internal problem which can be solved by communication. Men can be made of one mind in truth by communication in a pluralistic society: such a society is based on confidence resulting from insight into truths, understanding of others, and freedom for self-development. The one alternative to such communication is communication which builds a society based on fear, guided by guesses concerning the dominant direction or party, conformity to general expectations, and coercion to remove deviations.

5

Dialogue and Controversy in Philosophy

Philosophers have always welcomed dialogue if one is to credit the interest they profess in the interplay of arguments; and treatises on philosophy would be shorter, and probably less intelligible, if all references to other positions were deleted from them. This happy expectation that the restatement of distinctions and arguments will lead to agreement on principles and conclusions, and contribute to the advancement of knowledge, has, none the less, been thwarted whenever two voices have entered the dialogue. Controversy takes the place of dialogue when the philosopher whose position is reported and adjusted bursts into the conversation to restate what has been attributed to him and to rescue it from distortion. The recriminations, which form as large a part of the history of philosophy as the open-minded professions of willingness to consider other assumptions and approaches, suggest that it is not less difficult—if indeed it is even possible—for one philosopher to restate the position of another when he appropriates it to his own uses as a truth which he expresses somewhat differently, or even when he defends it as the doctrine of a beloved master who has been misinterpreted, than when he sets it forth starkly in all its weakness as the construction of an opponent to be refuted out of hand.

Many plausible reasons can be alleged to account for this failure of dialogue. Most of them have no direct bearing on the truth or falsity of the philosophical conclusions they account for. They are for the most part themselves intrusions into the dialogue which brusquely turn it into a jurisdictional controversy concerning the ultimate authority in treating philosophic questions: whether relations among the sciences

Reprinted from *Philosophy and Phenomenological Research* 17, no. 2 (December 1956): 143–63.

should be explored on philosophic assumptions concerning logical or dialectical proof, forms of experience or reason, or characteristics of phenomena or being, or whether, on the contrary, philosophic problems should be explained away on assumptions drawn from psychology, sociology, economics, history, the conditioning of man, or the claims of society. The nature of the failure of dialogue, even in its large reductive and pseudoscientific forms, is clarified, on the other hand, if the task which the philosopher undertakes is considered in general before failures in communication are accounted for as failures in proof. Like inquirers in other fields, the philosopher not only seeks truths; he also constructs arguments to relate the truths he finds to warrantable or defensible grounds, and he adresses his arguments to minds not yet enlightened or convinced. Unlike other disciplines, however, philosophy is synoptic and inclusive by design, not by occasional extension, and philosophic differences tend to focus on basic considerations about objects, arguments, and other minds.

Most of the extreme controversies in which philosophers abandon all pretense of dialogue and turn their backs on arguments can be traced to differences concerning the structure of arguments and their relations to objects and to minds. There have been, and there still are, philosophers who argue that these three tasks are inseparable, and that the discovery of truth, the construction of arguments, and the clarification of minds proceed pace by pace; methods which separate them fall into the error of constructing formal or subjective arguments unrelated to reality or into the error of constructing mechanical or partial conceptions unrelated to real processes or scientific principles. There have been philosophers, no less numerous and no less confident of their scientific pretensions and venerable antecedents, who argue that man is the measure of all things, that truth is discovered only in the free clash of opinions, and that plausible arguments can be found to support the contradictory of any proposition or doctrine; dialogue explores the plurality of positions, and it is transformed into controversy by dogmatisms which must therefore be refuted. At the other extreme throughout the long history of the opposition of dialecticians and skeptics, other philosophers have sought a method to construct arguments based on the nature of things without intrusion of imagination, emotion, or opinion; methods which fail to make this separation must be shown to be unsound and unscientific, since they do not penetrate to the nature of things, but weave verbal arguments to support meaningless statements pertinent only to unreal problems—although, it should be added, the verbal statements do express emotions, and the groundless arguments are often persuasive, and the unreal problems are consequences of artificial tensions, unexamined complexes, or persistent traditions. There remains a fourth possibility, which was developed by philosophers in antiquity and was further extended and applied at later stages of history, that each of these tasks presents a separate problem of method, that a logic should be elaborated for formal arguments, a method of inquiry for the discovery of truth, and a rhetoric and dialectic for communication among men, and that the use of these methods requires a metaphysics to explore the principles and organization of knowledge, a psychology or epistemology to explore the functions and powers of man, and a socio-political theory to explore the diversity of communities and circumstances; confusions among these methods must then be sought out and corrected.

1. As Plato conceived dialectic, it is the unique method of philosophy and science, precisely because it is suited to carry out all three tasks of philosophy simultaneously—the discovery of truth, the construction of arguments, and the clarification of minds. All other arts and methods are incomplete and dangerous unless transformed by dialectic. The dialectician is the true poet and interpreter of poetry, the best rhetorician and linguist, and the only sure mathematician, moral guide, and political ruler. Dialectic is a method of definition and argument, of division and collection, but far from being satisfied with verbal formulations, Plato is suspicious of the written word, which is dead and cannot answer back when questioned, and he seeks instead living words, which are planted and grow in living minds. The influence of dialectic on the mind, moreover, is due to the fact that it divides and collects real classes; dialectic divides at the joints of reality and to accomplish that purpose it assembles an intellectual alphabet for argument which, like the letters of ordinary alphabets, cannot be combined arbitrarily but only as they form syllables and words. Even in the *Cratylus,* where the subject of discussion is the nature of language, the proponents of the opposed theories of natural and conventional language come to agree in dialogue that they must give up seeking in words a knowledge of things, and instead turn their attention not to names but to things themselves, acknowledging the dialectician to be superior to the maker of language.

In order to form arguments and to treat things, dialectic must prepare minds. Socrates compares his art to that of a midwife, since it merely assists in bringing knowledge to birth, and he compares its effect to that of a torpedo-fish, since it shocks the mind free from unexamined attractions or polarities. The development of knowledge is a detachment, a reminiscence, an initiation which may have a divine or apparently accidental origin, but it may also be occasioned by method in discussion. The determining factor is not the concatenation of phenomena, the nature of mind, or the structure of argument, but the common source from which they all derive and to which they owe their interrelations. Education consists in turning the attention of the mind and enlarging the scope of its contemplation to a synoptic vision. Dialectic is the method of achieving this threefold purpose—it is a dialogue by which men come to agreement by means of argument concerning the nature and divisions of things.

The method of dialectic is dialogue in the sense that two or more speakers or two or more positions are brought into relations in which it becomes apparent that each position is incomplete and inconclusive unless assimilated to a higher truth. Phenomena may become the stages of History, and minds may become Spirit, without affecting the character of the argument as it operates in development of the dialogue. The processes of development of things, the levels of formation of knowledge, and the steps of synthesis of proof are fundamentally the same. Dialecticians, for the most part, do not refute, but rather assimilate other philosophers. Plato apparently found no need to differentiate his method from the method of Socrates or from the methods of the Eleatics, the Pythagoreans, the Heracliteans, or even at times the Sophists, who appear in his dialogues. Historians and scholars have not always been happy with the consequences of this assimilation of methods in dialectic and they have constructed the Socratic Question and the Platonic Question to recover distinctions Plato failed to make from the indications which he does give. For no one speaker expresses the truth, and all methods, even that of Socrates, show their weakness and incompleteness in some regions and on some questions.

Plotinus, using a similar dialectic, later adjusted the categories of Aristotle and of the Stoics to the Platonic categories, discovering that both have some basis in truth but that Aristotle's errors arose from seeking the categories of being in sensible rather than intelligible things and the Stoic errors from materialism. Porphyry transformed Aristotle's logic into a dialectic by writing an Introduction, an *Isagoge,* to the *Categories,* borrowing the "predicables" from Aristotle's *Topics,* in which the commonplaces of dialectic are treated, to loosen up the literal distinctions and univocal definitions of the Aristotelian logic, and the long line of Greek Commentators labored further to make Aristotle an acceptable, though imperfect, Neoplatonic dialectician. Saint Bonaventura found the formula of synthesis in the discovery that Aristotle spoke the language of science, Plato the language of wisdom, while Saint Augustine, illuminated by the Holy Ghost, used both languages. Hegel could trace the whole sequence of the history of philosophy evolving to its assimilation in his own philosophy; and Erdmann, who argued that Hegel's assertion that his system has assimilated all earlier systems is confirmed even by his opponents, is constrained by the passage of time and the continuation of the inevitable dialectic of history to add a final volume on the dissolution of the Hegelian system as appendix to his *History of Philosophy.*

This complex process of synthesizing is interrupted—and dialogue becomes controversy—whenever dialectic degenerates into sophistic or skepticism by neglecting content or into subjectivism and mechanism by neglecting argument. Socrates frequently notes the transition from dialectic to sophistic or eristic.

"What a grand thing, Glaucon," said I, "is the power of the art of contradiction (ἀντιλογική)." "Why so?" "Because," said I, "many appear to fall into it even against their wills, and to suppose that they are not wrangling (ἐρίζειν) but arguing (διαλέγεσθαι), owing to their inability to apply the proper divisions and distinctions to the subject under consideration. They pursue merely verbal oppositions, practising eristic, not dialectic on one another."[1]

The other form of controversy, due to neglect rather than misuse of argument and leading to partial conceptions of subject matter may take two forms. One is exemplified in the battle of the giants in which the aggressors break bodies and what they call truth into small fragments and talk about a kind of generation by motion rather than being, while the defenders proceed very cautiously with weapons derived from the invisible world above, maintaining that true being consists of certain ideas which are only conceived by the mind and have no body.[2] The other is the pragmatic empiricism which neglects scientific analysis to

1. Plato *Republic* v. 453E–454A.
2. Plato *Sophist* 246B–C.

concentrate on sensible effects and practical applications—as calculation or logistic (λογιστική) is adapted to commercial purposes but not, like arithmetic, to knowledge.[3]

Dialectic became the method of Christian theology and philosophy until the translation of Aristotle in the thirteenth century suggested the possibility of two methods and two ways; dialectic was also opposed during the middle ages because it is a purely verbal art and because it applies reason to matters that transcend reason. During the Renaissance the choice of methods lay between dialectic and rhetoric, and mediaeval logic was dropped out of the dialogue as verbal and as concerned with non-existent entities, like universals and transcendentals. The grounds of controversy are the same during the nineteenth century after the revival of dialectic attributed to Kant. According to Hegel three attitudes toward objectivity are found in logic and the formal doctrine of logic has three sides. The first attitude toward objectivity leads to metaphysics; the second is expressed in empiricism and the critical philosophy; the third is immediate or intuitive knowledge. The second of these attitudes was adopted by Hume and Kant. Thought is subjective and its most effective operation depends on abstract universality according to this attitude, but the logical development of empiricism is materialism (matter being an abstraction), whereas the critical philosophy of Kant separates the world of sensible appearances from the world of self-apprehending thought. The second of the three forms of logical doctrine is dialectic, which must be separated carefully from sophistry and skepticism. Modern skepticism partly precedes the Critical philosophy, partly springs out of it; it consists solely in denying the truth and certitude of the supersensible, and in pointing to the facts of sense and of immediate sensations as ultimate.[4] Engels is able to fit Hegel into this classification when he borrows and transforms the Hegelian dialectic. Philosophers are split into two great camps, idealists and materialists, on the paramount question of the relation of thinking to being, of spirit to nature. But the question of the relation of thinking to being has another side which separates Hegel, who asserts the identity of thinking and being, from Hume and Kant, who question the possibility of any cognition of the world.[5] These distinctions form the

3. Plato *Gorgias* 451B–C; *Republic* vii. 525D.

4. Cf. Hegel, *The Encyclopaedia of the Philosophical Sciences in Outline*, Part I, *The Science of Logic*, chapters 3–6.

5. Frederick Engels, *Ludwig Feuerbach and the Outcome of Classical German Philosophy* (New York, 1935), pp. 31–32. Cf. Engels, *Anti-Duhring*, trans. E. Burns (London, n.d.),

foundation of Lenin's philosophical argument,[6] but he traces the beginnings of immaterialism to Berkeley's arguments against matter and he encounters at every turn a variegated progeny descended from the "Humean agnosticism," not only Kant, but also Mill, Mach, Huxley, Cohen, Renouvier, Poincaré, Duhem, James.

11. The dogmatisms of dialectical history tend to overshadow the equally plausible—and, in the context of twentieth century dogmatisms, more attractive—version of the relations among philosophies set forth by the defenders of the antilogism and contradiction, the adherents of skepticism and sophistry, who find the method of philosophy in the interplay of doctrines and opinions, and who expose the consequences of dogmatism concerning the ultimate principles of knowledge and reality. Discrimination, not assimilation or reduction, is the method of philosophy, and dialogue proceeds by exploring the varieties of arguments and doctrines and testing assertions by their contradiction, not by adjusting all doctrines to a preferred position and refuting those which will not fit. In the course of controversy with dialectical and logistic philosophers all the names assumed by philosophers of this

---

pp. 28–29: "To the metaphysician, things and their mental images, ideas, are isolated, to be considered one after the other apart from each other, rigid, fixed objects of investigation given once for all. He thinks in absolutely irreconcilable antitheses. 'His communication is Yea, yea, Nay, nay, for whatsoever is more than these cometh of evil.' For him a thing either exists, or it does not exist; it is equally impossible for a thing to be itself and at the same time something else. Positive and negative absolutely exclude one another; cause and effect stand in an equally rigid antithesis one to the other. At first sight this mode of thought seems to us extremely plausible, because it is the mode of thought of so-called sound common sense. . . . Closer investigation also shows us that the two poles of an antithesis, like positive and negative, are just as inseparable from each other as they are opposed, and that despite all their opposition they mutually penetrate each other. It is just the same with cause and effect; these are conceptions which only have validity in their application to a particular case as such, but when we consider the particular case in its general connection with the world as a whole they merge and dissolve in the conception of universal action and interaction, in which causes and effects are constantly changing places, and what is now or here an effect becomes there or then a cause, and *vice versa*.

"None of these processes and methods of thought fits into the frame of metaphysical thinking. But for dialectics, which grasps things and their images, ideas, essentially in their interconnection, in their sequence, their movement, their birth and death, such processes as those mentioned above are so many corroborations of its own method of treatment. Nature is the text of dialectics, and it must be said for modern natural science that it has furnished extremely rich and daily increasing materials for this test, and has thus proved that in the last analysis Nature's process is dialectical and not metaphysical."

6. Lenin, *Materialsim and Empirio-Criticism: Critical Notes Concerning a Reactionary Philosophy* (New York, 1927), pp. 74–77.

tradition have been given a pejorative sense: they are sophists who were concerned with wisdom, skeptics who developed reflective thought and inquiry, rhetoricians who were skilled in the arts of communication, and academics who employed the method of Socrates and Plato.

Sophistic and rhetoric provided the counterpart, and a phase of the context, for the development of Plato's dialectic. They had themselves developed as practical instrumentalities in the democratic Greek city-states, and they provided arts by which opposed opinions might be brought into relation and confrontation. Plato gives Protagoras' aphorism, Man is the measure of all things, a relativist and sensualist interpretation which accords with the criticism attributed to Democritus as well as Plato in opposition to the doctrine ascribed to Protagoras, that all sensations are equally true for all sentient subjects.[7] Isocrates criticized speculative philosophers, who are in total disagreement concerning the nature of things and in even more confusing disagreement when they profess to attain scientific knowledge of moral questions. Philosophy is concerned to impart all the forms of discourse in which the mind expresses itself—not in abstract but in particular statements — and it should therefore bring the student into contact with the variety of opinions rather than inculcate a pretended or useless science.

Skepticism grew out of the exigences of dialogue at the very center of dialectic. Skeptics were prominent among the "Socratics" who set forth their philosophic positions in "Socratic dialogues." The Academy defended the position of Plato against the dogmatism and materialism of the Stoics by means of the skepticism elaborated by Arcesilas and the probabilism evolved by Carneades. Cicero, as a follower of the New Academy, interprets all the great philosophers as exponents of an identical truth to which they give only verbally variant expression, and he reserves controversy for the refutation of the materialism of the Epicureans and the dogmatism of philosophers who conceive truth to be susceptible only of a unique expression. Sextus Empiricus marshalls an encyclopaedic refutation of all dogmatisms, idealistic and materialistic, empirical and rationalistic. John of Salisbury in the twelfth century labels himself an Academic, and John Duns Scotus at the end of the thirteenth century elaborates subtle arguments to refute the Academics. The revived dialectic of the Renaissance is a battle ground between

7. Plato *Theaetetus* 151E–152E; Sextus Empiricus *Adversus Mathematicos* vii. 388–390.

Neoplatonists and Skeptics. Hume acknowledges the attraction which the academic philosophy had for him, and when Kant returned to dialectic he called it an art of semblance and disputation, an *ars sophistica disputatoria*, and derives the method he practices from the skeptics.[8] The modern exponents of the skeptical position tend, as Hegel pointed out, to be less thorough than the ancients and to favor one of the forms of dogmatism—empiricism—in their search for the useful and the practical among opinions.

Sophistic or the skeptical dialectic is an operational method. As expounded by Cicero it consists of two parts, a method of discovery and a method of judgment or proof, as contrasted to the dialectic of the Stoics which wholly neglects the method of discovery. This method is also called rhetoric, the art of discovering arguments and of organizing them in exposition. Properly employed it results in wisdom, and it should be employed only in conjunction with wisdom. In the history of philosophy, as Cicero recounts it, early philosophers combined eloquence and wisdom. Socrates unfortunately separated them and thereafter rhetoric and philosophy followed independent courses until the New Academy again undertook to join them. If men will equip themselves with the art of discovering and stating arguments, a dialogue is possible, since philosophers will come to recognize that truth is not acquired by a private and mysterious insight into reality, but by understanding the arguments by which truth may be distinguished from error in a given situation and application or an identical truth may be discovered by different means and be stated in different terms. Controversy results from inability to follow an argument and from dogmatic attachment to positions that are thought to be unique.

This conception of the relation between method and knowledge, between rhetoric and wisdom, has served as the basis for histories of philosophy. Philostratus wrote of philosophy in this sense in his *Lives of the Sophists*.

We must regard the ancient sophistic art as philosophical rhetoric. For it discusses the themes that philosophers treat of, but whereas they [the philosophers], by their method of questioning, set snares for knowledge and advance step by step as they confirm the minor points of their investigations, the sophist of the old school assumes a knowledge of that whereof he speaks.[9]

8. Cf. R. McKeon, "Dialectic and Political Thought and Action," *Ethics*, vol. LXV (1954), p. 12.
9. Philostratus *Lives of the Sophists* 480.

A few philosophers who were renowned for eloquence, like Carneades, Dio Chrysostom, and Favorinus, figure in Philostratus' history along with the older sophists from Gorgias to Isocrates; but the New Sophistic applied rhetoric to a wisdom that had little in common with the subjects treated by the philosophers, in spite of the interest which the philosopher-Emperor Marcus Aurelius, took in it. Eunapius' *Lives of the Philosophers,* on the other hand, begins with Porphyry, who is presented as skilled in rhetoric and in all branches of knowledge, and moves from the Neoplatonists to the sophists, pagan and Christian, to culminate in the iatrosophists, the healing sophists. Zeno of Cyprus was expert in both oratory and medicine, and his disciples were trained in one or both. The latter included Magnus, who was so able in rhetoric that he "used to demonstrate that those whom other doctors cured were still ill,"[10] Ionicus, Oribasius, and Chrysanthius, who was in turn Eunapius' master. The two traits which the sophist should cultivate— ability to discover and present arguments and willingness to listen to arguments—are found in a marked degree in the portrait Eunapius draws of his master, who possessed this disposition, according to Eunapius, either because the Platonic Socrates had come to life again in him or because his effort to imitate Socrates had led him to form himself from boyhood on the model of Socrates.

But it was not easy to rouse him to philosophical discussions (διάλεξις) or competitions (φιλονεικία), because he perceived that it is especially in those contests that men become embittered. Nor would anyone readily have heard him showing off his own erudition or inflated because of it, or insolent and arrogant toward others; rather he used to admire whatever they said, even though their remarks were worthless, and would applaud even incorrect conclusions, just as though he had not even heard the premises, but was naturally inclined to assent, lest he should inflict pain on any one. And if in an assembly of those most distinguished for learning any dissension arose, and he thought fit to take part in the discussion, the place became hushed in silence as though no one were there. So unwilling were they to face his questions and definitions and power of quoting from memory, but they would retire from discussion and contradiction, lest their failure should be too evident.[11]

The revival of the study of the history of philosophy in the Renaissance followed rhetorical rather than dialectical lines: exemplary uses of doctrines, aphorisms, and arguments rather than epochal successions of

10. Eunapius *Lives of the Philosophers* 498.
11. *Ibid.*, 502.

systems are emphasized in the lives of philosophers and the compendia of arts which followed the model of Hellenistic histories and Roman treatises and which showed a rhetorical tendency to refute dogmatisms and to seek the causes for the decline of the arts.

The importance of dialogue to the modern "skeptics," who are derived from Hume's agnosticism by their dialectical critics, is precisely in its encouragement and development of arguments. The advancement of science, the cultivation of values, and the resolution of practical problems all depend on the confrontation of arguments, the test of opinion by opinion, and the open possibility of innovation moderated by the stabilizing influence of tradition. Like the ancient skeptics and academics, John Stuart Mill bases the practical use of the free interplay of opposed arguments on the example of the theoretic use of the methods of rhetoric to advance toward truth in the natural sciences.

The peculiarity of the evidence of mathematical truths is that all the argument is on one side. There are no objections and no answers to objections. But in every subject on which difference of opinion is possible, the truth depends on a balance to be struck between two sets of conflicting reasons. Even in natural philosophy, there is always some other explanation possible of the same facts. . . . But when we turn to subjects infinitely more complicated, to morals, religion, politics, social relations, and the business of life, three fourths of the arguments for every disputed opinion consist in dispelling the appearance which favors some opinion different from it. The greatest orator, save one, of antiquity, has left it on record that he always studied his adversary's case with as great, if not greater, intensity than even his own. What Cicero practised as the means of forensic success requires to be imitated by all who study any subject in order to arrive at the truth. He who knows only his own side of the case, knows little of that. His reasons may be good, and no one may have been able to refute them. But he is equally unable to refute the reasons on the opposite side; if he does not so much as know what they are, he has no ground for preferring either opinion. The rational position for him would be suspension of judgment, and unless he contents himself with that, he is either led by authority or adopts like the generality of the world, the side to which he feels most inclination[12].

There are more proponents of this view than can be tabulated under any of the shining names—sophistic, skepticism, academicism, rhetoric, utilitarianism, liberalism—that have been attached to it and that have been tarnished by the contempt for "opinion," "sense experience," and "utility" expressed by its opponents. It underlies Justice Oliver

12. John Stuart Mill, *On Liberty,* chapter 2.

Wendell Holmes' vision of the free competition of ideas, James' pluralism, Bridgman's operationalism. Dialogue is statement and counterstatement, based on ordinary ways of life and ordinary uses of language, with no possible appeal to a reality beyond opposed opinions except through opinions about reality. Truth is perceived in perspective, and perspectives can be compared, but there is no overarching inclusive perspective. Meanings are defined in action and measurement, and there is no theory apart from practice. Method is the art of seizing and interpreting the opinions of others and of constructing and defending one's own. Virtue is method translated into intelligent self-interest and respect for others.

III. The Sophists used a method so similar to dialectic that Socrates could complain in the *Apology* that his critics mistook him for a sophist, and yet they denied dialectical absolutes beyond the relativities of perception and reduced dialectical certainties to opinions in the interchange of rhetorical argument. The ancient physicists and atomists, on the other hand, appealed to a truth based on reality so similar to the Ideas of Socrates that Socrates thought his position had been confused with that of Anaxagoras, although the physicists made no use of dialectic. Democritus' objection to Protagoras' sensationism is so like Plato's that the two were lumped together in antiquity. The special senses are false, since there is no counterpart to sensation outside the sensient subject. True born knowledge, as opposed to the bastard knowledge of sensation, is scientific knowledge of the atoms, and Democritus uses the same word as Plato—"ideas"—to designate these ultimate non-sensible realities. Aristotle judges the methods of Plato and Democritus to be balanced evenly in achievement and failure: Plato developed a theory of method in his dialectic but failed to apply it successfully to account for phenomena; Democritus developed a method which was faithful to phenomena, but he failed to formulate his method and overgeneralized it as a result of his misconception of definition and cause. The method of scientific knowledge is distinct from verbal logic or dialectic, and knowledge of atoms and their motions is distinct from the relativities of secondary qualities. Dialectic, in its transcendental no less than in its skeptical form, seemed to later atomists to be verbal and inapplicable to this scientific task, while the calculation of motions and combinations of elements was of so little interest to dialecticians, that Plato's silence concerning Democritus was a scandal in antiquity. Dialecticians who came after him found modest historical places for mechanistic materialists.

As later skeptics found it desirable to temper their doubts with some confidence in empirical aspects of experience and in the tautologies of thought and expression, so too later atomists provided a place in their rational methods for sensations and feelings. According to Epicurus there are three criteria of truth: sensations, anticipations, and feelings. The external world is known by perception. Sextus Empiricus reports the equivalence of truth and reality in sensation: "Epicurus said that all objects of perception are true and real: for it was the same thing to call a thing true and to call it existing. True then means that which is as it is said to be, and false that which is not as it is said to be."[13] But the method which Epicurus expounds in the *Canonic* has no place for dialectic or verbal arguments, and his critics are distressed by the contempt he expresses for logic which he criticizes as misleading. Cicero is shocked because "he abolishes definitions, he has no teaching about division and distribution, he does not tell how reasoning is conducted or brought to conclusions, he does not show by what means sophisms may be exposed, and ambiguities resolved."[14] The central problem of developing a method to construct truths from simple elements and their relations was however to receive impressive and suggestive embodiment in a field ignored by Epicurus. The long chains of proof which Euclid organized in his *Elements* were to provide inspiration for philosophers and scientists attracted by the hope to derive all truths from combinations and constructions, whether they begin with simple bodies, simple ideas, or even simple terms.

The geometric method has no necessary philosophic implications when it is employed to construct figures from their "elements" or even when it is used to make a transition from geometrical solids to physical bodies and motions. It is made into a philosophical method when it is generalized to cover all conceivable phenomena and all reality and when it is made to provide the test for truth and reality. When philosophers adopt the geometric or deductive method as the method of philosophy and construct deductive demonstrations (with or without recourse to the forms of geometric proof), they face a choice of starting point and subject: they may find their elements in things and make the world

13. Sextus Empiricus *Adversus Mathematicos* viii. 9.
14. Cicero *De Finibus* i. 7.22.

geometric, if primary qualities are distinguished from secondary; or they may begin with common notions or simple ideas and distinguish the combinations which yield knowledge of reality from fantasy and error; or they may start with symbols and their relations to atomic facts and separate the non-cognitive from the cognitive uses of symbols. They find themselves opposed in this effort to free philosophy of meaningless questions by philosophers (like Plato, Nicholas of Cusa, and Whitehead), who give mathematics a dialectical development, by philosophers (like Poincaré and Russell), who make the method of mathematics arbitrary and its subject matter indeterminate, and by philosophers (like Aristotle, Mill, and Dewey), who distinguish the methods of mathematics from the methods appropriate to other fields.

The geometric method has had many imitators in philosophy. Alan of Lille and Nicholas of Amiens used a mathematical deduction from "common notions" and "maxims" to rid theology of controversy in the twelfth century. Bishop Bradwardine used a geometric method to organize the sequence of proof from common notions in his *De Causa Dei* in the fourteenth century, while Richard Swineshead laid the foundations of a logistic philosophy in his *Calculator* by an exploration of variables homogeneous with the verbal logic on which his contemporaries engaged. But the great efflorescence of the geometric method came in the seventeenth century when treatises on mechanics, optics, and astronomy and all sciences that pretended to precision were thrown into the form of deductions from axiom sets, and the hope that psychology, ethics, and politics might also be made scientific was attached to the endeavor to deduce them from a few simple definitions and principles. Descartes' confidence in the long chains of mathematical reasoning contributed to this tendency by providing an analysis to justify it, for simple ideas cannot be erroneous since error arises in the combination of ideas and if one could proceed from indivisible ideas by indivisible connections, one could encompass the whole of human knowledge and achieve certainty in all sciences by avoiding the intrusions of imagination, emotion, and opinion which impede the development of science and philosophy. Spinoza used the geometric order in his *Ethics* to provide scientific demonstration of propositions which established morality and freedom on adequate ideas and on the minimization of the effects of the passions. Although his learning in Greek philosophy was slight he confessed an attraction to Democritus, Epicurus, and Lucretius as opposed to Socrates, Plato, and Aristotle. In the nineteenth and twentieth centuries the philosophic use of the geometric method moved slowly and indecisively from Laws of Thought to constructions built from simple sentences and atomic facts or from the elements of language and what they designate, for the vestiges of epistemology were attached to the symbolism borrowed from mathematics—science is the "cognitive" use of language as contrasted to a host of opposed uses, "emotive," "persuasive," "ejaculatory," "hortatory," "evocative," and new commitments to the theses of empiricism and physicalism seemed necessary if the cognitive was to be preserved from its old epistemological rivals.

The logistic or geometric method is better suited to controversy than to dialogue. What other philosophers conclude on other grounds can rarely pass as "cognitive." When it does, appropriate restatement is needed to make it precise. Much of traditional philosophy is found, therefore, to be devoted to the consideration of unreal problems, and the history of philosophy is a cumulative sequence in which sciences were separated one by one from the disorderly mass of conjecture, superstition, and insight until only logic and the theory of values stand in need of like reformulation for philosophy to be assimilated wholly to the sciences. The larger region of philosophic discussion is best treated by considering not the content of propositions but the state of mind of those who enunciate them. As dialogue it is non-cognitive. It may be brought to a conclusion by the discovery of truth, and the contribution of science to questions which involve only emotions is to remove superstition and fear, as the Epicureans put it, or to cure tensions and complexes and promote mental health, as the program is formulated in more modern terms. Discussion contributes to the discovery of truth and is cognitive when it takes the form of interchanges between men of different backgrounds and technical skill assembled in research teams. Controversy is a symptom of confusion, mental disorder, and drives to power.

iv. In the historical contexts in which dialogue concerning basic philosophic issues takes many forms—such as, (1) the synthesis of contraries and the assimilation of divergent views, (2) the development of differences and the examination of unresolved oppositions, (3) the reduction of all views to a basic thesis about the nature of physical reality and sense experience and the abandonment, as meaningless and non-cognitive, of statements which resist reduction—the desirability of making a series of literal distinctions among methods and meanings has appealed to philosophers repeatedly. It has seemed plausible that a method of formal proof common to all inference might be discovered and formulated, that this method might be distinguished from the method of examining the hypotheses and principles from which inference proceeds, that a dialectical method might be devised to treat opinions concerning particular matters and problems when agreement in statement is desirable and that it might be supplemented by a rhetorical method of constructing arguments to influence audiences when agreement is sought in attitude and action, that a method of solving sophistical arguments might be a useful adjunct to detect apparent inferences or apparent principles employed to reach demonstrably false conclusions, that a method of analyzing objects of art might be employed to separate esthetic characteristics from moral and political influences and doctrines adumbrated, and that, finally, methods of inquiry might be developed to treat the problems and matters particular to different fields.

The most obvious mark by which this effort to distinguish a plurality of methods may be recognized in its many employments and manifestations is a concern to apply a scientific method to all fields and yet to differentiate the use of science in three large areas—the theoretic, the practical, and the poetic or productive. Aristotle first made this differentiation recognizing the need, if methods are to be developed appropriate to the various tasks to which they are applied, of three master or architectonic sciences—metaphysics to treat the first principles of the sciences and to provide the grounds for a theoretical organization of knowledge, including not only natural sciences but also sciences of action and production; politics to treat the first principles of human actions and associations and to provide the grounds for a practical organization of common activities, including those which affect the advance of science and the cultivation of art as well as morals and politics; and poetics to treat the first principles of human production and to provide the grounds for an aesthetic organization of the products of arts, including those which set forth knowledge or affect action as well as the fine arts. Thomas Aquinas employed the same distinctions to rectify the controversies and confusions of mediaeval dialecticians and to separate philosophy and natural theology from the dialectic of the Augustinian formulation of revealed theology. John Dewey sought to extend the use of scientific method or the method of reflective thinking to the resolution of all problems, but he saw danger in the application of the method of the physical sciences to practical problems, and he treated philosophy itself as an art concerned with meanings rather than with truth and falsity.

The principles employed by philosophers in the development of other methods often lead them to differentiations similar to those based on the method of inquiry into problems and into problematic situations. Spinoza employed the geometric method in his *Ethics,* but since the principles from which his deduction flowed led to the conclusion that even the wise man does not live always according to the dictates of reason and that most men rarely do, an ethics based on adequate ideas must be separated sharply from a politics based on power and a religion based on piety. Kant was awakened from his dogmatic slumbers by a skeptical dialectic and separated the realms of pure reason, practical reason, and judgment with the aid of distinctions between general logic, transcendental logic and the uses of logic as organon and as canon. Aristotle's rejection of Plato's reduction of different forms of human association by the analogy between state and family finds echo in Locke's refutation of Filmer's use of a like analogy and in Montesquieu's study of the circumstances that determine the variety of systems of positive law.

Dialogue has a place in this distinction of methods according to the problems to which they are addressed. The problematic method, like the dialectical method, provides a place for each of the tasks of philosophy, but the methods proper to inquiry, proof, and persuasion are found to be different, when their respective problems are distinguished; like the logistic method, the problematic method requires univocal definitions and indemonstrable first principles, but there are many sets of such basic propositions, and they are not used to organize all knowledge in a single body of deductively derived propositions; rhetoric has an important independent place in the development of the problematic method, but is not, as in the skeptical or operational method, the whole method of science. Dialogue is preliminary and propaedeutic to the treatment of *theoretic* questions; other philosophic theories are studied in order to avoid errors already tried and exposed and to adapt truths already discovered and established. The treatment of *practical* questions does not permit like precision and their resolution depends on attitudes and communication bearing on what is best in various circumstances. The production of artificial objects must relate their proper perfections

to the natural objects they imitate and the proper pleasures they occasion. Politics and poetics, like metaphysics, employ a dialectical method
in inquiry concerning principles which are applied demonstratively in
deduction and induction. But it is a limited dialectic, concerned with
specific questions, like the nature of cause or sensation, earthquakes or
the origin of the Nile, property or slavery, rather than with large questions of philosophic systematization. On most questions numerous imperfect anticipations of the correct solution can be brought together.
Neglect of method or the improper use or extension of methods, however, leads to outright error: Democritus is betrayed into innumerable
inconsistencies and absurdities by his failure to examine the method
which he used successfully; the Sophists practise verbal trickery when
they ignore the requirements of substantive fact and formal argument
to extend methods derived from rhetoric; Plato attributes being to
separated objects constructed to provide grounds for dialectical analogies among things and dialectical extensions of reason and understanding. Controversy results no less from restatements of doctrine with partial approval than from refutations.

The methods elaborated by philosophers to treat materials and meanings fall into patterns which determine the forms of dialogue and controversy. The large forms of these opposed methods are easily recognized, and philosophers express their attitudes towards dialogue and
betray their proneness to turn dialogue into controversy in ways that
can be explained by those methods.

In significant senses dialogue is an inseparable part of dialectical or
operational methods. Both methods use opposed opinions or hypotheses directly as means of resolving substantive problems, but despite
occasional overlaps and some consequent confusion of the two methods by philosophers committed to other methods, the two uses of dialogue and their characteristic excursions into controversy are different.
In the large forms assumed by philosophies which employ the dialectical method, oppositions are found in fact as well as in opinion; and the
processes of nature, history, and thought are identical or strictly comparable since they all assimilate contraries to higher unities and
syntheses; for the dialectician any doctrine is both true (in one sense
and at one stage) and false (in many senses and at many stages). The
dialogue may have either positive or negative results without falling
into controversy; it is interrupted in controversy by the intrusion of a

verbal or skeptical method which separates thought from its object or by a partial conception of thought or its object which makes thinking subjective or nature mechanical. In the large forms assumed by philosophies which employ the operational method, on the other hand, the oppositions are found only in opinion, hypothesis, perspective, or measurements, and their basic irreducibility is itself an important trait to be observed in the methodological acquisition of theoretic knowledge and in the resolution of practical problems. Two possibilities are open to the operationalist—one of the opposed hypotheses may be inapplicable and the decision may be in favor of one of the opposed parties, or both hypotheses may account for or measure the same facts but in different ways, and different reasons based on opposed policies may be adduced for the same course of action. Dialogue is interrupted in controversy only by dogmatisms which refuse to submit opinions about ultimate reality or the compelling evidence of experience or thought to the test of other opinions and hypotheses.

Dialogue is not an essential part of logistic or problematic methods. Both methods use opposed opinions or hypotheses only indirectly in the solution of substantive problems, since both separate questions of opinion formation and communication from questions of inquiry and proof. In the use of the problematic method, dialogue is relevant to proof, and there is even place for a restricted form of dialectic to resolve differences of opinion and belief. Dialectic is a stage in the search for truth, but its methods are sharply separated from those of inquiry and proof. The examination of other theories and doctrines has a heuristic value in the treatment of any problem, for the assemblage of what has been said previously makes available existing knowledge at the start of investigations, but the balance of opinions does not contribute directly to the examination of data or the construction of suitable hypotheses concerning them. On the other hand, dialectic is the only method applicable to fundamental metaphysical questions. Controversy is directed against dialecticians (who invent fictive entities to make their propositions true), against sophists (who advance propositions which are indifferently true or false), and against methodless thinkers (who have no proof for their propositions even when they happen to be true). In the use of the logistic method, dialogue is avoided, since the truth is one, and the effort of science and philosophy is to achieve knowledge of truth. Dialogue enters into that effort when truth is not available and knowledge ceases in the balance of probabilities, preferences, and emotions and in the preparation for decision and persuasion. Acquisition of knowledge depends on exclusion of emotion, imagination, and opinion, and, consequently, of dialogue; and although none of these can be eliminated wholly from the lives of the many, science can control their deleterious effects by exposing substitutes for knowledge. Controversy is directed against philosophers who consider unreal questions, make meaningless statements, or construct proofs unsusceptible of empirical verification.

The primary purpose of philosophy is the discovery and demonstration of truth. But "truth" is differently conceived according to the principles of different philosophies, and philosophical methods are constructed to form and justify bodies of doctrines which express truths so conceived and so justified. Dialogue is part of all such methods since the justification of a philosophic conclusion must take into account other proposed analyses, yet the attempted dialogue does not extend beyond the limits of those who agree in method, and controversy arises both because the tenets of each method predestine certain methods to error and because the restatement which conclusions receive in the dialogue constructed by philosophers is seldom adequate or satisfactory to those who hold those conclusions. Differences of methods are seldom remarked, however, even in the case of philosophers who place great store on the novelty of their methods and explain and illustrate them in detail. In spite of the obvious differences in the large forms which philosophies take as a result of the methods employed in their construction—the massive progressions and syntheses of dialectic, the long chains of reasoning from primitive propositions of logistic, the skeptical pluralism of opinions and perspectives, the problematic pluralism of methods and principles—efforts at philosophical dialogue usually take the form of extracting isolated statements from the system of arguments by which they are justified to try them in the context of other principles and methods. Like the Cartesian "good sense," a sense of method is apparently thought to be equally distributed, for everyone thinks himself so well supplied with it that critics rarely pause to examine another method or to consider its possible cogency or validity before announcing the discovery of simple inconsistencies and fantastic absurdities, such as are seldom encountered in casual conversation, in the works of philosophers who base their statements on methods and principles which they have scrutinized meticulously.

Controversy has so far outrun dialogue in contemporary philosophical discussions that dialogue has all but disappeared except among the sects which have formed within particular philosophical traditions. This is no new phenomenon in the history of philosophy, and in a fundamental sense it is a natural consequence of the oppositions of philosophic methods. It has, however, taken on unusual importance today—as it did in the Roman Empire and again during the Renaissance—since the failure of communication and understanding in philosophy is a symptom of what is happening in larger communications in cultural relations and political negotiations. It might be argued equally plausibly that philosophy has come into new responsibilities and uses since the practical problems of our times may be traced back to an ideological conflict which is fundamentally philosophic, or that the integrity and effectiveness of the search for truth is destroyed by differences of philosophic tradition which simply reflect differences of culture and interest. In much the same fashion historians of Roman and Renaissance philosophy have argued equally plausibly that philosophy was freed from dogmas and superstitions in those periods and philosophers differed only verbally, and that philosophy disappeared wholly into the barren verbalism of rhetoric and the discouraged ineffectiveness of skepticism.

It is improbable that invitations to dialogue will lead to philosophic agreement or cultural uniformity, and it is doubtful whether such agreement or uniformity would be desirable if they were possible. But if controversy arises from the radical differences among the methods by which philosophers have sought truth, the possibility of dialogue is to be found in the similarities among the methods by which they have sought intelligibility and consensus. It is impossible to avoid controversy concerning what is true or probable, but controversy might be avoided without abandoning problems of the relation of arguments to the exploration of reality by turning attention to problems of the relation of arguments to elucidation of minds. Problems of communication are not wholly independent of problems of proof, but there are large regions of coincidence in the methods by which philosophers take into account the audiences to which their arguments are addressed. The controversies which grow out of differences of method are crucial precisely because they concern issues in which it is difficult to separate substantive differences concerning the nature and relations of things from verbal differences due to shifts of meanings of terms defined according to opposed methods and principles. Formal analysis of what is accepted as inference and what is accepted as principle should not only clarify meanings by separating fact from form of statement but it should also have material implications by giving objective grounds to the study of attitudes and audiences which has taken a skeptical and relativistic turn in comparative psychology, the sociology of knowledge, and the variety of studies in which the relations of cultures are treated. This large region is the field of what has often in the history of thought been called rhetoric, and since the four methods enumerated above have been described by considering four possihle positions concerning the relation of proof to persuasion, the possibility of cooperative study and mutual understanding of arguments of the second kind may be judged by considering the place of rhetoric in each of the methods.

The methods of rhetoric constitute the whole of philosophic method in the operational or skeptical method. Many of the efforts to reduce controversy and advance truth in the history of modern philosophy from Francis Bacon and Vico to Mill and some contemporary analytical philosophers have made more or less conscious appeal to the commonplaces of rhetoric. Ch. Perelman has urged a return to rhetorical considerations for a theory of philosophical argumentation.[15] The preceding analysis of dialogue and controversy was made from the point of view of the rhetorical or skeptical tradition in which the fundamental assumptions are that knowledge is advanced best by the free opposition of arguments, that a common truth may be given a variety of statements from different perspectives, and that there is an element of truth in all philosophic positions. In problematic inquiry, rhetoric or its counterpart, dialectic, is a methodological stage antecedent to the resolution of philosophic problems; it is not the method of philosophy, but any philosophical argument may be examined rhetorically or dialectically to disclose its assumptions and form. In the context of a dialectical philosophy, rhetoric is imperfect dialectic limited to subjective distinctions, but such distinctions and principles are susceptible of dialectical expansion and examination such as they receive in the "inconclusive" dialogues of Plato. In a logistic philosophy, rhetoric has no place as a cognitive method, but rhetorical arguments possess a structure which can be ana-

15. Ch. Perelman and L. Olbrechts-Tyteca, *Rhétorique et Philosophie: Pour une Théorie de l'Argumentation en Philosophie* (Paris, 1952).

lyzed in logistic semantics and which can be compared in structure to cognitive arguments.

Analyses of arguments for communication, separated from analyses of arguments for demonstration, may provide not merely the method by which to advance dialogue in philosophy but also materials by which to lessen tensions and oppositions between cultures. It is not to be anticipated that there will be agreement in the treatment of this common region of philosophy, since the approaches to it are affected by differences of method as much as the substantive problems of truth which are the center of philosophic controversy. But the different treatments will be comparable approaches to problems of communication—rhetorical enumerations of modes of expression adapting opinions or positions to audiences, problematic enumerations of methods adapting concepts to circumstances, logistic enumerations of constructions in which terms are defined and combined, dialectical enumerations of systems adapting principles to arguments—and they should make it possible to focus attention on the different structures of argument and the different presuppositions employed in different traditions and forms of philosophy. The basic problems of dialogue are, first, to find ways to make certain that there is agreement concerning what is in question and, second, to understand what is conceived to constitute a satisfactory answer to the question. Only when these problems have been resolved is it possible to decide whether proposed solutions are in agreement or opposed. Mutual understanding in the sense of agreement concerning what the question is and what is required in a satisfactory solution is necessary if philosophers are to resume their dialogue, or even continue their efforts to convince each other of the truth of their respective positions, and it is essential also to the solution of social and political problems—to make possible agreement on common courses of action for different reasons, appreciation of alien values, and confidence based on understanding.

6

Has History a Direction?

Philosophical Principles and Objective Interpretations

Essay, Oral Presentation, Reply to Queries, and Commentary

The problem of the direction of history is a counterpart of the problem of the objectivity of philosophy. The relevance of historical accounts to what actually happened depends on the relevance of philosophical formulations to what is actually the case. The question, What happened? may be distinguished from the question, What must happen? and then poetry, which sets forth what might happen, is more universal and philosophical than history; or the questions may coincide, and then the inadequacies and partialities of original history and reflective history find their completion in the necessities and rationalities of philosophical history. The difference between Aristotle and Hegel, however, is a difference of philosophic methods; it is not resolved by appeal to the facts of history or to the narratives of historians. Different kinds of history are determined by different philosophic principles, and the appeal to 'facts' and data in support of philosophic 'concepts' and conclusions does not provide independent confirmation, since the history is already homogeneous with the philosophy. Hegel and Croce can argue that history is the account of the development of freedom. Other philosophers can argue no less plausibly that history is the account of the accumulations and successions of power; or that it is an account of the conflicts and oppositions of freedom and power; or that it is an account of the interpenetration and transformation of the two. The differences are not differences of direction to the same or different goals, for 'freedom' and 'power' have different philosophic analyses which give meanings to four views of freedom and which find support in four histories.

Reprinted from *La comprehension de l'histoire: Entretiens de Jerusalem (4–8 avril 1965)*, ed. Nathan Rotenstreich (Jerusalem: The Israel Academy of Sciences and Humanities, 1968), 63–79, 87–101.

Whether history has a direction is a question of the interrelations of philosophic principles and objective interpretations.

History is an account of facts and of connections of facts. *Historia* meant inquiry and knowledge obtained by inquiry or, since it was probably derived from a verb meaning 'to see' in the perfect tense, knowledge of what has been seen. The data of history are selected existential simples, subject to enumeration, but the facts of history are interpreted complexes, stated in propositions. Data are given, but facts are made. There is always a connection in a fact, and there is always a direction in a series of statements of fact. In philosophy or science, inquiry or proof does not always follow the same consequences as the processes it treats. In history, interpretation or account seeks to trace the consequence of occurrences; but the facts depend on choice among connections, and facts are joined to each other in historical consequences only by preserving connections of meaning which are philosophical consequences. Natural history is continuous with human history and divine history. Facts are recorded about inanimate, animate, human, and cosmic things. Human history reflects this continuity: individual actions and social occurrences may evolve their meanings and connections against a transcendental background of intelligibility and reality which gives them an organic unity; or against the background of an underlying material structure—physical nature, human nature, 'natural law', relations of economic production—which provide them with 'elements' and 'laws'; or in the context of conditioning circumstances—biological, political, social, cultural—which give them circumstantial particularity; or in an interaction of impulsions and repulsions which give them an operational schema. The report of facts in any of these senses connects data by processes and functions. The direction of history depends on what history is about and how processes are conceived.

History, in one of its forms, treats the subjects and processes which provide the material and structure of the cosmic myths of the ages of man, of his origin and destiny, of the gifts of the gods, and of the development of culture. Analogies are found in the seasons of the year, in the sequence of birth, maturity and decline, in the four (or twenty-one) empires of the world, or in the being of the City of God (or the freedom of the classless society) contrasted to the becoming of the terrestrial city (or the repressions of the political state). This is epochal history, for it moves in ages—Hellenistic, Enlightenment, Baroque,

Romantic, Capitalistic—and each age has unifying characteristics shared by all activities in the age. Art, philosophy, science, commercial organization, geographic exploration, and life, in general, are baroque in a Baroque Age. The direction of history in epochal histories may follow stages of degradation from a golden age, of advancement to an ultimate utopia, of repeated cycles of initiation, fulfillment, and decay, or of emergence of order from chaos under the impulsion of reason and necessity.

History, in another form, is about processes, not about homogeneous cultural structures, and they are connected in lines of causal sequence, not in lines of organic transformation. The laws determining the sequences are taken from sciences like physics, biology, psychology, politics, economics, or military strategy; and the uniformity of human nature and human actions in all nations and ages takes the place of the uniformity of characters and processes in a people or an age. The basic analogy on which the connections are conceived is power, not culture. This is causal history, for it moves along thin lines of causes to which all other sequences and causes are reduced. The development of a political constitution, or of a philosophy, or of trends of aesthetic taste, of scientific speculation or of social, racial, or intellectual intolerance can, thus, be explained reductively by economic interpretation. Causal history gives prominence to the idea of progress, for some sequences are cumulative or progressive. The direction of history in causal histories may be random or progressive: the causal lines in transfers of political power are necessary, but the direction is random; while the causal lines in the accumulation and application of knowledge yield a direction or progress in knowledge and civilization, but paradoxical problems in the random use of knowledge and civility.

Epochal and causal histories determine the direction of history on patterns of reality which transcend or underlie the facts connected in historical sequences. A third form of history is based on denial that history is about forms or processes as such. History is about facts, and the connections of facts in the sequences of human history are established by the problems men have encountered and the actions they have undertaken to resolve, or to avoid, them. Experience, art and science, dispositions, habits, customs, and institutions supplement nature and natural ability as instrumentalities in the solution of problems. Human history is the account of problem-solving and of the development of means of solving problems. This is disciplinary history, for it moves from the solution of a problem to the utilization of what has been learned, and to the formation of new disciplines, to the solution of problems which arise from the solution or failure to solve the prior problem. Disciplinary history is used in histories of constitutions and institutions and in histories of arts and sciences. Polybius' history of the development of the Roman constitution and the peripatetic histories of the sciences in antiquity have been extended to other institutions and other disciplines in later disciplinary histories. The direction of history in disciplinary histories opens out like a fan at each juncture, for the solution of a problem is not an end of the historical process but the opening up of new problems some of which will be treated in deliberative and purposive activities, and problems which are ignored or not solved are likewise the source of new problems.

A final form of history is about acts, not facts, and the connections of acts is in their force in determining the actions of other agents or in their influence as models for modes of action employed. History teaches by examples drawn from the actions of great men and the operations of adaptable institutions. This is exemplary history, for the hero is recognized by all men despite differences in their cultures, in their scientific analyses, or in their problematic perspectives, and the balanced constitution provides for problems unanticipated in its formation; examples of both heroes and institutions move from one historical context to another. Machiavelli went to history in *The Prince* for the example of great rulers, like Moses, Cyrus, Romulus, and Theseus, in the interest of the unification of Italy, and to the history of Livy in *The Discourses* for the example of the division of powers in the constitution of Rome in the interest of the formation of republican virtues. The direction of history in exemplary history is determined by random interplays of external forces until they are coordinated by the initiative of a great man, or of a man who follows his example, or by an institution which brings powers into limitations and balances for productive operation.

The direction of history is discovered neither *a priori* nor empirically. It is neither an abstract imposition nor an objective observation. It is determined by philosophic principle and empirical fact much as philosophy itself is, and therefore, since philosophy too has a history, the history of philosophy is one of the least ambiguous examples of the direction of history. In epochal histories of philosophy, later ages synthesize the antitheses of previous philosophers. The historical sequence is cumulative, and the historian of philosophy seeks to preserve and develop in his history what was valid and efficacious in the contradictory philosophies of earlier antagonists. The tasks of philosophy and of the history of philosophy are fundamentally the same. In causal histories of philosophy, the whole of knowledge was once philosophy, and the historical sequence is the separation of the sciences one by one— mathematics, physics, biology, psychology, and the social sciences— from that whole. In any age, including our own, philosophy is the remnant of problems as yet unsolved or by nature insoluble. The history of philosophy is not directly relevant to the solution of philosophic problems. It is an account of how problems ceased to be philosophic when scientific methods were devised for them and of nonphilosophic reasons why philosophers considered meaningless problems and made odd or even absurd statements. In disciplinary histories of philosophy, the sequence of problems and of hypotheses for their solution is set forth. The philosopher may learn from the history of philosophy about past mistakes which he might otherwise repeat unaware that they had been shown false and past successes which he might otherwise fail to utilize in the formation of his own hypotheses. With the aid of history, progress may be made in the consideration of continuing or evolving philosophic problems. In exemplary histories of philosophy, the careers and achievements of great philosophers are set forth. They may open up the meaning and use of philosophy to a philosopher or a beginner who contemplates them, and they may teach him to pose his problems better and more completely by asking himself how Plato or Aristotle or William of Ockham or Spinoza or Kant would have framed them.

The example of the history of philosophy makes clear that the problem of the direction of history must be considered in two contexts or orientations. Since the facts of history depend on the philosophic principles according to which they are formulated, questions of the direction of history must be raised within the context of a single conception of history if they are to have objective meaning. To ask how the several conceptions are related to each other is to raise questions about the semantics of history, not about the directions of history. On the other hand, since the data of history are subject to formulation as facts according to any of these conceptions, history itself and historical narratives exhibit many conceptions of history and many directions.

In the first context or orientation, the directions of history must be differentiated and joined to their relevant philosophic principles. If you are interested in the problem of time, or of the criteria of truth and verification, or of the grounds of moral judgment and if you seek an account of past treatments of those problems and of past discussions of their adequacies and inadequacies, you will find that only in disciplinary histories of philosophy. If you are interested in the evolution from scholastic to baroque conceptions of time, you may find it treated in an epochal history which sets forth the evolution of thought from the Middle Ages to the eighteenth century. If you are interested in the transformation of the concept of time when it was put to scientific uses and analyses by Galileo and Huyghens, you should go to a causal history of philosophy. If you are interested in breaking from the aridities and abstractions of contemporary philosophies of experience and existence, you might see inspiration in the contemplation of how great philosophers faced like problems in an exemplary history of philosophy.

Once you have found the answer to the particular question adapted to your own philosophic preferences and commitments, however, you would do well to move to the second context or orientation. Philosophy is an enterprise carried out in all the philosophic formulations conceived by philosophers, and it has directions determined by all the objectives proper to those formulations—to new structures of reality and thought, to new truths and demonstrations, to new resolutions of old and new problems, and to new innovations of statement and action. Your problem in this context is not to decide which among these directions is truly the direction; your problem is to consider how the various movements and directions, which philosophy is asserted to have, may be made more effective by philosophic analysis and statement based on examination of their interaction on each other as supplementary and as mutually reinforcing rather than as contradictory and mutually exclusive. The directions of the history of philosophy are particularizations of the directions of history. The fruitful use of the directions of history, as mutually contradictory and mutually supplementary, is a particularization of philosophic problems of philosophic principles and objective interpretations.

R. P. McKeon:

The printed version of my communication, *Has History a Direction? Philosophical Principles and Objective Interpretations,* has been distributed. I shall not try to outline its contents. Instead, by way of introduc-

tion to the problems of the direction of history, I should like to discuss
three questions. In the first place, I shall explain how I came to conceive
the 'direction' of history as I do in my paper. We are now in the third
day of our discussions, and I shall therefore explain the distinctions
which I make in my paper by applying them to problems which have
emerged in the last two days. In the second place, having stated the
problem of the direction of history and having distinguished it from
the problems of the philosophy of history, I shall examine the distinction between historical data and historical facts, and the structure of the
distinctions which I use in treating historical facts. In the third place, I
shall state briefly some important problems of history and of philosophy which arise from these considerations and which I hope to introduce into discussion.

My first subject is the problem itself. As you know, the Organizing
Committee made a distribution of subjects. I found that it was necessary to make an adjustment or interpretation of my assignment when I
began to prepare my paper. My reason for this apparent deviation is
simple. I received two letters from the Organizing Committee, one in
English, the other in French. The letter in English stated the problem:
'Does history have a meaning?' My immediate answer to this question
was 'No'. The letter in French stated the problem: 'L'histoire, a-t-elle
un sens?' My answer to this question was 'Yes'. My two answers were
not contradictory. They were, rather, a recognition of the problem
which we face. The problem is not either of the two questions interpreted as if they were unambiguous. If the letter in English had stated
the problem: 'Does history have a sense?' I might have discovered that
basic problem in the pun on the word 'sense', but in French the two
meanings were perfectly apparent.

For philosophic purposes the two meanings and the two questions
open up the basic problem of the relation between two approaches to
history. My two answers to the questions were recognition of the fundamental opposition of two approaches. But both approaches to history have been widespread in history and in philosophy, and the relation between them poses a philosophic problem which might be lost in
a clash of controversial preferences in which one is taken to be true and
the other false.

The first approach to history has been all but pervasive in our discussions of the last two days. It is an approach in which *la conscience
historique* is fundamental precisely because only human deeds and ac-

complishments have a history. The other approach to history has been at least as widespread, but it has had fewer proponents among us to defend it against the first. It is an approach in which what occurs is viewed as events and movements, which are interpreted by human beings and arranged in orders appropriate to their interpretations. The meanings which men associate with events, and which influence their actions, give history a direction which is alleged as basic for the meanings. When I came to see this problem of the relation of different approaches to history, it seemed to me that my answer to the ambiguous question should not be thrown into the form it would take in one or the other of these two approaches. In other words, since I could now see the fashion in which history has a meaning, the philosophic problem of the meaning of history could not be treated adequately by limiting my consideration of it to the approach to history which I use in my historical studies—and which I think is most frequently used by English-speaking historians—in which history, strictly speaking, does not have a meaning. Since I wished to make provisions for both approaches to history I called my paper, 'Does history have a direction?' The direction of history may take the form of a direction which is interpreted into a meaning or of a direction which is already a meaning.

How should the problem of the relation of the meaning and the direction of history be stated philosophically, if it is a problem which can not be stated within the limitations of one set of philosophic principles or in the language of one philosophy? If history has a direction, it should be observable in the 'facts' of history; its discovery should not depend on viewing those 'facts' according to an antecedent philosophy of history. Delineation of the direction of history should be *propaedeutic* to the construction of structures of narrative accounts by historians, or structures of disputative argument by philosophers of history, for both structures have their bases in commitments to philosophic principles. Two tendencies operate to give the direction of history a meaning; to separate and relate them I proposed to discuss the meaning and direction of history by considering 'Philosophical Principles and Objective Interpretations', as is indicated by the subtitle appended to the question, 'Does History have a Direction?' The perception and even the indication of a direction depends on no appeal to philosophic principles; the presentation or account of movements of motivated people in directions which they observe, plan, and oppose depends on principles of selection, interpretation, and sequential inference which push back to philosophic principles. The objectivity of an historical account does not consist in the reproduction in statement of facts of occurrence: historical facts no less than narrative accounts of facts are selected and constituted; and the justification of the interpretation of what was the case and the account of what it was that occurred—the whether and the what—both depend on principles.

The two approaches to history which I have detected in our discussions are particular forms of these two tendencies. In both, philosophic principles are used to determine and to order facts. Statement of fact and interpretation of fact may be distinguished analytically, but they are not separate parts of a narrative or account; and therefore an approach to history is usually presented, not as an approach to, but as the nature of, history. The approach is forgotten or assimilated to the facts; the measure becomes part of the nature of the measured. In the opposition of the approaches, each is presented by its proponents as a statement of demonstrable and inevitable facts. Therefore the opposition is not resolved by interpretation but by appeal to the fact. According to the one approach, it is a fact that man is a natural being in a natural world. Human nature is a source and explanation of actions in a natural world which is the environment of man and the setting for his actions. History is the account of his actions and of events that affect them or follow from them. According to the other approach, only men have a history and a sense of history, and this reflexivity of history, which limits it to beings which perceive it, prevents the extension of 'history' from human beings, human intentions, and human realizations to natural history, natural functions and circumstances, and natural events. If the problem of the meaning and direction of history is to be considered, neither of these approaches can be taken as natural and inevitable, for the problem arises from the relations of the two. The principles which I take to be natural in my philosophical and historical studies could not be used as the ordering principles of my inquiry concerning the direction of history: those principles and other principles alleged to be natural are the subject of inquiry. Other distinctions are needed to order the principles, methods, and interpretations of philosophies. The fundamental distinctions which I use for that purpose are set forth and elaborated in my paper. I shall not repeat what I said in applying them; but an explanation of how they are derived and established may make clear their bearing on the problems we are now discussing.

My second subject grows out of the statement of the problem. Two sets of distinctions are needed to treat the problem of the meaning and direction of history, one to relate the data of historical experience to the facts of historical inquiry, another to distinguish the different forms of historical inquiry and the kinds of facts which are discovered and employed in each of the forms.

History does not occur in a world of pre-existent ready-made facts, constituted to fit metaphysical orders or epistemological forms and ideas. History is evolved from unordered or accidentally ordered immediate experiences. Experiences and testimonies of experience are the data, the given, with which the historian begins. How does a historian who inquires into and writes about the history of the Peloponnesian War or the history of the French Revolution or the history of Democratic Institutions or the history of Logic place himself with respect to his data and with respect to other actual or possible accounts of the processes and relations he investigates in treating his data? If he is writing a history of the Peloponnesian War he will share common data with other historians of that war, but he undertakes his history because he thinks the data have not been treated properly, or adequately, or truly. His history will treat common historical data, but present distinctive historical facts.

Several steps may be distinguished in the evolution of facts from data and in the differentiation of different histories of a common subject. First, there is a common conception which identifies the historical experiences which are the subject of investigation and presentation. The subject is the Peloponnesian War. It is an ambiguous conception defined by a rough circle drawn among data. The circle encloses an indefinitely large number of data from which an indefinitely large number of facts and connections may be discovered and formed. Second, each historian makes his selection among the data of the ambiguously identified subject. Data are not facts stated in propositions, but simples designated or named. The data are indicated persons, places, relations, events, concepts. They are not truths but categorical elements or commonplaces which may be used in the statement of facts. Third, statements of fact are constructed from the data. Data are the materials related in statements; they are presented in statements of alleged facts. Data as simples, are neither true nor false, and the presentation of truths about data is the transmutation of data into facts. Fourth, the

ordering of facts in sequences of occurrences or of discourse is the justification and verification of allegations of fact. It is only at this point
that the direction or meaning of history emerges.

The principles of history and of philosophy are guiding principles in
this transition from the ambiguously designated common data of experience to the unambiguously specified facts of an historical account.
They are principles of exploration or manifestation, of selection or discovery, of establishment or verification, and of coherency or justification. The principles of philosophy account for the evolution of facts
from data, but not for the differentiation of particular histories which
treat common data by giving different accounts of different facts. To
relate two approaches to historical research, distinctions are needed
which are not distorted by commitment to one of the philosophies
distinguished. The differentiation of the common data of experience
and the specific facts of accounts of occurrences provides such a distinction. Two histories of the Peloponnesian War are both about the
Peloponnesian War. But the available data relevant even to an event
long past and known through only a few surviving documents and material remains is indefinitely large, and new historians with ingenuity
will always be able to find new data and new approaches to the ambiguous common data they share with other historians of the common
subject. Different historians use different selections from the data; and
since the possibilities of selection are infinite, they will sometimes state
different facts and sometimes the same facts, interpreted in the same
way or differently, even to the extreme possibility of two histories of
the same subject which select totally different facts. Moreover, when
they differ, the different accounts are not necessarily in contradiction,
for a common fact interpreted differently is no longer a single fact;
statement and denial of it are equivocal, not contradictory, and it is
possible that both are true.

Any statement of the relation of the data of historical experience to
the facts of historical inquiry and historical narration must reflect the
inescapable ambiguity of 'data' and 'facts', even in meticulously precise
statements, for precisions of definition and meaning are introduced,
step by step, into inchoate materials and ambiguous statements. Our
statement of the relation began with the delimitation of a common
experience which was the potential source of infinite data, proceeded
to different selections of actual data by different historians, to the composition of the respective data of the different histories into facts and

statements of facts, and to the ordering of facts and statements into sequences of occurrences and discourse. As the ambiguities are removed, it becomes increasingly difficult, and eventually impossible, to express the distinction in philosophically neutral language. The question of meaning or direction therefore intrudes itself unavoidably at the fourth step when sequences of facts and statements are discovered and ordered. Ambiguity is congenial to discussion and research; precision promotes opposition and controversy. Consequently, when the common experience which the different histories shared as data is reviewed from the standpoint of the ordered sequence of the facts of a history or the truths of a philosophy, the ambiguous common data have shrunk to the particular data selected in the facts of the particular history and its philosophy. The same shrinking occurs in the common data which different philosophies share: once we begin to introduce some philosophic precision into statements about the 'common experience' investigated by different historians, we must decide what its status is and how it should be understood and described, and we are on the edge of philosophic controversy. Is it a common experience or a common series of events or a common sequence of statements or a common structure of meanings and values?

I do not think that we did justice yesterday to what Mr. Nikam said about recorded history. History as it enters our experiences and researches is not a brute fact or a collection of determinate facts. It is data known and conceived as a series of events only because they are stated; and in historical statements, of source documents or of historical accounts, facts are recorded facts. If the facts recorded are altered or questioned in interpretation and restatement, the change is justified by another record, including the record of the historian stating his interpretation of what took place. Whether the common element of the various accounts or interpretations is a common experience or a common series of events or a common sequence of statements or a common structure of meanings and values is a philosophical problem, which is faced by both historians and philosophers. To treat it requires the second set of distinctions, not between the data of experience and the facts stated in accounts of experience, but between the different forms of historical inquiry and the different kinds of facts that are relevant and definitive in each. The two approaches to history which I detected in our discussions may be placed in the matrix of the four forms of history which I construct in my paper. The four forms of history are not literally description as a catalogue of all actual and possible modes of historical inquiry and statement, but they are formally exhaustive as a matrix in which numberless particular approaches may be interpreted by specifying subdivisions under the four forms. I shall use the four forms of history in order to differentiate four answers to the questions, What has a history? How is the direction of history discovered? and What is the meaning or significance given to history?

One form of history seeks the meaning and direction of history in structures of meanings and values. History in classical dialectical philosophies was identified with myth, and we have rediscovered in our time the importance of interpreting myths to understand past civilizations and cultures. The transition from mythical narrative to dialectical argument is easy and natural—they are supplementary statements of the same truths; they are homogeneous statements of meanings and values. In history, meanings and values provide the connections and perspectives of sequences and synchronisms. I have called this form of history 'epochal history' because synchronous events and purposive activities share the common characteristics which define an 'age', and the sequences of history are successions of ages. History and philosophy employ different devices to set forth the same meanings and values: the complete history of an idea or an institution is the same as the philosophical analysis of it. Hegel emphasized this equivalence and made effective historical and philosophical use of it. There have been many modern epochal histories since those of Hegel and Marx, influenced by them or in reaction against them, but there were epochal histories before Hegel, in antiquity, the Middle Ages, and the early modern period. The approach to history which makes use of the epochal conception of the meaning of history and historical consciousness has been espoused repeatedly in the course of our discussions. But the dialectical equivalence of history and philosophy, which seems obvious and natural in epochal history, does not hold for any of the other approaches to history. I have questioned its extension to history as such, while recognizing its meaning and appropriateness in epochal history.

The second form of history has also been espoused or assumed in our discussions. In this form history is a sequence of events, of occurrences, and therefore of movements. The causal sequences are determined by causal laws which fix the order and direction of the sequences, and the laws of motion are often stated in sciences like politics, psychology, economics, or military science. I have called this form of history 'causal history'. Nature and human nature have important functions in causal history. The sequences of human attitudes and activities are kinds of motions, and the meanings of history depend on the motions and orientations of speech and thought, including the choice which the historian makes of the laws of motion which will govern his account of historical occurrences. Hume's observation, that to know how ancient Greeks or Romans acted one has only to consider how modern Frenchmen or Englishmen act, is an appeal to the common laws of human nature which are unchanged from antiquity to the present. The motions of bodies and human bodies environing a man are known and interpreted by the motions and associations of ideas and emotions in the man.

Since the case for causal history has not been stated as emphatically in our discussions as the case for epochal history, let me analyse two examples of this approach. Paradoxically the historians who have used this form of history have stated its philosophical principles clearly, while the philosophers who have defended it have been clear in their use of historical data. I shall therefore choose an ancient historian and an ancient philosopher. Thucydides says at the end of the first book of the *Peloponnesian War* that he will seek to state the real causes of the war and that he will place those causes in the context of the grounds alleged. The underlying causes, what really happened, were affected by what men thought and said. Therefore Book One is devoted to tracing the development of a unity and a community in Hellas, and after its emergence to the development of the power of Hellas. But the sequence of events is not limited to oppositions of power and the action and reaction of forces. The Lacedaemonians were alarmed by the growth of power of Athens, and the speeches play an important part in forming the alignments, deciding on policies, and initiating the actions which led to hostilities. In the fifth book of the *De Rerum Natura* Lucretius gives a cultural history of the world. It begins with the nature and origin of the world, goes on to the development of vegetable life and living creatures, then to man and the development of his mode of living from the solitary life of primitive man through the stages of civilization—fire, clothes, and shelter, the beginnings of language by experimentation, the discovery of gold, the institution of government and laws, the origin of religion and the development of metals, the cultivation of the arts and of civilization and warfare.

The third form of history has its philosophical basis in the denial of the forms of epochal history and the matter of causal history. When Aristotle abandoned the ideas of Plato and the atoms of Democritus, he continued to use history as an inquiry into facts. His *History of Animals* is a history; his *Constitution of Athens* is a history of the development of the constitution and the institutions of Athens; he prefaces many of his treatises with a history of the science and of the problems he proposes to treat. The direction of history is fixed by the problems men have treated, the solutions found, and the further problems faced as a result of those steps. The meaning of history is encountered in the present problems which have resulted from the cumulative, cyclic, or fortuitous attention given to problems and their past solutions and ensuing consequences. Common experience includes problematic situations. The available means to solve problems, like the problems themselves, is determined by historical, social, and cultural circumstances. I have called this form of history 'disciplinary history'. Disciplinary history includes 'natural history' in sciences which begin with an inventory and ordering of natural facts. It includes 'constitutional' histories of political institutions, like Aristotle's *Constitution of Athens,* the sixth book of *The Histories* of Polybius, Fustel de Coulanges' *History of the Political Institutions of Ancient France,* and Maitland's *Constitutional History of England.* It includes histories of the arts and sciences, which took their origin in the peripatetic histories of biology, psychology, poetry and the organization of the arts and sciences of the Hellenistic period. It is a history of facts and functions, of problems and resolutions, of the formation and operation of habits and institutions, of the formation of kinds of things and kinds of associations and the mutual adaptation of their parts.

The fourth form of history is based on phenomena without recourse to prior metaphysical entities—form, matter, or essence, idea, body, or substance. The account of history and the argument of philosophy treat a subject matter which is made, and they interpret it in the perspective of the agent or the interpreter. The 'facts' of history are 'acts'—deeds and words, *facta* and *verba.* There is a cultural history of mankind in Plato's dialogue *Protagoras* in which the sophist who conceived man as the measure, that is, the maker, of all things, presents history as it is made by gods and men. The facts of Protagoras' cultural history are different from those of Lucretius' but the common data are the same: the origin of the world and of man is traced to the actions of the gods rather than to the motion of bodies, and the stages of the acquisition of the arts are not presented as the acquisition of powers over kinds of things and of motions but as the formation of skills to satisfy needs and to build security. Prometheus gave man wisdom in the arts and the art of fire; Zeus gave him wisdom in daily life and in civil life. Men acquired religion, articulate speech, skill in inventing shelters, clothing, and food; they also acquired civic art, including the art of warfare, and justice, temperance, and law. Rhetoric has played a prominent place in the development of history. The disciples of Isocrates wrote histories; and Cicero, at the beginning of his dialogue *The Laws,* makes the transition from the discussion of political constitutions in the *Republic* to the consideration of political institutions in the *Laws* by way of a discussion of history and poetry in which he recounts the arguments of his friend Atticus and his brother Quintus urging him to write the history of Rome because history is closer than any other branch of literature to oratory. I have called this form of history 'exemplary history'. The example is the basic method of argumentation in deliberative oratory. Past actions are a guide and a source of discovery in planning future actions, and the orator forms himself by following the words and actions of great orators as models. The direction of history is determined by planning and prediction, and the meaning of history is found in the actions undertaken to achieve desired ends.

My third subject grows out of the differentiation of kinds of historical facts. If facts were given unambiguously, the problems of historical objectivity would be problems of fitting statements to facts, and philosophical principles would have a simple relation in history to objective interpretations. But if fixed facts are formed from ambiguous data, and if historical accounts select a finite number of facts from the infinite possibilities of data and justify one interpretation among numerous possible interpretations, philosophic principles have a wider function than providing the rules for matching statements to facts, for facts must be determined as well as statements, and the determination of the two are closely interrelated. Two problems should be distinguished. Since 'fact' has many meanings and since each of the facts alleged in statement has a like number of meanings, the different kinds of facts should be distinguished: this is the problem of philosophic semantics. Since what is a fact and what is relevant in one form of history is dubious or false, irrelevant or misleading, in another form of history, the methods of verification, justification, demonstration, and systematization in history should be examined in the light of the diversity of methods disclosed by philosophic semantics: this is the problem of philosophic inquiry.

The application of philosophic semantics to the facts of history is apparent from the sketch of the four forms of history. Facts are structures of meanings and value; or they are motions of bodies; or they are functions of natures and institutions; or they are actions of formation and opposition; and each of the four varieties of facts may be used in a variety of ways in historical accounts. In any of them, allegations of fact may be shown to be mistaken, and criteria of objectivity and truth are available for use. But the facts of one form of history are not facts in another form: their relations are not relations of contradiction or falsification but of ambiguity or irrelevance. The relations among the facts of the different forms of history may be illustrated by an example from intellectual history. If one is interested in the history of 'time', one may find it treated in a variety of histories of thought and culture. Epochal histories will sometimes include a presentation of the 'classical', or the 'baroque', or the 'modern' conception of time in their delineation of the characteristics of such ages. Causal histories sometimes trace the evolution of the use of time in the analysis of motion and the development of instruments of precision in the measurement of time. Disciplinary histories sometimes set forth different conceptions of time, problems presented by each, and their resolution in new conceptions of time with new problems. Exemplary histories sometimes set forth the creative readjustments in which a great thinker transforms, as Galileo, Newton, and Einstein did, the approach to and formulas of motion and the concept of time. Since philosophic semantics applies to the ideas of philosophy as well as the facts of history, a philosopher who goes to history for factual confirmation of his ideas usually has little difficulty in finding that the facts support him, since he takes to his history the same philosophic semantics as guided him in his philosophy.

The application of philosophic inquiry to the ideas and methods of history has in the past opened up new perspectives of historical inquiry. The problems of the meaning and direction of history today, the problems of facts and interpretations, have new dimensions and complexities which are the proper subjects of philosophic inquiry. The multiplicities of meanings of historical fact disclosed by philosophic semantics have appeared in philosophic discussion in the past primarily as a controversial opposition of schools. The cultural history of the world has moved through these oppositions, and continuous themes have emerged which provide the common context of the disputations and the continuous links to the stages of evolution and progress. The themes are not of battles and refutations but of meanings and amplifications. They depend on communication rather than debate. The cultures of the world have entered into universal communication which involves in turn contacts of the philosophies of the world, past and present. It is not a simple opposition of cultures or of philosophies. A pluralism of cultures and a pluralism within cultures are increasingly apparent and operative. The simple opposition of a spiritualistic East and a materialistic West loses its persuasive power when one places spiritualism and materialism in their context in East and West. In Greece the voluminous writings of Democritus have all but disappeared and we know about his materialistic philosophy from the refutations of his adversaries and a few fragments of his works. In India the early materialistic philosophy of the Carvakas suffered the same fate. The communication among cultures is not a clash of opposed meanings and values but a broadening to world scale of alternatives and oppositions which had formed the philosophic basis of interpretation and motivation in each of the major cultures. The facts of history and the directions of accounts of facts differ because they are selections based on a diversity of philosophic grounds, but they are selections from common data, and the inquiries of philosophy and of history take place in a common social and cultural context. The ambiguous themes which cross from one sequence to another in occurrence and discourse and provide the continuities of problems of inquiry and discussion are possible sources of insight by which to enrich our penetration into historical facts and our realization of the possibilities of action. If the apparent oppositions of direction and meaning in history which result from oppositions of the forms of histories and their facts, were clarified by philosophic semantics, historical inquiry could turn to the real complementarities which are found in the pluralism of historical forms and could explore the themes to which the various accounts are specifications and particularizations.

R. P. McKeon:

I am grateful to the speakers who have reflected on what I have written. I am grateful both because they have suggested ideas to me and also because their remarks have illustrated the pluralism which I have found in philosophical speculations concerning history. I want consequently to take advantage of both aspects of their interventions in my reply, to develop the ideas they suggest and to place their criticisms in the context of my treatment of the direction of history. In so doing, I shall try to rectify some of the statements attributed to me and some of the statements made in interpretation of what I have said, and I shall try to show how the resulting distinctions are broad enough to include treatment of the issues that have been raised.

First, Mr. Van Breda has raised a question concerning degrees of objectivity in history. I have argued that the problem of discovering what is objective is extremely difficult, whether objectivity is sought in science or in history or, finally, in philosophy. I have not, however, advanced or defended a relativism. I have not suggested or held that whatever is said is necessarily true. Data are before us, and facts can be discovered and established by methods which make use of criteria subject to explicit statement and rational criticism. What one seeks and finds as a fact does not depend on one's preferences; it does however depend on one's philosophic assumptions, and these include one's assumptions about the nature of things and the nature of human actions. Such assumptions direct one's attention to what is observed and noticed. The observation is guided by principles, but it is not determined exclusively by principles. I have stated, and I have argued in defense of the statement, that there is a direction in history but that direction or meaning can neither be perceived *a priori* and imposed on historical occurrences nor be discovered empirically and derived without assumptions from historical occurrences. Consequently, my reply to Mr. Van Breda is that each of the many kinds of history, which I treated under four heads, seeks objectivity in a different way. It is important that distinctions be made among different criteria of objectivity because what is objective fact in one historical account is not objective or a fact in another: if the alleged fact is considered at all, and it may be omitted without mention because it is irrelevant, it is shown to be fantastic, mythical, abstract, or simply untrue.

Let me run through the criteria of objectivity employed in the four forms of history. Hegel wrote epochal history. In the *Philosophy of History*, he distinguished three methods of treating history: original history, reflective history, and philosophical history. In philosophical history, history in the true sense emerges for the first time. The philosophy of history is nothing but the thoughtful contemplation of history. In causal history this is nonsense. History is concerned with events and actions as they are and as they have been, and any reflection or contemplation of what has happened must be based on an objective account of the events. In the epochal history of Hegel, objectivity is encountered because reason is the law of the world and things have come about rationally in world history. The positions of many of the speakers in our discussion have made use of a conception of objectivity close to Hegel's. In causal history, objectivity is encountered in occurrences, perceived and observed clearly, and in sequences, justified and tested by notions or laws of motion and process and of cause and effect. In disciplinary history, objectivity is encountered in the discovery of facts: natural facts in natural history; facts of habits and institutions, second natures which are sources of future actions, in political and social history; facts of thought and creation in intellectual, aesthetic, and cultural history. Objectivity is attained in disciplinary history by avoiding the accidental and discovering the continuing sources of future action. In exemplary history, objectivity is the result of action. The results of the actions of great men, of heroes, of groups of men, and of nations are objective, and in exemplary history one can learn from history by taking the accounts of past deeds as models to guide one's future actions.

Mr. Polin suggests that the four forms of history that I distinguish are not philosophies of history, but should be called philosophies about history and be related to a philosophy of history. In the third part of my oral report I argued that questions of philosophic semantics should be distinguished from questions of philosophic inquiry. From the semantic point of view, there are as many 'philosophies of history' as there are meanings attached to the words 'history' and 'philosophy', that is, there are as many philosophies of history as there are intelligible philosophies or defensible histories. My distinction of four forms of history is a semantic differentiation of four kinds of history based on four sets of broad philosophic assumptions. Philosophic inquiry is undertaken by use of one set of philosophic assumptions, chosen among possible approaches to philosophic problems and, therefore, in opposition to other possible philosophies. The pluralism of approaches to philosophy disclosed by philosophic semantics usually yields controversial oppositions among philosophies in philosophic inquiry. The alternative to controversy in a pluralism is not synthesis but communication or dialogue. In controversy the assumptions of the alternative approach are denied and the facts supporting the assumptions are questioned; in discussion the consequences of the alternative assumptions are examined for the light which they throw on facts not considered under one's own assumptions. The semantics of philosophy and of history convinces me that no inclusive agreed-on synthesis or *mélange* or syncretism is possible. If one is engaged on causal history, one cannot pause to do a little epochal history of the age, a little institutional disciplinary history, or a little exemplary sketch of a great man for emulation. But one can treat the facts bearing on the character of an age, the operation of a constitution, and the actions of influential men by breaking them up into elements which fit in the causal lines one traces and which are reducible to the causal laws which govern the sequences of occurrence.

The semantics of history, moreover, suggests the answer to the question whether the forms of history should be called 'philosophies of history' or 'philosophies about history'. 'Philosophy of history' has a proper and strict sense only in dialectical philosophy and epochal history. I used it in that sense when I sketched Hegel's philosophy of history. The other three forms of history are opposed to a philosophy of history in the dialectical sense. I myself am not a dialectician, and it was for this reason that I dwelt on the causal form of history in which history does not have a meaning and philosophy does not have a separate branch, or philosophy of history, devoted to contemplation of that meaning. Philosophy has a function in the other three forms of history, but they do not have philosophies of history in the dialectical sense. Whether 'philosophy of history' is given other senses applicable to the uses of philosophy in these forms of history or whether other expressions like 'philosophy for history' are found for them is a matter of indifference, provided it is not assumed that one over-riding dialectical philosophy of history is the point of reference and the ground of more limited philosophies about history, or that the principles of the philosophies about history can be synthesized in one common philosophy of history. There are four forms of history, not merely because of differences in ways in which accounts of what has occurred are written, but also because of differences in the facts and relations and sequences which constitute the historical processes which the historian investigates and recounts. Our problem is how these different sets of facts and processes have fitted together in the past, how they eventuate in the present, and how they provide background for our understanding of the ongoing world of the future.

I have already replied in part to Mr. Aubenque's accusation of relativism in answering Mr. Van Breda's question about objectivity. There are facts, and facts are the object of inquiry; but there are many methods and devices by which to determine what the facts are, and the facts stated in any account of an occurrence or a subject are selections from an indefinitely large number of facts which can be discovered, formulated, and constructed from the common data of inquiry. The pluralism which I presented is a pluralism of different conceptions of fact, not a pluralism of allegations of fact indifferently accepted as true. This pluuralism is recognized in the words which have been used in antiquity (*pragma, facta*) and in the modern languages (*fait, Tatsache, Tat, Handlung, fact*). A fact is something done or made. It is not something made arbitrarily. Facts have objective bases, but they are determined by active and inquiring minds. They do not exist preformed like grains in a pile of sand. They take on their characteristics in the process of inquiry, and the facts available to an inquirer at one time and in one set of cultural circumstances may be different from those known and recognized by his predecessors or successors.

Mr. Aubenque has asked me what the proper task of philosophy is. My answer is based on consideration of the tasks undertaken in the history of philosophy and the tasks undertaken by philosophers today. Philosophy has had and still has many proper tasks. I have a conception of the proper task of philosophy based on my conception of the principles and methods of philosophy. That is philosophy as I engage in it, but it would seem to me improper and arrogant for me to say from that philosophic point of view what other philosophers, particularly those who do not share my philosophic orientation, should undertake in philosophy. There have been many revolutions in philosophy, including several in the twentieth century. In my youth, there was a revolution against idealism in the United States and England, and the proper task of philosophy became some form of realistic philosophy; and realisms merged into naturalisms, neo-positivisms, neo-scholasticisms, and linguistic analyses. There was another revolution against psychologism in which the proper task of philosophy became phenomenology which merged into various forms of existentialism. There have been controversies among all these tendencies, in which the opposition against predecessors and opponents has been that they do not engage in the proper task of philosophy but ask meaningless questions. The proper task of philosophy, it seems to me, is not to make one conception of the task of philosophy prevail until all philosophers share it, but rather to understand the different tasks which philosophers have meaningfully undertaken and to treat the new problems and richer facts which emerge from that pluralism of inquiries.

Mr. Aubenque says that I propose a synthesis. The opposite is the case. I have argued that a synthesis of diverse philosophic approaches is impossible and that even an eclecticism is impossible. All philosophers quote from other philosophers and use their predecessors and contemporaries in their own arguments. But positions are transformed in restatement, favourable or unfavourable; the most devoted disciple departs from the teaching of the master, and the synthesis of two positions is a third independent position even when the joining is done with little originality. I have argued that philosophers remain faithful to their philosophic principles and methods, except when they contradict themselves, and that we should therefore seek a clearer understanding of our philosophic assumptions and those of others. We can understand the task of philosophy in that context. Instead of saying, what I am doing is the proper task of philosophy, one may take into account what other philosophers are doing and the 'facts' which are brought to light by their approaches, and one may then be able to raise questions which one would not otherwise consider and open up the way to discussion and cooperative inquiry. Scientists frequently make such use of pluralism of approaches to the statement and treatment of problems. The cooperative volume *Albert Einstein—Philosopher-Scientist* edited by Paul Schilpp contains the story of a group of scientists who differed radically in their basic scientific and philosophic principles and who used their differences to make crucial contributions to the development of quantum physics. Their opposed principles provided alternative hypotheses. If they had conducted their discussions in the manner of the discussion of philosophers at the time, they would have accused each other of talking nonsense. Instead they applied their opposed hypotheses to investigate the facts and relations relevant to them. Discoveries made according to one hypothesis could be recognized to be true by the proponents of the opposed hypothesis, but to be in need of restatement and reinterpretation, which in turn led to new problems and the discovery of new facts. This is philosophic communication without synthesis, as opposed to philosophic controversy in the interest of establishing a synthesis.

Mr. Aubenque has raised specific questions concerning the history of philosophy. Does the history of philosophy have a unity and a reality in itself which imposes itself on us? Are we the creatures of our time?

Can we do philosophy as it was done twenty years ago? Yes, we are influenced by the history of philosophy and by the place of our times in the history of philosophy, but there are many histories of philosophy in every age, and every age rewrites the plural histories of philosophy which influenced earlier ages. Many philosophers were influenced by Plato, including his followers who called themselves Academics or Platonists, but the history of Platonisms has a unity of pluralism which does not impose itself on us in any one form—Platonism is in turn a supple dialectic, a skepticism, a neo-Platonic hierarchic metaphysics, a dogmatism, a mysticism. The history of philosophy in which Platonism is a strand is an even more complex pluralism. Descartes was a creature of his time, and he was influenced by the history of philosophy. He developed a method of analysis, a *mathesis universalis,* an analytic geometry. The history of analysis runs from Plato through Euclid, Apollonius, and Pappus to Descartes. Descartes took as his initial problem in *The Geometry* one which Pappus reports that neither Euclid nor Apollonius nor any one else had been able to solve completely, and with the solution of that problem he initiated a new branch of mathematics, which has become part of the history of science and of philosophy. Descartes was a creature of the seventeenth century, and he was a creature of the history of philosophy and mathematics of the fourth century B.C. to the fourth century C.E. But he was a unique creature of his times, and if the history of philosophy has a unity and reality they imposed themselves on him differently than on other readers of Euclid and Pappus. In a lesser way, we historians of philosophy are evidence of the pluralism rather than the fixity of the history of philosophy: we write interpretations of past philosophers primarily because we have formed a different and new interpretation of their thoughts and their times, that is, because the reality of the history of philosophy has imposed itself on us differently than it has on other historians.

Mr. Arieli raised questions concerning the relation of the conceptual frameworks of historical reflection to the historical process itself. He raised three questions about that relation: (i) how the present concepts of the history are brought to bear on the past concepts current and effective in the period treated, (ii) how the emergence of new concepts of structure affects the history of the past, and (iii) how the variety of frameworks are brought together as modes of treating common historical facts.

Mr. Arieli frames his first question in Huizinga's terms, in which history becomes the reflection of a present age on its own past. The terms of the question throw it into the form of epochal history in which both the present and the past have conceptual frameworks. This formulation is true only of epochal or dialectical history. Let me state the reasons for this and its consequences more fully. In some approaches to history, an historical account of a development is also an analysis and establishment of the nature of what is developed; in other approaches, there is no relation between philosophic or scientific analysis and historical investigation of sequences and relations. In epochal and exemplary history, the formation of concepts and the development of processes are related at all stages of analysis and evolution, and ultimately they are the same. In causal and disciplinary history, the sequence of occurrences is distinct from the structure of laws employed in ordering them and the assemblage of facts is distinct from the problems encountered in them by the inquirer.

Epochal history is based on a dialectical philosophy; and the contact of conceptual frameworks results from some form of the assimilation which Hegel states in the principle that reason is the law of the world and that what happens takes place rationally. Exemplary history is based on an operational philosophy; and conceptual frameworks are made, as facts are made. Rousseau went to history to examine the degradations brought about by developments in the arts and sciences; Sartre argues that existentialism is a humanism because we make not only papercutters but ideas, ourselves, other minds, and the world itself. Causal history is based on a logistic philosophy; and conceptual frameworks result from scientific analyses which are cognitive, while historical occurrences are the results of intentions and preferences which are emotive. Buckle goes to the physical sciences for the framework of his *History of Civilization in England,* and James Harvey Robinson goes to the social sciences for the ordering principles of *The New History.* Disciplinary history is based on a problematic philosophy; and conceptual frameworks order the common data of experience according to the relations established among facts determined from those data and according to the problems encountered in examining those facts and relations in different sciences. When Aristotle wrote his natural histories in the biological sciences and his histories of doctrines in all the sciences, he differentiated them according to the facts of different sciences derived from the data of common or particular experiences; when Janet and Séailles wrote their *Histoire de la philosophie—Les problèmes et les écoles,* they ran through the history of philosophic positions on problems ranging from those of psychology, animal life, and sense perception through reason, memory, and language to liberty and habit.

Mr. Arieli's second question is concerning the effect on the objectivity of history of using present conceptual frameworks and even new ideas in treating what happened in the past and in understanding what was thought of in different frameworks and without awareness of ideas which were to develop later in history. I have argued that many different frameworks are used by historians in the present and that a like plurality was operative in the past. I have therefore argued that the dialectical philosophy of history should not be treated as if it were a universal philosophy or an independent reality, and I have argued that even in epochal or dialectical history a present and a past conceptual framework can be synthesized without distorting historical objectivity. But the introduction of a new idea to control ideas and actions, which had originally been conceived and carried out without benefit of that new idea, introduces a problem of a different sort. Once the Renaissance was named, and once it was studied as a rebirth, the concept of the Renaissance not only affected the interpretation and statement of historical facts of the 'Renaissance' but also made the preceding period a 'Middle Ages' during which actions, institutions, and thoughts were developed without consciousness of the fact, later apparent, that they were mediaeval. There are other new concepts, which are not merely names given to epochs or ages, and therefore adjusted to and controlled by the historical materials to which they are applied, but which are general organizing principles, like 'social system' or 'culture', developed during the last century or two and now applied to the study of historical materials to determine the characteristics of societies and cultures centuries or millennia ago.

The second question, like the first, is framed in the epochal mode of history, but the problem which it raises is a problem in all four forms of history. Let me illustrate ways in which the problems occur by considering the history of 'culture'. I serve on the Editorial Board of the *Encyclopaedia Britannica*. One of the functions of the Editors is to point out lacunae in the Encyclopaedia. Some years ago I called attention to the fact that there was no article in the work on culture. There was an article on 'Civilization and Culture' written by the historian James Harvey Robinson in 1929. He wrote about 'civilization' as a new word and about the revolutionary effect of the study of civilization, which was not more than 50 or 60 years old. Culture was the accumulated product of the development of civilization. Robinson's article was retained in the *Encyclopaedia,* but it was supplemented by an article on 'Concepts of Civilization and Culture', by the anthropologist David G. Mandelbaum. According to this article all tribes or societies have 'cultures', but civilization is a particular kind of culture. Both terms came into their current use in the eighteenth century. The two articles did not seem to the Editor to provide an exhaustive treatment of culture. I was therefore asked to do a third article on 'Culture and Humanity'. Its orientation, like the orientations of the other two, was modern, but it found the beginnings of the terms and the discussion of culture in antiquity and in speculation concerning *paideia* and *cultus* and *cultura.* The three articles are not controversially opposed; they treat different aspects of culture and different meanings of the word; the history of culture has different scope, contents, and a different relation to civilization in the three approaches.

Mr. Arieli suggests as answer to his third question that the different frameworks of different forms of history meet in historical action itself. I agree with him and I should like to use his answer to restate the distinction which I have made between facts and data. In my oral presentation I distinguished four stages from the data of common experience with which the historian begins to the ordered facts of historical accounts in which the problem of the direction of history is encountered for the first time. I distinguished these four steps in order to relate the four forms of history, which are distinct at the fourth stage, to the common beginning which they share. The first two steps have to do with common data and with selected data; the last two steps have to do with stated facts and with ordered facts. As I used the words, 'datum' and 'fact' have radically different meanings. A datum is something that can be designated or named; it is a simple, encountered immediately in experience; it is neither true nor false. A fact is what is signified by a true proposition. Philosophies of radically different kinds are in remarkable agreement concerning the relation of propositions and facts—that propositions are true or false, and that facts are signified by true propositions. In some philosophies there are atomic facts and atomic propositions, but in most philosophies facts are complexes. I have used the word 'data' to apply to the simples which are put together in a statement of 'fact'. Philosophers do not agree further about the nature of facts or of simples. In problematic philosophies, like Aristotle's, facts tend to be substances and their qualities and functions; and data are essences, properties, and accidents. In logistic philosophies, like Hobbes', facts tend to be occurrences understood according to their underlying physical laws; and data are bodies and their motions and reactions. The data of dialectical philosophies are appearances, and the facts are truths; the data of operational philosophies are impressions, and the facts are acts. For this reason I distinguished two stages in the treatment of data: the potentially infinite data of common experience and the selected data of directed inquiry; and there are two stages also in the treatment of facts: the formulation of facts in true propositions and the ordering of facts according to the methods of the four forms of history in the directions of history.

Mr. Spear asks particularly for an explanation of the sense of 'causal history'. Are not the characteristic distinctions of causal history made also by the other forms of history? In what sense is 'cause' used in causal history? What is its relation to the history of nature?

Mr. Spear is correct in his fundamental insight. The fact that I have called one form of history 'causal history' does not imply that the other forms of history do not treat causes and cannot distinguish between causes operative in science, philosophy, and history. The basic characteristic and the defining terms of each of the forms of history reappear in other meanings as subordinate considerations in the other forms. Causal history is history which seeks its facts in events which are ordered according to underlying laws of nature, or of cause and effect. Causal history therefore traces thin lines or chains of sequences rather than delineating large inclusive ages or communities, or specifing facts and problems and their solutions, or recounting acts of men or groups and their purposes and consequences. Political histories, economic histories, military histories are causal histories when they treat of a series of events selected from the rise and fall of a nation or a ruler in terms of the accumulation of political power and its employment, or the formation of economic powers of production and their direct consequences and indirect manifestations, or the development of armaments of aggression and defense and the use of strategic and tactical devices. Causal history is reductive: the history of culture is not omitted in political or economic histories, but it is treated in terms of the social, political and economic forces which enter into the determination of taste and the complex of values which in turn influence political and social institutions and economic production and distribution. The fundamental relations of politics, economics, or military strategy which provide the laws of causal history may be treated in epochal, disciplinary, or exemplary history but not in the thin lines of cause and effect which characterize causal histories.

Perhaps the best way to indicate these relations and differences is by means of the history of philosophy to which Mr. Spear made reference in his questions. It is the characteristic of causal histories of philosophy to trace the line by which philosophy once constituted the whole body of sciences from which the sciences one by one were separated as they attained scientific precision, while philosophy remained at each stage the remnant of problems which were still unsolved or which had not yet been treated by a scientific method. Bertrand Russell's *History of Western Philosophy* is such a causal history of philosophy. This conception of the subject matter of philosophy and of its relation to the sciences is not shared by any of the other forms of history. In disciplinary histories of philosophy the sciences are separated from each other according to differences of subject matter: and the basic problems, or the problems of principles in every science, are philosophic. Mathematics is one of the theoretic sciences, and the philosophy of mathematics has had a continuous history, to which indeed Russell has made contributions. In epochal histories of philosophy, the evolution of philosophy is not from a broad scope in the past to a narrow range of problems in the present; it is a cycle, or an advance or a decline measured in terms of ideas or ideals, not in terms of subject-matter covered or omitted. In exemplary histories of philosophy, the evolution is in terms of perspectives and orientations, of arts and skills subject to study and emulation; the subject matter of mathematics might or might not be relevant to the actions recounted.

Mr. Wahl has made many critical and witty observations concerning my differentiation of four forms of history; but as he moved along in his reflexions, I have the impression that he agreed with me in the uses to which I put the distinctions. He said that I was too analytic, but he conceded that I made synthetic use of my analytic distinctions at the end of my presentation. He argued that my analytic tendencies led me to treat facts without connections, acts, or meanings. He agrees that poetry is more universal and philosophic than history; but he doubts that philosophy is more philosophic than history, and I suspect that he would doubt that history is more philosophic than philosophy. He disbelieves in the simples which I find in the data from which history begins; and he moves from the connections between facts and the connections within statements of facts, to question the simplicity of the data from which statements of fact are composed. He notes that the ages of epochal history are named and characterized after the event; he is convinced that disciplinary history and exemplary history are not history properly so called; he does not like 'cause' or 'law' as designations of causal history, but he is convinced that what I call causal history is history in the true sense. He closes his reflections by returning to Mr. Van Breda's question about the objectivity of history, and he gives point to his question by the example of Koyré's work in the history of science which is excellent history but is not, despite the approval which we both expressed of causal history, an exercise in causal history but an examination of scientific problems in the mode of disciplinary history. These are all criticisms and reflections which I find very sympathetic, for one makes distinctions to use them and Mr. Wahl has used my distinctions as I had hoped they would be used. To answer his criticisms therefore would be to misunderstand them, and I must therefore answer his questions on a lower plane by defending, somewhat pedantically, the distinctions which are the basis of our agreements.

Mr. Wahl is right. I have been analytic. I have distinguished four kinds of history and four stages from the common data of immediate experience to the ordered facts of historical discourse. This is an analytic schema constructed to distinguish the senses in which history may be said to have a direction or a meaning. I arranged the distinctions in a matrix to facilitate the analysis. But the use of such a matrix does not hypostatize meanings, or make distinctions of sense into separations of existence, or pigeonhole dynamic facts in static compartments. A matrix does not function as a picture or map of a real world; it provides a system of possible interpretations of what is under discussion and of what is the case. The matrix I have been using is fourfold: history has a different structure and 'history' a different meaning in each quadrant. Among other things, each quadrant provides history with a different direction and a different meaning. But since these are differences of interpretation, each kind of history and what I have said about each kind, may be interpreted in the meanings of the kind. A preference for epochal history or for causal history may make all histories seem imperfect forms or approximations to the one history. Recognition of the diversity of views men have had of 'facts' is in itself a contribution to historical objectivity.

Poetry is more philosophical than history in the disciplinary history and problematic philosophy which Aristotle employed when he made the observation. But poetry and history are philosophy in epochal history and dialectical philosophy; concrete history is more philosophical than abstract philosophy in exemplary history and operational philosophy; and history is in no sense philosophy or comparable to philosophy in causal history and logistic philosophy. In much the same fashion the distinctions apply to the observation that ages are named after their occurrence, since the designation of ages and the sequence of their occurrence is proper to epochal history alone. Ideas of later ages are applied in the histories of earlier occurrences, but the narrative of history is not always an account of relations ordered in temporal sequences. My simples are analytic simples—the parts of sentences—and if they are conceived in this way they may be put to useful employments without arousing ontological fears in analysing history and its direction. 'Randomness' is of importance only in the perspectives of exemplary history, and since Jean Wahl has no belief in exemplary history, randomness need be of no concern to him.

Mr. Löwith, finally, returns to the question of direction and meaning in history. He says that my change of title from 'the meaning of history' to 'the direction of history' is without meaning or, if it has a meaning, it is impossible. This is true for dialectical epochal history. But, as I said in my oral presentation, I am not a dialectician. I expounded causal history in some detail in order to make clear a philosophic approach to history in which to talk about an objective meaning in historical occurrences, as dialecticians do, is nonsense. It is possible to indicate a motion, to measure it accurately and unambiguously, and to interpret it, so designated, in a variety of ways and give it a variety of meanings. There is a great difference between supposing that a freely falling body has a direction and successive positions and accelerations, and supposing that the motion has a meaning. A causal historian would be interested in presenting the successive interpretations which Galileo, Newton, and Clerk Maxwell gave to the phenomena of falling bodies, and in the account he would treat the meaning of 'acceleration', 'mass', 'inertia', 'force', and 'energy'. I made the distinction between epochal and causal history because it seems to me important to include in the examination of the philosophy of history philosophies which give history a meaning and philosophies which do not. Neither position is nonsense. When I write intellectual history, however, I do not use either the epochal or the causal form of history. Like Koyré, I write disciplinary history; disciplinary history, like causal history, recognizes directions in history but finds meanings in the interpretation of those directions.

Mr. Löwith reinforces his argument that direction implies meaning by analysing the temporal structure which he finds implicit in direction, for he argues that direction implies an end and a meaning. He quotes the passage in my paper in which I say, 'The historical sequence is cumulative, and the historian of philosophy seeks to preserve and develop in history what was valid and efficacious in the contradictory philosophies of earlier antagonists. The tasks of philosophy and of the history of philosophy are fundamentally the same.' The passage is my description of epochal histories of philosophy. It is true of epochal histories, but it is untrue and demonstrably false in other forms of the history of philosophy. In particular, the tasks of philosophy and the tasks of the history of philosophy are radically different in causal and disciplinary histories of philosophy. It is not true that a process which has an end has a meaning, or that all processes have unique and determinate ends. It is not true, even, that historical accounts are all or necessarily accounts of temporal sequences. There are disciplinary histories which are accounts of fact and function, problem and resolution, and in disciplinary history there are other meanings of 'prior' and 'posterior' than those derived from the temporal relations.

Mr. Löwith raises a second question concerning the pluralism of approaches which he reduces to a relativism. My pluralism is based on a pluralism of facts which are objective. It is a recognition that no finite account of an infinity of facts can be exhaustive. Mr. Löwith's account of the meanings of history omit the facts which I find to be the matter of all history, and he encases other facts with meanings given them by philosophers whose principles and methods I do not accept. I can understand epochal histories, and I am content to read them according to the meanings they assign to statements and facts. My refusal to take them as unique and exhaustive accounts is a result, not of relativism, but of heuristic methods of inquiry adapted to search for historical facts in all the senses in which facts have occurred and have been recognized. The opposite of pluralism is not the presentation of one account or interpretation as necessarily true and inclusive. I cannot imagine what the true perspective of the history of philosophy is or could be. I have encountered a number of statements of the true perspective in the course of the history of philosophy, but they have all turned out to be false or incomplete. The recognition of the regularity of the process by which certainties have become doubtful is not an argument for or a statement of relativism. Facts must be discovered; allegations of fact must be tested and controlled; the process of historical inquiry, even into facts long past, is continuous and open-ended. I hope that by the cooperation of scholars and philosophers we shall be able to construct more reliable and more comprehensive accounts of historical occurrence, and I hope that by devices such as we are now using we shall be able to establish communication among different approaches and turn from controversial oppositions to philosophic discussions in the philosophy of history.

Mr. Löwith's final question is concerning communication among philosophies of history and between history and philosophy. He states the question, however, by attributing to me a statement that philosophy and history are homogeneous. As I have already pointed out, this statement was part of my description of epochal history, and I do not hold it to be true in my own philosophy of history. In the final pages of my paper and in the final paragraphs of my oral presentation I discussed the present situation in philosophic semantics and in philosophic inquiry: semantically we are coming to recognize the plurality of meanings and approaches in philosophy; in philosophic inquiry it is necessary to commit oneself to one of the methods of philosophy distinguished in semantics, but it is possible that the tendency to philosophical opposition may yield to philosophic discussion and understanding of differences. That understanding of differences need not be a synthesis in the manner of a dialectical philosophy of history. My exposition of semantics and inquiry was in the disciplinary mode, but it could be restated in different terms and meanings in accordance with the epochal, causal, and exemplary forms of history.

I am convinced that there are true approaches to history, that there can be agreement on facts despite differences of method, and that there are ways of doing history which take into account the variety of ways of approaching and interpreting data and facts. If what I have said is correct, we must learn the semantics of the variety of meanings, and we must guide the methods of inquiry in ways that take into account other methods and their results. Philosophers and historians have been refuting each other since the beginnings of philosophy and of recorded history. We shall begin to listen to each other, not by translating statements into the errors that they would be if they were given the meanings we attach to words and facts, but by reconstructing their proper meanings. If, instead of opposing our positions in controversy, we used the opposed principles to which we adhere as hypotheses for the discovery of facts which might be supplemented by facts discovered by the opposed hypothesis, new progress could be made in the discovery and interpretation of historical facts. We shall not, I hope, carry our efforts to convert each other to our forms of thinking to the point of securing agreement on a single monolithic philosophy. Instead we shall concentrate on facts and relations of facts, rather than on intentions and imputed meanings, and we shall test other allegations of facts and, if they turn out to be facts, fit them into the facts we have established and interpreted; and we shall go on, as we have in the past, each writing his own mode of philosophy and his own form of history, but in a new fashion which may have a cumulative effect and contribute to the progress of truth without distortion of objective facts or departure from testable truths.

7
Freedom and History

1. Historical Background and Theoretic Assumptions

The discussion of basic theory and philosophic principles in different times and places shows the marks of changing modes and fashions. Changes in the matter or manner of analysis are advanced and advertised by their proponents as revolutions of perspective based on newly acquired knowledge and calculated to avoid the confusions and unreal problems of preceding modes. Fashions in thought and presuppositions make their appearance as the tenets of a school, the attitude of a sect, or a party, or a people, and the characteristics of an age; yet, like other fashions, those of the mind do not await justification from examination of theoretic or practical consequences. We abandon philosophies as we abandon styles of dress, and conceptions of truth and right seem false and wrong when they are outmoded. The spread of fashions in doctrine, however, has consequences in thought and action, and its effect may be deleterious or disastrous if statements of difference and claims of superiority have no more relation to what is said and done than is found normally in philosophic disputes or in ideological conflicts. Doctrinal fashions have consequences in theory which affect even what is accepted as science. They have consequences in practice which affect statements of purpose and communication among people situated in common conditions and faced by common problems. Even the analysis of these fashions and their consequences, to be effective in thought or action, must be conducted within the accredited fashion.

Originally published as *Freedom and History: The Semantics of Philosophical Controversies and Ideological Conflicts* (New York: Noonday Press, 1952). Copyright 1952 by Richard P. McKeon.

The dominant intellectual tendencies of our times turn discussion of basic questions to considerations of action or of language. In the United States this tendency takes form in a variety of operational analyses and a variety of semantic systems. Action and language have been associated as sources of principles whenever basic principles have been derived from practical effects or symbolic relations to resolve puzzles about the nature of things or about the processes of thought or to demonstrate that such inquiries are unnecessary or impossible. Cicero's recurrent formula—"words and deeds"—gives evidence by its frequent echo in later rhetoricians of the force of this combination. Yet action and language are basically opposed in analysis: when principles are operational, language does not provide principles but is explained by operations; when principles are linguistic, action is consequent on language. Pragmatic and operational analyses today seek the test of meaning in action, and the definition of words is possible only after experiment and the solution of problems; semantic analyses, on the contrary, construct structures of words and languages on which meanings can be conferred, and "pragmatics" adds the further dimension by considering the effects of signs on people. In Great Britain, the tendency to seek linguistic or practical principles takes form in the "analytical" philosophy, which resorts to "ordinary" language and "commonly accepted" meanings rather than to scientific language and arbitrarily assigned meanings. Analytical philosophy goes back to the method which G. E. Moore used in refutation of idealism, and the treatment of moral problems associated with the method—under the influence of Moore's argument that "good," like "yellow," is indefinable—differs likewise from the related American conclusion that practical uses of language, like poetic uses, are "non-cognitive" and "emotive." On the continent of Europe, the tendency has taken form in a variety of dialectics which throw emphasis on action or the practical and seek to avoid the formal and the verbal. The Marxist dialectic is directed to a fusion of theory and practice, and opposition to Marxism is stated in terms of dialectics which find a chief source of error in pure theory and verbal formalism. Phenomenology, which derives in part from Kierkegaard's reaction to Hegelianism, and Hegelianism, from which Marxism and Phenomenology borrowed assumptions and devices in their opposition, place their emphasis on the concrete and the practical; Existentialism is committed to the "engagement" of the thinker and the artist in practical issues; and even in the tradition of Catholic philosophy the system of Blondel rests on a Philosophy of Action and a Philosophy of Thought.

It was plausible, when the current fashion came into vogue in revolt against idealism, to suppose that ideas might be clarified by asking what they mean in action or that misunderstandings and meaningless questions might be avoided by defining terms. At the height of the fashion, however, a double conflict has arisen. A basic rift has developed, in the first place, between protagonists of linguistic and practical principles— between those who seek to ground the scientific method in a formal logic without commitment to ontology or to the nature of things and those who seek to ground science in the operations employed in inquiry or in the devices by which human action, guided by experimental or dialectical analysis, influences natural processes. Principles can be found both in action and in language by a large number of different techniques and methods; however, conflicts have arisen, in the second place, at each pole of the first basic opposition. The operational and the dialectical statements of the need to translate ideas into actions are similar, yet they are put into effect by different techniques, and there are many forms of operationalism and of dialectic. "Language" also, like "action," is subject to many different kinds of treatment: philological semanticists trace the evolution of meanings in the actual language spoken by men, philosophical semanticists seek the determination of meanings in the systems and formal languages constructed by logicians, and literary semanticists—critics and propaganda analysts—explain, or explain away, the influence and effects of metaphors and arguments; and in each, in philology, philosophy, and literary criticism, there are many factions. As theories are elaborated and as refutations are constructed, moreover, many of the problems—including the unreal and insoluble problems—which were avoided by appeal to action and language, are rediscovered in new forms and have the effect of further solidifying the oppositions of schools and parties.

The temptation to revolt against the confusions and verbalisms of this fashion in thought is tempered by the recognition that the predicament is not new and that a successful revolution would provide a basis on which a similar logomachy would eventually be fought after the fashion of past philosophic innovations and revolutions. The alternative to attempting to institute a new fashion in principles is to use the current fashion in order to analyze the causes of difficulties and disputes. The following essay undertakes such an analysis of meanings and actions. Language is a human activity, and common understanding of actions is possible only by communication. Theories about action and language can be made concrete by two interrelated means: by historical inquiry into how men have acted and spoken and by theoretical inquiry into action and language as human functions. The nature of the semantic predicament becomes apparent as soon as an effort is made to employ either means to give existential content or practical bearing to the analysis of language. "History" itself has many meanings, and the history of human action and speech is the history of "freedom" conceived in as many senses as those employed in the discussion of "action," "language," and "history."

The study of the co-variations of these interrelated terms—"semantics," "history," and "freedom"—is a proper study for historical semantics. Historical semantics, in this broad sense, differs from philosophical semantics which places emphasis on formal principles and institutes rules for the determination of meanings and truth. It differs from philological semantics which places emphasis on roots and traces the evolution of the meanings of cognate terms and the meanings shared by non-cognate terms in the languages employed by men. It is the study of meanings which important words carry over from the systems of philosophers into the program of politicians, the preachments of moralists, the discriminations of poets, and the distinctions of ordinary speech. It supplies a structure which is relevant both to the rigidities and oppositions of philosophic systems and to the wandering meaning and ambiguities of common speech. It is the one structure by which the circularities of both—of systematic analysis and of common usage—may be brought to direct attention. The following essay, thus, is an exercise in historical semantics conceived as the examination of the presuppositions of systems of philosophical semantics. Since the history of the meanings of the terms in philosophical systems varies with the basic assumption concerning the nature and activities of man, the meanings of "history" are found to vary with the meanings of "freedom" according to the basic principles found in philosophy for processes and natures, including the processes and nature of language. But the differences of principles exemplified in the history and assumed in the freedom of human actions may in turn be explained by differences in the philosophical "semantics" employed in various systems of philosophy. There are, then, as many meanings for the "semantics" by which the meaning of history and freedom is explained as there are meanings of "history" and "freedom" by which the nature and operation of speech and communication are determined.

Historical semantics follows the fashion of the times by treating metaphysical problems in terms of language and theoretical problems in terms of action. The method employed in this essay, while conforming to that fashion, is designed to focus attention on it by making explicit the historical background and the theoretic implications of basing systems of analysis on linguistic and practical principles.

The history of the fashions of philosophizing may be sketched briefly by tracing the subject matters in which philosophers have found their basic distinctions. Problems of science and of practical action were related to each other in ancient Greece by principles found in the nature of things: the atoms of Democritus, the Ideas of Plato, and the substances of Aristotle were all existences which provided principles for science and had a bearing on the problems of morals and politics. The philosophers of the Hellenistic period professed to take over and to reconcile all or most of what their predecessors had said but to find more basic principles in the nature of thought: the Stoics, the Epicureans, and the Academics turned their attention to the perception or judgment by which truth or probability might be achieved. Philosophers in the late Roman Republic and in the early Empire found epistemological differences as complex and unfruitful as metaphysical disputes and sought the principles of practice and science in words and deeds: Cicero argued that all the differences of philosophers would be seen to be merely verbal if wisdom were joined to eloquence and if theoretic questions which had no consequences in action were abandoned, and Sextus Empiricus disposed of the errors of the dogmatic philosophers in the various sciences by examining their use of signs.

The coming of Christianity had the effect of reorienting doctrines about principles found in the nature of God, man, and the universe. This reorientation received its systematic formulation in the West in the philosophy of St. Augustine. Boethius, a century later, professed to follow all the doctrines of Augustine, but he thought it desirable to find new arguments for them and to translate and reformulate portions of Aristotle's logic in terms which emphasize the processes of thought. Cassiodorus in the sixth century related the trivium of grammar, rhetoric, and dialectic as linguistic disciplines to the interpretation of Scripture, in his *Institutes of Divine and Secular Letters,* and Isidore of Seville reduced the whole of knowledge to an encyclopedia arranged on linguistic principles in his *Etymologies*. The practical problems involved in the application of Christian doctrines to a community led to the early efforts to systematize canon law under Charlemagne. When Alcuin set forth the principles of morals for that monarch he stated them in a dialogue *On Rhetoric and the Four Virtues,* while the followers of Eriugena encountered nominalism in the discussion of the problem of the universal. The methods used in the codification of canon law influenced the methods of theology in the numerous books of Sentences of the twelfth century, among which the compilations of Peter Abailard and Peter Lombard were particularly influential, arranged according to questions on which there were contradictory or apparently contradictory positions. During the same century nominalism again became prominent in the discussion of universals, while John of Salisbury found in the rhetoric of Cicero the principles of a practical Christian humanism. The new translations of Aristotle's works provided the philosophers of the thirteenth century with a vast body of scientific information and a systematic discussion of scientific method which they labored to relate to the principles of theology wherever the two bodies of doctrine met in the discussion of the nature of God, man, and the universe. Duns Scotus sought to avoid the complexities of doctrine and the dangers of heresy encountered in these explorations of the nature of things by seeking the principles of truth and certainty and by refuting, in a manner reminiscent of the Stoics, the positions of the "Academics." The late Middle Ages was the great period of the development of nominalistic philosophies and logical subtleties, and the Renaissance based a new Humanism largely on rhetoric and on the philosophy of Cicero.

The beginnings of modern science turned the attention of philosophers, once more, directly to the nature of God, man, and the universe, and they emulated the method of science to discover new philosophic principles in the nature of things. By his "Copernican revolution," Kant made man the center of philosophic attention and started the fashion in which philosophers for more than a century sought the principles of philosophy in the examination of the categories, forms, and intuitions of human thought or of transcendental ideas. In our own times we have witnessed a revolt against idealism which has led to the quest for philosophic principles in action and in language. There are obvious similarities between the contemporary fashions of philosophy and those in vogue during the last century of the Roman Republic and the first centuries of the Roman Empire and during the end of the Middle Ages and the beginning of the Renaissance. These similarities have led recent historians of logic to rewrite the history of those periods in order to give prominence to the propositional logic which Sextus Empiricus found in the Stoic doctrines and which grew out of the late Medieval interest in the intentions and the impositions of terms. It has led to new recognition of the influence of rhetoric on literary criticism and on the manipulation of motives in mass communications. Yet a more striking analogy than those which our present fashions bear to Roman or to Renaissance thought is found in its similarities to the fashions which arose in the period of Charlemagne. Then a body of religious doctrines which had taken theoretic form and which had stimulated practical expectations encountered difficulties both of theoretic order in the contradictions found in doctrine and of a practical order in the political chaos and institutional corruption threatening the community which shared the doctrine. The method of canon law was designed to remove the apparent contradictions in the statements of Scripture and of church Fathers, the decisions of popes and of councils, and the doctrines of philosophers. It applied to problems of interpretation of texts to remove contradictions, to problems of persuasion to prevent factions and to adjudicate differences, to problems of power employed to enforce decisions, and to problems of formalization of doctrines and methods. Today a body of scientific doctrines, which seemed to have taken definite theoretic form in the nineteenth century and which had stimulated practical expectations of the control of nature and the improvement of the conditions and the relations of men, has encountered difficulties which can be stated again either in terms of theoretic contradictions in the interpretation of science and of its effect on human life, or in terms of the social chaos and the political and economic inequities which threaten the world community consequent on the advance of science. The world is divided into parts by basic differences in policy which reflect basic differences in whatever is said about science, morals, politics, or art. These differences of meaning are insuperable unless they are treated in their practical dimension. The fundamental problem of communication and cooperation is whether common action to common ends in a world community depends on doctrinal agreement or whether common understanding can determine to what extent doctrinal differences are merely different modes of stating mutually consistent positions and to what extent they entail mutually exclusive objectives and manners of action.

The fundamental problems which are encountered when the fashions in philosophic discussions shift and principles are sought in different subject matters—in things, in thoughts, in actions, or in signs—change their form and quality but seldom disappear. The problems which had been most difficult are usually resolved easily as the result of a change of subject-matter. Yet the recurrent expectation that a revolution in philosophy will free speculation and life from questions branded meaningless and from actions thought useless or ineffective proves always to be elusive. What is significant and what is practicable are both dependent on assumptions—on postulates and purposes—and on methods by which initial principles and definitions are elaborated and by which prospective principles and ends are achieved. The oppositions among methods and principles are not resolved by changes in fashion which turn philosophers to different subject matters in applying their methods and in establishing their principles, and many abandoned problems of philosophy turn up in the new fashion once philosophic disputes and ideological conflicts are resumed in the terms newly constructed to treat the new subject matter.

The recurrent differences which survive changes in fashion may be grouped under the persistent oppositions of three fundamental methods and three kinds of principles appropriate to those methods. The numerous forms which each of these methods take are easily recognized in their present fashion of semantic statement.* "Dialectical" methods employ words in broad analogical meanings which permit the comparison of things different in kind and the reconciliation of oppositions. In all ages, the advantages claimed for the dialectical method in its various forms have included the provision of a foundation for science in the identity established between thought and things and between theory and practice. The principles required to accomplish these scientific and practical purposes are "comprehensive" principles which bind all things ultimately into one organic whole. "Logistic" methods are

---

*The characteristics of the three kinds of methods and the three kinds of principles are stated more fully and in broader applications to questions beyond the scope of semantics, freedom, and history in my essays "Philosophy and Method," *Journal of Philosophy,* XLVIII (1951), pp. 653–82; "Philosophy and Action," *Ethics,* LXII (1952), pp. 79–100; "Semantics, Science and Poetry," *Modern Philology,* XLIX (1952), pp. 145–49.

employed to construct systems of proof on the model of the mathematical deductions of geometry by giving simple terms literal and univocal definitions, by establishing simple relations among them, and by proceeding in long chains of deductive reasoning to the construction of more and more complex wholes. It has been assumed in all ages that knowledge would be more precise and the grounds for its truth would be more easily ascertained if conclusions were deduced logically from postulate sets, and that the problems of human action and association would be solved more easily if a science of man were constructed on the model of the science of mechanics. To accomplish these scientific and practical purposes the sciences must be derived in increasing complexity from basic "simple" principles. "Problematic" methods or methods of inquiry define terms relative to the problems under consideration and to the circumstances by which the problems are determined. They avoid alike the dialectical assumption that science is concerned with an organically interrelated universe in which the effect of each part on all others must be taken into account in each inquiry and the logistic assumption that science is concerned with a model or a construct in which effects are explained by the operations and interrelations of least parts. Science and practice alike consist, in the various forms of the problematic method, in the solution of problems; and the principles required for the use of the method are "reflexive" principles which determine the character and the extent of the problematic situation and the methods and hypotheses employed in its treatment.

The fashions of philosophy are reflected in ordinary speech and discussion as well as in the constructions of philosophers and in philosophical disputes. It is a characteristic of our times that people all over the world are concerned deeply with action and with language, with what can be done on the basis of our resources, our knowledge, and our technology and how men come to agreement or are persuaded, coerced, or deceived by argument, communication, art, and propaganda. Moreover, the differences of philosophic methods and principles are as widely apparent as the similarity of philosophic fashion. In the United States, current attitudes of mind are affected by the problematic method employed by pragmatic philosophers and the logistic method developed in our schools of symbolic logic; what Americans mean when they think of themselves as practical in action and precise in statement reflects distantly the peculiarities of those methods. On the continent of Europe all the dominant schools are dialectical, or tinged with dialectic; and art, politics, and morals have taken on a dialectical mode. There are basic differences in British and American attitudes which are not uninfluenced by differences of current philosophic methods: English "analytical" philosophy derives from the same roots as American speculation in philosophic semantics, but it is relatively untouched by the practical turn which the problematic method of pragmatism has made part of American theories and practice in education, the social sciences, and even the natural sciences, while its concern with the significances of ordinary speech gives British analytical philosophy a dialectical turn which distinguishes it sharply from American semantic analyses of the requirements of artificial and formal languages. Much of the rest of the world has learned a language that has been influenced by Marxist dialectic. Communication is difficult between Americans and other people, since all forms of dialectic sound the same to American ears, and all are suspect alike on theoretic and on practical grounds, while to men who have accepted something of the dialectical method and who have credited its presuppositions, American propositions make a dubious appeal both to the sciences on which it is professed they are based and the practical objectives to which it is professed they are directed.

The rifts and oppositions which underlie the present fashion of philosophy, both in its technical and in its more widely diffused forms, are full of dangers to theoretic understanding and to practical cooperation. In their practical form they contribute to the division of the world into two irreconcilable parts, and they threaten to extend and harden that division. Yet the differences of methods and principles are not differences of peoples in the various parts of the world. Until the second decade of the twentieth century, idealism and the dialectical method were the dominant forms of philosophic thought in the United States. The American revolt against idealism borrowed elements from British utilitarianism, Scottish common sense philosophy, Comte's positivism, and the eighteenth century enlightenment, and it developed and preserved modes of thought which had ceased to be widely influential in the countries in which they originated.** The basic differences are not differences which divide the peoples and the parts of the world, but

** For the relations between recent traditions in French and American philosophy, cf. my essay, "An American Reaction to the Present Situation in French Philosophy," in *Philosophic Thought in France and the United States,* ed. M. Farber (Buffalo, N. Y., 1950), pp. 337–62.

alternative attitudes and modes of thought that are found in all peoples and in all parts of the world. In most parts of the world they have found practical reconciliation in the habits of life and social institutions in which they are translated into common courses of action; in some times, in some places, and in some applications they are irreconcilable.

The problem of the interrelations of basic methods and principles is treated in this essay as a problem of "historical" semantics. The data of that problem are found both in the meanings which are given to terms systematically in the philosophies of a given period and of successive periods, and in the transfers of meanings in actual language under the stress of theoretic developments and practical problems. Since it is an examination of contending philosophic systems, historical semantics is involved in problems of truth concerning the nature of things and of man, and concerning the nature of science and action, but it is also, for the same reason, an examination of the effects of those differences in the conflict of ideologies and of the effects of thought and statement on action. The present essay raises the practical rather than the theoretic issues of "historical" semantics, that is, the problem of the grounds of meaning found in action and the possibility of common action based on different principles elaborated by different methods, not the problems of the grounds of meaning found in science and the contribution of different principles and methods to the advance of knowledge by inquiry and proof. Different programs of action find their justification in the history of past action and in the nature of man and his freedom of action. But "history" and "freedom" have many meanings which throw light not only on the differences of philosophies and of human attitudes but also on the possibility of agreement concerning the facts of the past on which future action is based and concerning the conditions of the future which will permit the fullest realization of the potentialities of the present, including the exploration of the promise of freedom in its variety of meanings.

2. Historical Semantics and Philosophical Semantics

Doctrines, knowledge, and belief influence the associations of men in groups in two different ways. Religious sects, political parties, and schools of philosophy, of science, and of art are held together, in part at least, by common adherence to doctrines, by common use of knowledge, or by common methods of validating or applying theories. Conversely, groups in which men are associated by the accident of common origin, location, condition, race, class, nationality, sensibility, or interest seek knowledge and construct theories and doctrines in order to understand their common situation, to increase their effectiveness in common action, and to elevate the objectives made practicable by their association. These two uses of thought and philosophy supplement each other: doctrines and methods form groups among men, and the cohesion of groups is strengthened by doctrines and methods. Moreover, groups enter into opposition and conflict in either employment of knowledge: since theories are often contradictory, the groups which seek to advance rival theories are opposed to each other; and since the interests and aspirations of groups are in conflict, factions are formed which construct antithetical doctrines to advance their incompatible actions.

These are not, however, simple oppositions, such as might arise if groups were formed and were preserved uniquely by the doctrines which unite them—or which seem or ought to unite them—or if doctrines were determined only by the conditions of the group which holds them—or which professes or ought to hold them. The thinker, who uses a method or credits a body of doctrines and principles, belongs to other groups as well as to the school of those who agree with him in his methods and assumptions. When he turns his thought in scientific or philosophic generalization to include all things, all thoughts, and all actions, he is frequently led to modify methods and principles without abandoning adherence to his church, his party, or his school. The member of a family, or trade union, or nation who is conscious of the solidarity of his interests with those of other members of his group is also associated with other men in a great many other activities and communities which are sometimes in agreement with each other, sometimes mutually irrelevant, and sometimes in conflict. When he meditates on the conditions, the objectives, and the proposed policies of action of any of the groups to which he belongs he finds a variety of doctrines and methods purporting to account for those conditions and to secure those objectives.

The oppositions of thought and doctrine, which assume their intellectual form in philosophical controversies, may therefore be accounted for by oppositions of groups constituted by other forces than the intellectual reasons advanced by their protagonists; and philosophic doctrines and principles may be explained by the political, social, or economic conditions and purposes of philosophers. Conversely, the oppositions of groups may be accounted for by differences of doctrine and conception, which assume their practical form in ideological conflicts, and any attempt to state or to account for the nature and conditions of groups employs doctrines whose methods and principles may be examined. In either of its forms, this process tends to gravitate—despite the efforts in philosophy of empiricists, positivists, and naturalists who seek to limit speculation by appeal to some form of facts and despite the efforts, in practical action, of realists who seek to restrain utopian speculation by recourse to some species of forces in operation—to a purely theoretic level both in the philosophic examination of ideas and in their practical use in action. The reasons for this tendency toward oppositions based on theories are not far to seek, for any exposition of a problem or analysis of a subject matter is brought into faithful and fruitful relation with issues and facts by means of the method employed in the exposition and analysis, and the oppositions between rival philosophies and rival policies, even when they are stated in terms of issues and facts, are the results of differences of methods and principles. Nor is this tendency due to any indeterminacy in the facts or ambiguity in the issues or to any dependence of facts and issues on the constructions of thought. Facts are discovered and issues are encountered, but no situation is made up of a simple fact or of a unique agglomeration of facts, nor does it present a single set of issues oriented to one ideal resolution or its possible frustrations. The philosopher and the man of action are therefore free to select among facts and issues. They invent hypotheses to be tested by the facts and to lead to the discovery of new facts. They initiate policies which relate means to ends and permit the formulation of new ends. The refutation of philosophies is consequently a simple process, although it may be practised with elaborate ingenuity applied in the invention of technical details. Since the doctrine refuted is the doctrine of another and different philosophy, it is presented and analyzed for purposes of refutation according to a method different from the one by which it was established, or it is made to depend on different principles, or it is related to a different subject matter. So presented, the fundamental terms in which the doctrine is expressed are never found to be clearly or relevantly defined; its principles are always arbitrary and in some respects poorly chosen; its method is haphazard and committed to obvious fallacies; and the final doctrine elaborated is never adequate, seldom important, and usually false. These transformations which facilitate the refutations of philosophies assume a practical form in the official pronouncement of heresies, in the prohibition of doctrines thought dangerous to the state, in the social disapproval of forms of ideas, convictions, and disbeliefs, and in general in the suspicion of philosophy and thought in religion, in practical action, in social groups, and in the arts.

The polemical oppositions of ideas, despite the distortions to which they are subject, have important uses both in theory and in practice. The examination of opposed theories affords both a check on accuracy in the statement of doctrines and their grounds, and a source of suggestions for expansion and invention in the development of theories. One may learn from the thought of others to avoid their errors, to adapt what they have done well, and to go beyond them in comprehensiveness, accuracy, and innovation. The presentation and examination of antithetical proposals is the only means by which action can be planned rationally. Yet polemics about ideas are dangerous because it is easy to pass from the facile refutation of one philosophy by another to the earnest conviction, based on arguments and principles, that false philosophies should be suppressed, that the lines of party, school, or sect should be preserved, at all cost, against external criticism and opposition, and that wise policies should be imposed, if necessary, by force. These are practical dangers which affect at once the meditations of philosophers by the restriction of their freedom of speculation and the activities of all men by the establishment of a frame for thought and action. The statement and analysis of these dangers are, however, theoretic and philosophic. They are new philosophic problems, not because similar dangers have never occurred previously nor because they have passed unnoticed in their previous occurrences, but because the influence of the conditions and the associations of men on the forms and the exercise of thought and expression has increased today to the point that the development of knowledge and its communication are endangered. Meanwhile, the effects of knowledge and its applications have attained a power capable of wholly transforming the conditions and associations of men. Knowledge, together with all the goods of living and life itself, is threatened with extinction by the arbitrary use of power, and the chief source of the increase and concentration of power is knowledge.

There is a middle region in the treatment of principles between the dogmatism that is implicit in any commitment to a method of thought or to a doctrine and the use of power which is necessary in any commitment to a plan or to a course of action. This middle region, in which differences of basic principles are recognized and discussed without resorting to force when reason has failed to produce consensus, and in which agreement in a common way of action and a common life are harmonized with individual differences and rational criticism, depended in the past on the external conditions of philosophizing rather than on the efficacy of philosophic analysis itself. Heterodox thinkers formerly, even in periods of extreme dogmatism, had at least the hope of exile or the possible protection of a friend powerful enough to resist the central or common dogmatism, and even in a despotic regime there was some place for criticism from within and some consequence of influence from without. Those conditions have changed with the increase of knowledge and the concentration of power, and no defense remains for either intellectual or practical analysis and criticism except such as can be derived from rational analysis. Philosophers and sophists, preachers and demagogues, have tried with only limited success for centuries to produce a uniformity of doctrine to serve as basis for a coherent and universal community. Meanwhile scientists and engineers have produced instruments which have so transformed the conditions of men that some form of world community is inevitable, and the problem for philosophers—not only for the theoretic philosophers who analyze doctrines but also for the practical philosophers who enunciate national and international policies—is whether the forces making for world community will be so directed that they will involve the imposition of uniformity of doctrine. If ideas are important in the formation of a community, dangerous ideas may be prohibited by the community because they have been shown to be incompatible with its philosophy. There are three steps in this process which, unless they are carefully distinguished, can be taken unawares by hasty, or frightened, or practical philosophers. They are the steps in which ideas are opposed, first, in alternative programs of political action, second, in alternative definitions discovered by semantic analysis, and, third, in alternative conclusions disposed of by philosophic refutation. If ideas are politically dangerous, semantic analysis and philosophic refutation supply only additional reasons in any polity for repressing what endangers the polity. Or, moving in the opposite direction, since it is easy to refute other philosophers within the framework of one's own philosophy, it is also easy to take, first, the step from the refutation of other doctrines to the conviction that the definitions and meanings employed in those doctrines are quite without conceivable foundation and, then, the step of suppressing doctrines not only because they are shown to be false but also because they are thought to be dangerous and therefore presumed to be false.

The relations among ideas apart from their organization in the systems of philosophy—and therefore the relations among ideas brought into relation in the contacts of heterogeneous systems—may be viewed in three different ways which serve to distinguish three different problems in the non-systematic relations of ideas. The relations of ideas may be viewed *philosophically* in the course of the establishment of a system, a doctrine, or a method; other ideas are then adapted to the system, doctrine, or method and are altered, supplemented, or refuted. The relations of ideas may be viewed *semantically* when comparable concepts, principles, and methods are examined in relation to identical or similar problems and subject matters. The problem of semantic analysis differs from the problem of philosophic refutation in the relation which basic principles have to derived concepts in the two, for the examination of concepts in semantic analysis may guide the philosopher in his selection of principles, whereas basic principles determine the significance of concepts in philosophic analysis and refutation. Semantic analysis has always served as a critical propædeutic to philosophic method, and its new importance today consists in the fact that it might also serve as a means of mutual understanding among groups and peoples adhering to different philosophies. Semantic analysis, therefore, affords an alternative to the impossible task of discovering and expounding an overarching doctrine to include whatever is good in all doctrines while avoiding what is false, or incomplete, or meaningless, or unessential. The polemic powers of ideas become dangerous only when they are used for purposes which escape criticism from other points of view and control by independent criteria of truth.

Finally, the relations of ideas may be viewed *politically* when alternative purposes and methods are examined relative to the same practical problem and social situation. The problem of political debate and political opposition is a problem of relating divergent ideas to possible courses of common action, whereas the semantic problem is a problem of understanding divergent meanings attached to common terms as their definitions are determined by divergent principles, and the philosophic problem is a problem of reconciling divergent ideas and their implications to the requirements of one set of principles and a single method. Political debate, which is an extension of the opposition of political forces, has always in some form and to some degree influenced the common action of groups of men, and its new importance today is derived from the need to formulate and establish the conditions which will govern the discussions and agreements of men who differ in philosophic doctrines, political forms, cultural values, and economic systems. Political debate affords an alternative, therefore, to the promulgation by force of a conformity in doctrine and action to promote security, preserve peace, and save souls. The power to impose decisions concerning ideas is dangerous whether it is motivated by the benevolent intention to extend benefits to all or by the factional intention to preserve or secure benefits for a few; but even arbitrary power is justified by its apologists as the one practical means of applying the rule of right reason.

Problems of doctrinal orthodoxy are separated from problems of political action by semantic analysis. The varieties of philosophies and of basic attitudes might be made intelligible by semantics. An understanding of basic differences would provide grounds both for the insight which furnishes criteria for philosophical analysis and the confidence which is essential to agreement in political and practical discussion. But an obvious difficulty faces any effort to distinguish semantic analysis from either philosophic or practical considerations, for the distinction is involved in the problem it is intended to solve. Semantic analysis cannot treat meanings in isolation, since ideas have intellectual relations and practical consequences which are interdependent. Since meanings depend on the external conditions of the analysis as well as on its principles and methods, semantic analysis, like philosophic inquiry and proof, requires a subject matter, principles, and a method. No subject matter is available for semantics which has not been explored by philosophies, for nominalisms and philosophies of words and symbols have been elaborated, and the examination of meanings is part of any philosophy. No novel principles can be found in semantic analysis, for the principles of language are either comprehensive principles which treat language as an organic whole in which meanings change and are determined by context, or simple principles which determine the meanings of individual terms and the rules of operation by which they are combined, or reflexive principles which assign meanings to terms as a result of inquiry into the subject matter and the problems to which the terms are applied. The methods of semantics, finally, are limited to the methods of thought, expression, and action which have been generalized in philosophies—the dialectical, logistic, and problematic devices which philosophers have constructed and have combined with each other to give signs concrete meanings, systematic relations, and novel contents and to justify and improve symbols in applications to objects, in inferences from principles, in communications of meanings, in forms of expression, and in influences on action. How can semantic analysis avoid being another form of that amiable and sympathetic or of that destructive and critical exposition of the advantages and shortcomings of other philosophies which is part of the statement of any philosophy?

Meanings are treated at two points in the formation of any philosophy and in the use of any method of acquiring, proving, and organizing knowledge. Preliminary to the selection of principles and to the choice of a method, meanings that are possible and meanings that have actually been developed and accepted operate as influences which are sometimes expounded in a preliminary examination of other doctrines and sometimes only implied in the methods, assumptions, and possibilities more or less explicitly excluded. In the course of the development of a philosophy, in the second place, meanings are established according to the requirements of the method of that philosophy whenever definitions are proposed and whenever the significance and implications of conclusions are examined. Historical semantics, like linguistics, usually takes the first form of inquiry with a minimum of concern with the philosophic assumptions to which it is committed or the philosophic consequences to which it leads. Philosophic semantics usually takes the second form of inquiry with a minimum of concern with the relation of philosophic meanings to common meanings or with the historical grounds of the meanings it constructs in usages of language in society, art, or science. Moreover, political institutions and political debate influence the formation of philosophies much as semantic traditions and constructions do, and they likewise are explained in turn by the principles of philosophy. In smaller compass within the history of thought and meanings, the history of political institutions provides a propædeutic to political theory, and political theory orders the treatment of political institutions and of the forces which determine them.

Semantic analysis does not differ from philosophic refutation and political debate by a radical difference of methods, principles, or subject matters. Philosophic semantics, indeed, is a part of philosophy, and its functions are determined by the characteristic method employed in the philosophy. In dialectic the varieties of meanings emerge relative to particular stages and phases of evolution or of argument, and semantics in the sense of a purely formal examination of meanings is an abstraction from the concrete determinations of dialectic, while politics is a limitation of dialectic to the particular determinations of times and circumstances. In the employment of the logistic method a philosophic semantics is needed because the meanings of terms and statements are not the same as the things they designate, and they are not determined uniquely by the system in which they occur. The logistic method consists in the isolation of elements and the determination of laws regulating their combination, such as the elements and the laws of motion of an atomism, the ideas and their relations of an associationism, or the vocabulary and syntax of a universal language or combinatory art. The development of a philosophy according to the logistic method depends on the knowledge which sets the requirements of a language and which is expressed in the language; that knowledge is available in the sciences. Philosophic semantics as developed according to the logistic method serves the function of a lexicon setting forth the meanings of terms and the conditions of true statements, as distinguished on the one hand from the syntax of the rules of their combination and on the other hand from the encyclopedia of available knowledge. In so far as politics and practical action depart from knowledge or are incapable of scientific statement, they escape logistic treatment and are assimilated in logistic statement to the demonstrations of biology, psychology, anthropology, or sociology. In philosophies developed by use of the method of inquiry, finally, meanings are developed in the course of the solution of problems and the adequacy of solutions is tested by the operations in which they are put in effect in that process. Problems are solved by action, but the consequences of hypotheses and the implications of meanings established by the solution of past problems may be examined in reflective thought apart from overt action, and the problems of politics are problems which depend on accepted meanings and on communication.

There is therefore no general statement of philosophic semantics. Like the philosophies of which it is a part, philosophic semantics may be universal, in the sense of being adapted to treat all problems, including the problem of refuting other semantic theories, without being general, in the sense of precluding or decisively subsuming other methods. Dialectical semantics is equivocal and dogmatic by the criteria of logistic and problematic semantics; logistic semantics is arbitrary and abstract by the criteria of dialectic and inquiry; the semantics of inquiry is unsystematic and vague by the test of dialectical development and logistic proof. Yet despite the differences of philosophic semantics, philosophies not only treat, in some sense, the same problems and the same subjects but also are affected by the same conditions and even influence each other. If the differences of methods set systems of philosophic semantics in opposition, the interrelations of those methods, when they are adapted to comparable problems and purposes, should permit the statement, without commitment to one philosophic method, of the problems of meanings posed in the varieties of philosophies and by the varieties of methods.

Semantics is an examination of statements. The difference between the philosophic semantics which is part of a philosophy and the historical semantics which is preliminary to the formation or choice of a philosophy is that the one is an examination of meanings determined by the relation of statements to truth while the other is an examination of meanings determined by the relation of statements to what they were intended to signify in a context of related and opposed meanings applied to related situations and objects. Not only is there a place for such a semantics in dialectic but it serves a useful function in counteracting the tendency of dialectic to rigidify into a set of fixed meanings presented as uniquely related to the whole, dynamic, concrete truth, as the final product of historical development, and as the sole determinant of the next stage of evolution and action. Plato practised such a historical semantics in presenting the philosophy of Socrates, which scholars have tried in vain to separate from his own, in elaborating the philosophies of the Eleatics, the Pythagoreans, and the Heracliteans, which he seldom thought it necessary to disavow or refute, or even in restating the philosophy of the Sophists prior to refuting the assumptions and inferences he thought in error. A semantics of actual or historical meanings has a similar function in the logistic method as part of the preliminary examination of the simple elements and combinations from which the system is to be constructed and as corrective of the arbitrary formalisms which often render the precisions of systems devoid of scientific applicability or practical use. The method of inquiry, finally, stands in similar need of an historical semantics both as a propædeutic to its statement of problems and of hypotheses and as corrective to its tendency to innovation without system.

In each case universality can be achieved and criteria can be found by means of the principles from which the method starts: dialectic can be employed to create a variety of doctrines dependent on comprehensive principles which establish in each case the system of those doctrines; logistic can form a variety of languages and constructions composed of simple principles or elements arranged according to rules of combination; and inquiry can be employed to investigate the conditions of meaning and communication determined by reflexive principles discovered by inquiry into the character of the inquiry. In each case the subject matter is terms and concepts, statements and judgments, and the method is employed to examine meanings derived by different methods from different principles relative to the common subjects to which they apply. The present analysis, thus, employs a method of inquiry: its subject matter is concepts and statements and their various meanings; its method is to state and to analyze the problems presented by the non-systematic relations of statements to other statements or to other expressions, embodiments, or applications of ideas; and the principles of the analysis are sought in the commonplaces of the relations of ideas in their explicit statement as ideas to their operation within communities—apart from and even prior to abstract statement—in practical actions, in cultural values, and in the use of resources to satisfy needs. In such an inquiry, historical semantics is distinguished from philosophic semantics and from political debate by differences among the problems they present. The problem of historical semantics is the problem of relating differing sets of meanings to the divergent principles which justify those meanings, while the problem of philosophic semantics is to relate one compendent set of meanings to its proper principles, and the problem of political discussion is to relate many meanings to a common subject matter and a common course of action. Neither historical semantics nor political agreement requires the same commitment to one method or to one set of principles that is essential to the use of the method of inquiry in philosophy. Yet the peculiarities of each method permit its extension to other methods and systems of meanings. Thus, the method of inquiry depends on discovering principles in the state of things by trying hypotheses in application, and it therefore employs as subordinate methods both the examination of principles in the opinions of men, apart from considerations of fact (and this examination fixes the meaning and use of "dialectic" in inquiry) and also the examination of the principles of symbolic uses and symbols apart from considerations of actual meanings or actual facts (and this examination fixes the meaning and use of "logistic" in inquiry). In inquiry, therefore, historical semantics assumes the form of a dialectic employed to state the problems of the varieties of philosophies encountered in philosophic discussion and political debate, and a similar dialectic is employed critically, preliminary to the commitments of philosophic semantics in dialectical and logistic philosophies. It is not a substitute for philosophy nor an adequate statement of the varieties of philosophies but a means of communication among philosophies on particular points of definition and problem which, by increasing mutual understanding, contributes also to enriching philosophy and to facilitating agreement in action.

Historical semantics occupies, accordingly, a middle ground between philosophic controversies and ideological conflicts. The oppositions of ideas in doctrine and in action depend on a minimum communication and a minimum recognition of common conditions and common problems. The problem of *historical* semantics is not a problem of ambiguity (although *philosophic* semantics tends to turn on questions of ambiguity in those philosophic methods which seek univocal definitions), but rather a problem of the persistence, recurrence, and transformation of problems under different verbal forms. Historical semantics is therefore a first step, essential to any effort to place thought and philosophy in the circumstances that condition its forms and development. The differences of meanings explored in historical semantics are differences of objects to which symbols are applied and of influences which determine the meanings of symbols in those applications, and once thought is recognized to be effective in theory and practice because ideas operate under other forms than their expression in words, the differences of meanings of words can be treated in relation to the other forms of differences of meanings which constitute the whole of the environment of man insofar as it affects any of his sensibilities or impulses. The relations of philosophies are an integral part of the relations among the aspects of reality recognized by men, and any statement of the conditions of thought and action is therefore involved in the problem of historical semantics. The conditions of men can be stated either in the historical account of the evolution of institutions, cultures, arts, and sciences or in the analytic account of the influences and forces which have operated and continue to operate in that evolution. But what "history" is and what constitute the conditions of "freedom" in action and thought vary according to the meanings given those terms, and the study of the conditions which determine the efficacy of thought, in theory and in history, is in large part a study in historical semantics.

The forms which history has taken reflect the basic differences of methods. Dialectical history is based on the assumption that the processes which operate in historical evolution and the processes of proof are fundamentally the same. Whatever basis of rationality is found for knowledge is therefore also the basis of process in concrete reality, and history is the account of the relations and reconciliations of contraries in processes schematized in epochs which pass and in civilizations, cultures, peoples, periods, or empires which rise and decline. Dialectical history is therefore "epochal" history, since it depends on discovering traits which characterize organic wholes—peoples, nations, or periods—and which apply to all activities of the group or of the time, including the characteristic forms of morals, political practices, religion, philosophy, and scientific inquiry. The periods, the peoples, and the civilizations may be chosen differently in different dialectical histories (Jerome and Augustine describe four empires and seven ages, Joachim of Floris elaborated three ages, Hegel three, Marx five, Spengler eight, and Toynbee twenty-one), and they can be set in different chronological relations to each other—as successive stages of degradation from a more perfect state, or as progressive stages of evolution to a better or a perfect state or to a community of men without need for the external controls of a state, or as cycles like the seasons of the year or the ages and generations of man, or simply as successions of growth and decline. History tends to be universal in dialectic, since it treats of the characteristics of the whole and attributes characteristics to smaller groups or to internal movements because of their places as parts of the whole.

Logistic history is based on events and on the effort to discover and set forth the relations among them. These relations are recorded originally in annals and chronicles as the temporal succession of events within a limited area or affecting a limited group or community of men, but as events become more complex and their consequences more far-reaching, causes must be found, which are attested and expounded, if possible, in some "human" or "social" science, to relate events to each other in the order and succession of their development. This transition from simple temporal succession to causal influences is rendered easier in the logistic tradition since philosophic speculation on the nature of causation in that tradition tends to reduce causes to constant conjunctions of objects in a regular order of succession and contiguity. Logistic history is therefore "causal" history, and it tends to become "scientific" both in the sense of applying regularities discovered in a science to order and to explain the contingencies of human development and in the sense of employing scientific method to accumulate, classify, and test the materials related in history. Logistic history differs from dialectical history in its basic theory, since the regularities and causes of natural processes and human actions may be applied to particular cases without assuming that processes or actions are rational or inevitable because they are intelligible. Indeed, the relation between general laws and their particular exemplifications which has suggested to some historians the ideal that history be made scientific has also been reflected in the philosophic discussion of necessity and probability in science, for as historians turn from the formulation of probabilities to the search for necessary historical laws, scientists turn from the quest for universal and certain laws to the calculations of the contingencies of probability. Logistic history is not universal. It begins with particular data—the forces relevant to a great event, the occurrences of a particular period, the accomplishments and sufferings of a particular group, people, or nation—and with the lines of causal relations or with the probabilities of consequences—the evolution of political forms and political power, the development of military instruments and tactics, the influence of geographic environment, the elaboration and extension of tools, technology, and industry, the alteration of economic conditions, moral influences, and social forms and customs. Logistic history tends to become general history in the form of history of civilization based on the progress of knowledge and its consequences in the lives and relations of men, but logistic history even in its most general form differs from dialectical history even in its most material form, not only in the nature of the scientific laws discovered in or applied to historical processes, but still more strikingly in the practical consequences derived from that application. Thus Buckle could apply, in his *History of Civilization* in England, laws which he found expressed in Adam Smith and Ricardo to demonstrate a progressive and justified tendency toward the extension of free trade, while Marx and Engels could apply the laws of the science of the history of society in their historical study of revolutions to discover an inevitable movement to the common ownership of means of production and to the controls of a planned economy.

Problematic history, or history conceived according to the method of inquiry, is based on an evolution in the recognition and statement of problems, in the solutions found for them, and in the human activities made possible by the successive solutions of problems. It is no accident that the scholars of the Hellenistic period who classified the disciplines and the sciences often bear the designation "peripatetic" as part of their names, for when the method of inquiry which was developed by Aristotle was applied to the analysis of data such as he ordered in his philosophic speculation, philosophers trained in that method wrote histories of biology, physics, mathematics, astronomy, logic, rhetoric, poetics, literature, and philosophy. Problematic history is the account of the achievements of men and of groups of men in the treatment of a subject matter or in the solution of a related series of problems, and it usually takes the form of tracing the development of individual disciplines in histories of literature, art, science, philosophy, and theology, or the development of methods, operations, and organizations in histories of inventions, techniques, and tactics, of political, economic, and social forms, and of doctrines, methods, and principles. Problematic history is therefore "disciplinary" history. "Disciplinary" history differs from "epochal" and "causal" history in its basic theory, since inquiry suggests that human history is not explained simply by natural processes, whereas dialectic discovers a fundamental identity between science and process, and logistic projects a science of human action. The history of problems and of their solutions does not depend, therefore, either on assuming that nature is rational in any other sense than that the results of actions are predictable to a degree once the problematic situation has been analyzed or on assuming that the solution of problems by human intervention is a science in any other sense than that it may employ a method similar to the scientific method of the natural sciences. The particularity or the generality of problematic history is determined by the scope of the discipline whose history is treated and the extent of the influence of the problems to which the discipline is applied, and universality can be achieved by tracing the history of theory, or practice, or art, since each, in its way, is an architectonic history in which the others may be treated as aspects or influences.

The differences among these three forms of history cannot be stated in terms of a unique claim of any one to be scientific or in terms of a superior power or a greater inclusiveness proper to any one of them. Each makes use of knowledge and science to discover a rational order, and no historical fact accounted for in one order escapes explanation by the other methods, nor is any sequence unassimilable to other accounts. Yet the significance of the data, and even the entities which undergo change and the processes involved in the change, are radically altered as they are interpreted according to different methods. The order or rationality that animates dialectical or epochal history is an order in nature which is indistinguishable from the order of knowledge. The development of man's environment and of his actions forms an organic whole in which all parts and aspects share common characteristics, and history is concerned with the development of mankind as a whole and with the realization of the essence of man conceived as spirit or producer, as wisdom or love, or, in a word, as free. The order or rationality found in logistic or causal history, on the other hand, is an order of causal succession or influence which traces lines of development through the complex sequence of events by applying available knowledge and science insofar as they bear on the nature and actions of men. The development of man is a reaction to his environing circumstances, and history is concerned with the actions of individuals and of the groups which they form and with the progress which emerges in the large as the progress of knowledge makes possible freedom from superstition, fear, oppression, and want. The order or rationality developed in problematic or disciplinary history, finally, is a result of the application of reflective reason to the statement of problems, the ordering of their solutions, and the recognition of the emergence of new problems. The development of man is a consequence of his ability to solve problems, and history therefore traces the sequence of the use of rational analysis or effective action in a series of related problems in the sciences, the subject matters, or the actions to which it is relevant. The subject of dialectical history is mankind or even the universe; all parts of mankind, including individuals, and all actions are treated as they are known, by science or dialectic, to be interdependent or mutually supplementary aspects of that whole. The subject matter of logistic history is any coherent group of men, whose coherence and whose actions can be analyzed and explained by causes known, if possible, by a science of man; insofar as the development of knowledge enters into consideration in logistic history, it is attended by concomitant progress in other

aspects of human life. The subject matter of problematic history is neither a whole (since universal wholes transcend human experience and
knowledge) nor an interaction of parts (since the complexes of intellectual development, social action, and esthetic experience cannot be explained by reduction to the causal interaction of parts) but rather the
problems and hypotheses by which the human mind has approached
the conditions of a reality not otherwise known than by the hypotheses
men have constructed and by which men have approached associations
with other men for the solution of common problems and for common
action.

Any statement of the distinction among the kinds of history is open
to misinterpretations and countersenses, since each of the varieties of
history not only takes into account all the facts and the processes treated
in other versions but also, in the light of its own principles, treats them
more fully and better. Dialectical or epochal history treats causes and
disciplines, but its basic principles determine the organic unity and
succession of periods which it treats, and all forms of knowledge
and expression and all formulations of problems are found to be appropriate to their periods as determined in this fundamental historical and
scientific pattern. Causal and disciplinary histories, from the point of
view of dialectic, commit the error of abstracting sequences and problems from the contexts by which they are determined. Logistic history
treats epochs and disciplines, but its basic principles are universal laws
of human action which are the same for all mankind, for all periods,
and for all problems, while the characteristics of periods and peoples
are the result of the operation of those laws under particular circumstances, and the formulations of problems are functions of the state of
knowledge. Dialectical and disciplinary histories, from the point of
view of logistic, are defective in their lack of scientific basis, which leads
dialectical historians to construct myths of the characters of races,
peoples, and periods and their inevitable succession, and disciplinary
historians to trace the discussion of unreal problems unrelated to the
advancement of the sciences. Disciplinary history treats epochs and
causes, but its basic principles are canons of inquiry and method appropriate to the variety of problems which mankind has faced, while it
treats periods and peoples by examining the diversity of doctrines,
problems, and characteristics which enter into the formation of any
homogeneity that they present, and it examines the causes of action in
individual terms which are not reducible to universal laws and proba-

bilities and the development of knowledge in terms of hypotheses and trials which are not reducible to simple cycles or simple programs.

The dialectical history of philosophy, to take one instance of the variety of historical accounts of a single subject, is indistinguishable from universal history, except in the dialectical sense that the philosophy of history and the history of philosophy treat different aspects of the same succession of ages, and that philosophy is at once one of the traits by which ages are characterized and one of the ways in which the characters of ages are expressed. The logistic history of philosophy, on the other hand, is an account of the development of knowledge, and it tells some form of the familiar story of an evolution in which philosophy once embraced the whole of knowledge, from which branches and departments were separated as they became scientific, until the residue consists in part of unreal problems which are therefore insusceptible of scientific treatment (except indirectly insofar as psychopathic or social reasons are found for their occurrence) and in part of the science of man or of language which will, once it is perfected, reduce the whole again to a unified science. The problematic history of philosophy, finally, treats the problems and doctrines which philosophers considered. It is an account of the succession of schools, of methods, of subject matters and of problems, which form a continuity with, and afford suggestions for, the treatment of philosophic problems still under consideration. From the point of view of dialectic, other histories treat philosophic thought in abstraction from the conditions by which it is determined and which in turn it influences; from the point of view of logistic, other histories treat philosophic thought without differentiating fancy from knowledge, myth from truth; from the point of view of inquiry, other histories treat philosophic thought without fidelity to what was said or meant by adjusting the development of philosophy to a dialectic of what philosophers must have meant at that time, whether they realized it or not, or by selecting among what they said bits and phrases that may be interpreted as anticipations of later truths.

Or, to take a phase of history that might seem less susceptible to later intellectual manipulation: the history of military strategy and tactics may be written by a dialectical historian in terms of the spirit or the material conditions of ages and the fundamental law may be found in the character and succession of societies or ages; it may be written by a scientist technician in terms of the development of arts of offense and defense and then the fundamental law may be found in the development of tools with the progress of knowledge, science, and technology; it may be written by an inquirer-soldier in terms of the problems of deploying troops and then the fundamental law may be found in relations of armament and mobility which were basically the same for Alexander, Caesar, Napoleon, and the strategists of the last war. Each of these histories of strategy is based on a rational conception of events and of human actions, which the defenders of each may choose to call scientific, and on a conception of the efficacy of rational action: in dialectical history the basic historical law determines periods, and military strategy at once shares the intellectual and cultural characteristics common to the activities of the period and is numbered frequently, when changes occur in strategy, among the signs of the beginning of a new period; in logistic history the basic historical law isolates causal relations or probabilities in human actions, and military strategy at once enters the causal sequences which make war a continuation of political policy or social purpose and shows the consequences of progress which results from the advance of science and technology; in problematic history the basic historical law isolates situations in terms of problems, of hypotheses by which they are solved, and of new problems to which the solution leads, and the history of military strategy presents at once basic problems which recur in a variety of forms and a progressive accumulation of knowledge pertinent to the solution of more complex forms of the problems. But once the distinction is recognized obscurely or made explicit, each variety of history undertakes to treat the basic law of the other varieties as a consequence of its own basic assumptions: periods can be treated in terms of the operation of laws of human nature in particular circumstances or the assemblage of characteristic problems; the laws of human action may be found to be particularized to periods or to the solution of problems; and problems may be determined by the circumstances under which they occur or by the laws of human action and reaction. Nonetheless the books written on strategy by the historian *qua* dialectician concerned with the succession of cultures, *qua* technician concerned with the development of instruments, and *qua* soldier concerned with the disposition of troops continue to differ, and the one variety of history will not serve except incidentally the purposes for which the others are conceived.

Variant conceptions of freedom are implicit in the various conceptions of history, and they vary according to the same principles as determine the species of history and the forms which each of these species assumes. Conceptions of freedom, however diverse, have a common core in the notion of absence of external control or restraint, as conceptions of history have a common objective in the purpose to recount the facts relevant to the sequence of situations and processes. What constitutes external control, nonetheless, is different in the different theories of freedom and in the different histories based on dialectical, logistic, or problematic methods and principles. If the development of man is part of a rational or necessary process of universal development, as it is in dialectical history, freedom is found precisely in the dialectic of that development. Freedom is then a power based on conformity to the truth, wisdom, spirit, or circumstances that rule all things; it is not a self-determination or a contingency due to the action of objects or persons or groups according to the laws of their own nature rather than according to the impulsion, influence, or determination of external causes or due to the interplay of kinds of causes or of independent lines of causal influence, or due to a radical indeterminacy in the operation of all things; nor is it a region of choice left to the individual man by the nature of his associations with other men and delimited only by consideration of the effects of free action on the freedom of others and on the maintenance of free institutions. It is an ability to choose the better and the right in the absence of external controls which deflect choice to the erroneous, the partial, or the bad, and the conditions of freedom for the individual are analogous to the condition of freedom for the state, for the free man is the wise man whose irrational impulses are controlled by reason and the free state is the well-ordered state ruled by a wise elite. The free man may indeed rise superior to the contingencies of his natural and social environment, but his actions will be directed to the ideal of a society in which all men will be as free as their nature and the circumstances which environ them permit.

If the development of man is the result of the operation of causes whose regularities are or may be known by science, as it is in logistic history, freedom is a cause operating according to the necessary laws of the individual body, person, or group in counterdistinction to causes operating according to the necessary laws of external agencies influencing operations and actions. Freedom is achieved by action in accordance with the laws of one's own nature (and the motion of a freely falling body is then the basic example of freedom from external restraint) or in accordance with a basic contingency found in complex processes and actions despite the necessities of the laws of mechanics, or in accordance with the laws of thought or of logic or even in accordance with a basic contingency in the operation of simple elements, such as the swerve of the atoms of Epicurus, the principle of indeterminacy of quantum mechanics, the experiences which supply the origin and the contents of simple ideas, and the choice of terms and postulates in analytical logics. Freedom is then a self-determination subject to necessary laws or an indeterminacy subject to probability calculations, and absence of external control consists in the operation of the individual in his individual character and according to his individual habits undetermined by external necessities. To that freedom must be added the freedom of man based on knowledge of necessary laws and probabilities— a freedom from ignorance, superstition, fear, and domination —which may be extended to include knowledge of the operations of the individual according to the laws of some science of human nature or according to the laws of probability.

If the development of man is the result of reflective thought applied in the solution of problems, as it is in problematic or disciplinary history, freedom is found in the institution of conditions in which actions which do not affect the freedom of others to act are tolerated and protected by the recognition of duties and the imposition of laws to control or prohibit actions which destroy, endanger, or limit freedom. Freedom, so considered, does not have a metaphysical basis in the nature of things or in historical processes to which human actions are made to conform by wisdom or group affiliation, nor does it have a scientific basis in the laws of motion and operation, but it has a social and political basis in the actions and associations of men. The conditions of freedom are not found in the action of the wise man choosing what is right or in the motion of an unhindered body or of an electron determined only by its own nature or statistical averages, but in the political institutions by which free men separate a region of agreement under law and a region of freedom for doctrine, statement, and action. The differentiation of the two depends on reflective thought, and the progress of that differentiation is the history of the development of democratic institutions, since democratic institutions are possible only in communities in which free men predominate and have as their end the extension and preservation of freedoms. Democracy depends, in turn, on the institution of conditions in the community under which men may come freely to agreement concerning common courses of action and on the development in the individual of reflective attitudes applied in the examination of alternative hypotheses prior to choosing a course of action which will affect, to some extent, the condition of the individual and which might affect the condition of other individuals and the structure of the community which unites them.

There is no necessary contradiction between a conception of freedom which makes it depend on a rationality or order in nature to which man approximates in successive ages while realizing in so doing his essence by means of wisdom, or action, or production, and a conception of freedom which makes it depend on the differentiation of internal and external causes of motion and on knowledge of laws of motion and of probability, and, finally, a conception of freedom which makes it depend on the relation of individual rights and actions to social and political duties and controls. Yet the discussion of freedom reduces to large questions determined by the decision to consider freedom relative to dialectical, scientific, or political bases, and refutation is almost automatic when the absence of external restraint is sought in principles other than those admitted in some one philosophy. Neither a freedom of self-determination and probability such as is normally evolved in logistic analyses nor a freedom of reflective thought and choice suited to the method of inquiry is easily restated to answer dialectical questions concerning how indeterminacy or choice can be reconciled with necessity and the laws of nature or concerning how free actions escape the control of external forces which determine the selection between apparent alternatives, unless there is some rational accord in freedom between human action and natural order. Neither a freedom of natural order, ideal or material, and of rational action, evolved in dialectic, nor a freedom of reflective thought and of choice, adapted to inquiry, is invulnerable to questions suggested by the logistic search for efficient causes, for when the causes of reason or of choice are sought, they are found in the necessary or probable laws which govern human behavior. Finally, neither a freedom of natural order and of reason, dialectically elaborated, nor a freedom of indeterminacy and of probability, logistically calculated, can escape the arguments which flow naturally from the method of inquiry against conceptions of freedom that seek in the necessities and contradictions of nature or in the indeterminacies and motions of particles the foundations of a power resulting from the foresight made possible by human language, reason, and society. The discussion of freedom, on bases so radically different, degenerates frequently, in the exchange of criticism and philosophic refutation, to a

lengthy and violent logomachy. The differences in the conceptions of
history are no less radical and the confusions no less verbal, although
less effort is devoted to the communication of ideas and their clarification among historians than among moral philosophers. History is
treated, in the large, either as a dialectic worked out in epochs and
civilizations and characters of times and of peoples, or as a science discovering and applying laws and probabilities to situations, persons, and
processes, or as an art and a science providing insights and explanations
of the emergence and resolution of problems, the development and
elaboration of statements, and the planning and execution of actions.

The differences concerning freedom and history, which lead to confusion in the discussion of the nature of human action and in the interpretation of what has been done, frequently have disastrous effects in
practice, for conceptions of the conditions of human action and of the
past sequence of human actions under those conditions influence the
conditions imposed in the present on actions anticipated or planned for
the future. Differences of conceptions of freedom may become threats
to freedom and, in the interests of preserving freedom, temporary restrictions may be placed on freedom, in each of its senses, which may
lead to the extinction of freedom in all senses, including the sense in
which it was thought to be endangered and in which it was thought to
be protected by the limitations imposed. In support of measures of
control or in recognition of necessities, the fixed determination of past
events treated in any version of history can be extended a little or far
into the future by dialectic, by science, probability, and extrapolation,
or by analysis of likenesses and differences of problems. The contribution of historical semantics to the discussion of philosophic problems
of freedom and history should be to introduce on a common level the
meanings proper to the opposed positions in order to prevent discussion from becoming merely captious and refutation merely verbal, and
its contribution to political action in the interests of freedom and in the
light of history should be to make apparent the dangers that arise from
the degradation or misuse, due to fears of the consequences of actions
based on rival theories, of conceptions and doctrines which have defensible significances and pacific uses.

3. The Dialectical Analysis of Freedom and History

In dialectic, freedom and history are closely interrelated because both
are expressions of the nature or essence of man. The history of the
development of men, institutions, and cultures is inseparable from or

even identical with philosophy, for history recounts a movement toward freedom and philosophy is an expression of freedom. Since the essence of man is sought in dialectic by use of comprehensive principles which present the full man in all his contradictions and in all his relations to his circumstances, the characteristic form which freedom takes in dialectical analyses is a kind of knowledge, truth, or wisdom adequate to encompass such contrarieties; and the characteristic form of history is the account of a succession of periods, peoples, or civilizations, each with characteristic philosophies and freedoms which determine the nature, the life, and the actions of men. However, since there is room for dialectical differences concerning the essence of man, there have been many expressions of the truth on which freedom depends and many formulations of the nature and succession of the cultures of men.

What has been called, since the nineteenth century, the philosophy of history has been for the most part variant constructions of the dialectical method, and almost all the forms it has taken have been strongly influenced by Hegel. The history of the world, according to Hegel, "is nothing but the development of the Idea of Freedom."[1] Since Spirit is self-contained existence, the essence of Spirit is Freedom. The three stages of historical development are determined by the gradations of the growing consciousness of Freedom. The Orientals did not attain to the knowledge that Spirit, man as man, is free; they knew only that *one* is free, and the one becomes a despot, not a free man. The consciousness of freedom first arose among the Greeks, according to Hegel, but they and the Romans knew only that *some* are free, not that man as such is free. The German nations, under the influence of Christianity, were the first to attain the consciousness that man, as man, is free: that it is the freedom of the Spirit which constitutes its essence.[2]

Freedom in this sense and the history of the periods in which it is developed depend on differentiating kinds of freedom and kinds of history. Real or objective freedom must be distinguished from the subjective freedom which is illusory except when it is joined to real freedom.

But Objective Freedom—the laws of *real* Freedom—demand the subjugation of the mere contingent *Will*—for this is in its nature formal. If the objective is itself Rational, human insight and conviction must correspond with the Rea-

1. *Lectures on the Philosophy of History,* trans. J. Sibree (London, 1861), Part IV, sec. 3, Chap. iii, p. 476.
2. *Ibid., Introduction,* pp. 18–19.

son which it embodies, and then we have the other essential element—Subjective Freedom—also realized.[3]

Spirit is defined in terms of its opposite, matter, for matter has its essence outside itself, while Spirit is *self-contained existence,* which is precisely the definition of Freedom.[4] The comprehensive principles of dialectic therefore combine principles which are opposite and contradictory in the logistic and problematic methods: the internal causes opposed by external causes in the determination of human action and the freedom which is a right (*jus*) opposed by the regulation of duties and laws (*lex*). Freedom in its full sense is a coincidence of internal with external causes and of rights and duties.

The bond of duty can appear as a restriction only on indeterminate subjectivity or abstract freedom, and on the impulses either of the natural will or of the moral will which determines its indeterminate good arbitrarily. The truth is, however, that in duty the individual finds his liberation; first, liberation from dependence on mere natural impulse and from the depression which as a particular subject he cannot escape in his moral reflections on what ought to be and what might be; secondly, liberation from the indeterminate subjectivity which, never reaching reality or the objective indeterminacy of action, remains self-enclosed and devoid of reality. In duty the individual acquires his substantive freedom.[5]

Similarly, what Hegel calls Philosophical History is distinguished from more empirical varieties of history by recognizing its concern with thought and its commitment to the hypothesis that the history of the world presents us with a rational process.[6] The comprehensive principles of dialectic, which join all aspects of reality, find expression in philosophical history which is universal history and in which freedom is realized in activity which expresses man's true essence in a rational universe in which all aspects of his activity are interdependent: consciousness of freedom is inseparable from freedom, and freedom results

3. *Ibid.,* p. 476.
4. *Ibid.,* p. 18; cf. also *ibid:* "The nature of Spirit may be understood by a glance at its direct opposite—*Matter.* As the essence of matter is Gravity, so, on the other hand, we may affirm that the substance, the essence of Spirit is Freedom. All will readily assent to the doctrine that Spirit, among other properties, is also endowed with Freedom; but philosophy teaches that all the qualities of Spirit exist only through Freedom; that all are but means for attaining Freedom; that all seek and produce this and this alone. It is a result of speculative Philosophy, that Freedom is the sole truth of Spirit."
5. Hegel, *Philosophy of Right,* trans. T. M. Knox (Oxford, 1942), par. 149, p. 107.
6. *Lectures on the Philosophy of History,* p. 9.

from a conjunction of reason and will which joins politics to ethics, history to philosophy, and all to theodicy.[7]

The conception of freedom and history constructed in dialectical materialism is built about a different conception of man elaborated at the opposite pole of the dialectical antithesis between Matter and Spirit. The essence of man, what distinguishes him from an animal, is not conscience, religion, or spirit: men began to distinguish themselves from animals when they began themselves to produce their means of existence and so to condition their physical organization and their life itself. What men are coincides with their production, with the nature of the production as well as with the mode of production. What they are depends on the material conditions of their production.[8] The history of society is a science. Indeed, there is only one science—the science of history—whose two parts, the history of nature or the science of nature properly so called and the history of man are inseparably connected. Any other version of history is an "ideology" and is either a false interpretation of this history or a total abstraction from it. With the transformation of material productive forces, economic relations are altered and, as a consequence, the social, moral, and political situation of nations is changed. The material changes of economic conditions of production, which are known by means of the natural sciences, are therefore to be distinguished from the juridical, political, religious, artistic, or philosophic, that is, the ideological forms by which men become conscious of the conflicts those changes involve and carry them through. Five major stages in the development of society are so deter-

7. *Philosophy of Right*, trans. T. M. Knox (Oxford, 1942), Addition 152, p. 279: "The state in and by itself is the ethical whole, the actualization of freedom; and it is an absolute end of reason that freedom should be actual. The state is mind on earth and consciously realizing itself there. . . . The march of God is the world, that is what the state is. The basis of the state is the power of reasoning actualizing itself as will." *Philosophy of History*, p. 477: "Philosophy escapes from the weary strife of passions that agitate the surface of society into the calm region of contemplation; that which interests it is the recognition of the process of development which the Idea has passed through in realizing itself—i.e., the Idea of Freedom, whose reality is the consciousness of freedom and nothing short of it. That the History of the World, with all the changing scenes which its annals present, is this process of development and the realization of Spirit—this is the true *Theodicaea*, the justification of God in History. Only *this* insight can reconcile Spirit with the History of the World—viz., that what has happened, and is happening every day, is not only not 'without God,' but is essentially His Work."

8. *Die Deutsche Ideologie* B. A. 1. "Die Ideologie überhaupt, spezial die deutsche" (Karl Marx), *Der Historische Materialismus: Die Frühschriften* ed. S. Landshut and J. P. Mayer (Leipzig, 1932), vol. II, pp. 10–11."

mined—primitive communal, slave, feudal, capitalist, and communist. The danger to freedom in the course of this development is from alienation. Man appropriates his essence to many aspects of many objects in many fashions—by senses, sentiment, thought, contemplation, passion, and activity, that is, by the organs of his individuality as well as by social organs. The appropriation of human reality and its relation to the object is the accomplishment of human action. By the sentiment of possession, private property has led to the alienation of all physical and moral sentiments. The abolition of private property is therefore the complete liberation of all sentiments and all human attributes.[9] But dialectical materialism, like Hegelian dialectic, differentiates two kinds of history and two kinds of freedom. The history of society is a basic science, while any other form of political, social, artistic, or philosophic history is the expression of an ideology. The realm of freedom begins, in actuality, where labor determined by necessity and external purposes ceases. Freedom is possible in the realm of necessity determined by purely material production to the extent that the associated producers govern their material rationally instead of being governed by it as by a blind force. Beyond the realm of necessity begins the development of human powers which is an end in itself, the true realm of freedom which comes to flower only if it is rooted in the realm of necessity.[10]

The influence of the Hegelian and the Marxist conceptions of history has been considerable and various. It is apparent in a tendency to identify reason and history by means of freedom. That identification can be accomplished in one of two ways: either by arguing that the only adequate knowledge of any thing or event is knowledge of its genesis or evolution and that its history is the account of the development of freedom, or by arguing that the historical process is a development of freedom as it becomes more rational and self-conscious. Benedetto Croce follows the first course and modifies Hegel's dictum that history is the history of liberty, arguing that the dictum is misinterpreted when it is used to distinguish the oriental, the classical, and the Germanic worlds according to the formula one, some, or all free. He adopts the dictum "with a different intention and content"

. . . not in order to assign to history the task of creating a liberty which did not exist in the past but will exist in the future, but to maintain that liberty is the

9. *Nationalökonomie und Philosophie* "Vorrede," *ibid.* vol. I, pp. 299–300.
10. *Capital* III, 2, p. 355; quoted by A. D. Lindsay, *Karl Marx's Capital: An Introductory Essay* (London, 1925), p. 36.

eternal creator of history and itself the explanatory principle of the course of history, and on the other the moral ideal of humanity.[11]

So complete is the identification of reason and the knowledge of origins that philosophy becomes an antiquated idea except as it is identified with the methodology of historiography.[12] "The concept that concrete and true knowledge is always historical knowledge has the obvious consequence that the knowledge or qualification or judgment of an event cannot be separated or distinguished from the knowledge of its genesis, nor can that which is a single act be made to appear as two successive moments, still less as two divergent or successive acts."[13]

Harold Laski follows the second course and borrows from Marx the conception of the economic as the basic force determining the evolution of freedom. The history of freedom is divided into two major moments since its beginnings in the period of the Reformation. The first moment is the period of a struggle to free the individual from subordination to a position, religious, political, or economic, in which he has been placed by an authority superior to himself. Liberty is related only negatively to justice and equality; privilege is attacked—religious privilege, political privilege, the privilege of birth, or sex, or race. The second moment of the development of freedom is coincident with the growth of the modern proletariat and consists in the discovery that the negative liberty does not give freedom to the masses. This is a period of social emancipation and paternalistic government, the regulation of the behavior of groups and individuals in the interest of an increasing equality in their lives. It involves the transference from the plane of political to that of economic rights, and the aim of regulation is an increasing approximation to equality. Freedom is defined, not only as absence of external restraint, but also as "the affirmation by an individual or group of his or its own essence."[14]

The practical consequences drawn from these dialectical differences concerning history and freedom are as extreme as the practices attached to the Hegelian and the Marxist dialectics: Croce argues from his principles that the acquisition and extension of freedom depends on the

11. Benedetto Croce, *History as the Story of Liberty,* Eng. trans. of *La Storia Come pensiero e come azione* (New York, 1941), p. 59; cf. p. 53 for a similar criticism of the Marxist formula.

12. Croce, *op. cit.,* p. 147.

13. *Ibid.,* p. 151.

14. Harold Laski, "Liberty" *Encyclopedia of Social Sciences* (New York, 1933), IX, 442–46.

reaffirmation of liberalism; Laski concludes from his that they depend on its abandonment.

The Hegelian and the Marxist conceptions of freedom and history are far from exhausting the varieties of freedom and history that have been discovered in dialectical analysis and investigation. On the contrary, Hegelianism and Marxism are restricted and comparatively rigid forms of dialectic, for they relate philosophy to history in such fashion that history is made to afford apparent evidence for the truth of one philosophy, and philosophy is made the ground for the inevitable occurrence of an age described as the final stage in the historical evolution of freedom. Dialectical conceptions of history and of freedom depend on fundamental relations posited between knowledge and action or (in the terminology of an older discussion) between reason and will. Those assumptions require a world which is fundamentally rational or at least ordered, both in the sense that processes occur in it according to principles accessible to the human mind in some fashion, though not necessarily as a result of the activity of the human reason, and also in the sense that a human being achieves the fullest realization of his own essence by conforming to the principles that govern the world. That relation between man and the world in which he lives, and acts, and knows can be stated in two fundamentally different ways which lead to two types of dialectics of history and freedom: according to one, the principles governing the order which man encounters in the world are distinct from the principles governing human reason and are therefore accessible to man by some other means than rational evidence alone; according to the other, the rational principles in the world are the same as the rational principles in man, and freedom and history present common problems of subordinating other principles to reason and of bringing the causes of human action into coincidence with the reason that rules things. In the first form of dialectic, will or some other source of attachment and action tends to be emphasized, and then freedom may be a gift of grace, a characteristic of human nature, or an innate right distinct from, opposed to, or transcending reason. In the second form of dialectic, reason or some other source of wisdom and understanding tends to be emphasized, and then freedom may be identified with knowledge inasmuch as truth influences love, animates nature, and guides action. It is apparent that dialectical materialism is a development of the first variety of dialectic since the essence of man is identified with his production and philosophies are ideologies which are not reliable as knowledge of the conditions which they treat or as guide in actions which they inspire, while Hegelianism is a development of the second variety of dialectic since the essence of man is spirit and spirit is freedom. Both varieties of dialectic tend to require a differentiation between two kinds of freedom similar to that which Hegel and Marx employed.

St. Augustine, Rousseau, and Kant are among the philosophers who relate freedom to concepts which in some fashion transcend theoretical knowledge and rational processes. According to St. Augustine, God is the supreme law and the immutable nature above the rational mind. In all its processes, reason judges according to this law, but it cannot judge the law itself. The first life and the first essence of man and the universe are where the first wisdom is. To know that truth which is above the mind is to love it, and our freedom consists in subjugation to it, since it frees us from death, that is, from the condition of sin.[15] The law of freedom is the law of charity,[16] and charity is the love of God as contrasted to cupidity, which is the love of temporal material things without the mediation of wisdom and charity. Augustine distinguishes sharply between free choice or free will (*liberum arbitrium*) and freedom (*libertas*): free choice leaves open the possibility of doing evil, whereas freedom is the good use of free choice. The will is always free, in the sense of possessing free choice, but it is not always good, and therefore is not always free in the sense of possessing freedom.[17] The more the will is subject or slave to grace the more sound it is, and the sounder it is the freer it is. True freedom is to be subject to Christ: Augustine develops the dictum of Paul that to be free is to be slave or servant (*servus*), free of sin, but slave to justice. The progress of mankind to freedom is the process of differentiating the terrestrial from the celestial city which will be realized fully beyond this life. Bossuet discovered the foundations of "universal history" in the history developed in the *City of God;* the history of Augustine is a history of periodization, differentiating the characters of eras sometimes according to the differences between Pagan and Christian, sometimes according to the pecu-

15. Augustine, *De Vera religione* 31. 57–58; *Patrologia Latina,* XXXIV, 147–48. Cf. *De libero arbitrio* ii. 13. 37; PL, XXXII, 1261, trans. *On the Free Will,* Richard McKeon, *Selections from Medieval Philosophers* (New York, 1929) I, 53.

16. *Epistola* 167. vi. 19; PL. XXXIII, 740.

17. For a discussion of the relation of *liberum arbitrium* and *libertas,* cf. E. Gilson, *Introduction à l'étude de Saint Augustin* (Paris, 1929), pp. 208–9.

liarities of the Four Empires mentioned in the Book of Daniel, sometimes according to the succession of seven ages of man based on the
schematization of Eusebius.

Rousseau argues that man is distinguished from other animals not
as a "rational animal" but as a "free animal." Other animals have ideas,
inasmuch as they have senses, and all to some extent are able to combine ideas, but man alone is characterized by freedom. The brute obeys
nature when it commands, whereas man is conscious of his freedom to
acquiesce or to resist an impression, and the spirituality of his soul is
most clearly manifested in this consciousness. This difference between
man and animal, however, is subject to dispute unless it is joined with
another distinguishing quality concerning which there is no dispute,
that is, man's faculty of perfecting himself. Moreover, in spite of what
moralists say, it is precisely by the activity of the passions that the
understanding is perfected.[18] Rousseau put to radically different uses
the same commonplaces as Augustine used: freedom consists in choice
conjoined with the possibility of using free choice well, but for Rousseau that possibility is a mark of nature rather than of grace; passions
are contrasted to understanding, but the recognition of material needs
and the activity of the passions are stimuli to self-perfection rather than
possible sources of cupidity and distractions from charity; finally, love
and the passions are the basis of the sociability of man, and in the
history of states inequality increases among men with the progress of
the arts and the sciences.

Since man is by nature free, the state likewise is determined by liberty. The mistakes which Rousseau found in his predecessors' treatment
of the social compact result from ignoring this fundamental fact, for
they suppose the compact to consist in the surrender of rights and liberty into the hands of a sovereign, in spite of the fact that to give up
liberty is to surrender one's character as man.[19] The problems of political philosophy are determined by the nature of man: rights and duties
are not arbitrary things to be put off and taken on at will, and liberty
in particular is inalienable. Man cannot return to the state of nature, for
he is already corrupted, but he can establish a rule of administration,

18. J. J. Rousseau, *Discours sur l'origine et les fondements de l'inégalité parmi les hommes,*
Part I (*Oeuvres complêtes* [Paris, 1824], I, 238–41).

19. *Ibid.,* Part II (*Oeuvres,* I, 303–5). Cf. *Du contrat social,* Livre I, chap. iv: "Renoncer à sa liberté, c'est renoncer à sa qualité d'homme, aux droits de l'humanité, même à ses
devoirs."

legitimate and sure, that utility and justice may not be divided. Freedom and equality are the two great goods which are the object of every system of legislation,[20] and the basis of legislation is a pact of free and equal men. The pact does not destroy a natural equality but rather substitutes a moral and legitimate equality for natural physical inequalities, and men who are unequal in force or genius are made equal by convention and law.[21] By the social contract man loses his natural liberty, which is limited only by the power of the individual, and gains civil liberty, which is limited by the general will. With civil liberty he also acquires moral liberty, which alone renders him truly master of himself, for the impulsion of the appetite alone is slavery while obedience to the law which one prescribes to oneself is freedom.[22] Neither the progress of man in the development of the arts and sciences, nor his consequent regression in the corruption of morals and in the increase of inequality, has an inevitability based on the rationality of nature or the force of material conditions and economic relations such as characterizes history in the Hegelian or the Marxist dialectics, for the growth of inequality may be checked by political means uncontrolled by either the development of Spirit or the relations of production. Yet, as Augustine's *City of God* has influenced the writing of history by providing a scheme by which events might be ordered to an end beyond time, so Rousseau's conception of man has influenced the writing of history by providing schemes by which to order the events both of man's progress and of his degradation.

The concept of freedom, according to Kant who joins to a dialectical conception of the overarching and comprehensive function of freedom a problematic conception of the distinction of theory from practice, is a conception of pure reason and is therefore transcendent in respect to theoretical philosophy. Freedom is not the object of theoretical knowledge. It is not constitutive of knowledge but regulative of action, and is conceived only negatively in speculative reason. In the sphere of reason, however, the reality of freedom can be demonstrated by practical principles which, as laws, prove a causality of the pure reason in the process of determining the activity of the will, which is independent of empirical and sensible conditions. It is possible, thus, to establish in us

20. *Du contrat social,* Livre II, chap. xi.
21. *Ibid.,* Livre I, chap. ix.
22. *Ibid.,* chap. viii.

the existence of pure will as the source of all moral conceptions and laws. Freedom is the key-stone of the whole system of pure reason, including speculative reason, and it is the only one of the ideas of speculative reason of which we know the possibility *a priori*, even though we do not understand it, for it is the *ratio essendi* of the moral law which we do know, while the moral law is the *ratio cognoscendi* of freedom.[23] Again the commonplaces employed by Augustine and Rousseau are put to still different uses: freedom of choice, which distinguishes man from the brute, is an empirical freedom found in the capacity to choose between two opposing things, including the lawful and the unlawful, as contrasted to the transcendental freedom by which man as noumenon legislates for objects of choice and with respect to them is free but has no choice. Kant also adds a third kind of freedom which he finds in the activity of the faculty of judgment mediating between the phenomenal and the noumenal world.

Freedom is the one innate right which follows necessarily from the humanity of man.

> Freedom is Independence of the compulsory Will of another; and in so far as it can co-exist with the freedom of all according to a universal law, it is the one sole, original, inborn Right belonging to every man in virtue of his Humanity. There is, indeed, an inborn Equality belonging to every man which consists in his Right to be independent of being bound by others to anything more than that to which he may also reciprocally bind them. It is, consequently, the inborn quality of every man in virtue of which he ought to be *his own master by Right (sui juris)*.[24]

Such patterns and such progress as are found in history follow from the activity and development of freedom. In his *Idea for a Universal History with Cosmopolitan Intent* Kant finds the universality of history in the progress of freedom toward a community consisting of all men. "History allows one to hope that, when history is considered *in the large* the play of the freedom of the human will, it will be possible to discover the regular progressions thereof."[25] The scheme of universal history will show the progress of human rationality which is brought into existence according to a plan of nature by passion, ignorance, and selfishness,

23. Kant, *Critique of Practical Reason*, trans. T. K. Abbott (London, 1898), Preface, p. 88.

24. Kant, *Philosophy of Law*, trans. W. Hastie (Edinburgh, 1887), p. 56.

25. Kant, *Idea for a Universal History with Cosmopolitan Intent*, trans. C. J. Friedrich, in *The Philosophy of Kant* (New York, 1949), p. 116.

and which is to lead to the achievement of a civil society which administers law in general. The achievement of that society will be furthered by a philosophical attempt to write a general world history. Different means of achieving such freedom were elaborated according to the various forms of dialectic by which Fichte, Schelling, Hegel, Lotze and Marx made similar identifications of history with the development of freedom.

The second form of dialectic, which finds the basis of freedom in the possibility of establishing rational principles for human action which are identical with the rational principles governing the universe, leads also to the differentiation of two kinds of freedom. When the essence of man is found in some form of activity and when the principles of his actions are thought to exceed reason, as in the case of the first form of dialectic, true freedom which is beyond the realm of necessity is contrasted with the freedom which is possible in self-alienation, in choice, in the passions, in the regulations of law, each of which may be a means either of the self-assertion of the individual or of his control by external forces. When the essence of man is found in some form of reason and when the principles of his action are thought to be directly accessible to rational analysis, as in the case of the second form of dialectic, true freedom is identical with wisdom as contrasted to the domination of the passions. Since, however, few men are wise, freedom is also achieved by the rule of law which may, like wisdom, be based on the law of nature.

Plato, the Stoics, and Spinoza are among the philosophers who identify freedom in varying ways with wisdom acquired through the rational processes employed in the theoretic and practical sciences. For Plato the basic contrast is once more between freedom and slavery, but only the virtuous are truly free, and virtue is knowledge. In the individual and in the state, freedom is self-mastery, and the two senses of freedom arise from the two senses in which a man may be master of himself, i.e., when the better or rational part is in control of the emotional or, conversely (as the drunkard or sluggard might claim), when reason is conquered by the passions. In the *Republic* Socrates explains the apparent absurdity of the expression "master of oneself" in terms of the rule of the better and the opposed possibility of becoming "slave to oneself." There are in this sense men who are by nature and education free and men who are by nature tyrants or slaves.

It is also true that the great mass of multifarious appetites and pleasures and pains will be found to occur chiefly in children and women and slaves and, among free men so called, in the inferior multitude; whereas the simple and moderate desires which, with the aid of reason and right opinion, are guided by reflection, you will find only in a few, and those with the best inborn dispositions and the best educated."[26]

The ideal freedom in the Republic is that of the good man, who has organized the faculties of his soul in proper relation and subordination to one another, and since all virtues are one, virtue and freedom in such a man is wisdom. In the perfect state the rulers are those who are capable of that freedom and of the dialectical propaedeutic to it. The freedom of the democratic man and of the democratic state, on the other hand, is a freedom of license which puts all appetites on the same level and assigns a kind of equality indiscriminately to equals and unequals alike.[27]

Since there are few wise men and since the ideal state never did and never will exist, Plato also examined the operation of freedom in the conditions of second-best or actual states. In default of the freedom which might be possible if philosophers were kings, he recommended a mixed form of government directed to three objectives: freedom, wisdom, and the unity of friendship.[28] The three are treated in a relationship which suggests the dialectic employed in later discussions of liberty, fraternity, and equality. Freedom is conditioned by a bond of unity (philia or "friendship" serving in the place of "fraternity") and by a quality in the elements which makes the relation possible ("wisdom" serving for "equality"). The mixed constitution is a combination of monarchy and democracy: monarchy in its pure form can for a time maintain a balance between freedom and slavery and democracy can prevent freedom from becoming license, but eventually freedom is lost in both unless provision is made against their respective weaknesses. The Athenians, who had received all freedom, consequently, were brought to the same predicament as the Persians, who were reduced to utter servitude. The discussion of freedom is consequently never far from history in these dialectical turns and vicissitudes, but history is, without derogation, myth for Plato. The defense of the mixed constitution in the *Laws* is based on a brief history of the world; the ideal

26. *Republic* iv. 431C; cf. *ibid.* iii. 395B–C.
27. *Ibid.,* viii. 557B, 562C, 564A, ix. 572E.
28. *Laws* iii. 693B–E.

state is given metaphysical foundation at the end of the *Republic* in the myth of Er which extends the story of man for thousands of years before his birth and after his death and it is given concrete verisimilitude in the historical details of the myth of Atlantis in the *Timaeus;* and the history of the development of the virtues in the societies of men is traced repeatedly in forms of historical development such as those recounted in the myth of Prometheus in the *Protagoras* or the myth of Cronus in the *Statesman*. In these myths the familiar historical devices of progress from primitive forms of culture, of degradation from a golden age, and of cycles of growth and decay are all used, and the background of that history is the freedom exemplified even in the life to which we are bound by necessity inasmuch as virtue owns no masters.[29]

The commonplaces which underline the doctrine that only the wise man is free and only the fool is a slave reappear in greatly altered form in the Stoic philosophy. Cicero gives a succinct statement of the Stoic argument that no one is free except the wise man:

For what is freedom? the power to live as you will. Who then lives as he will except one who follows the things that are right, who delights in his duty, who has a well-considered path of life mapped out before him, who does not obey even the laws because of fear but follows and respects them because he judges that to be most conducive to health, whose every utterance and action and even thought is voluntary and free, whose enterprises and courses of conduct all take their start from himself and likewise have their end in himself, there being no other thing that has more influence with him than his own will and judgments: to whom indeed Fortune, whose power is said to be supreme, herself submits—if, as the wise poet said, she is moulded for each man by his manners. It therefore befalls the wise man alone that he does nothing against his will nor with regret nor by compulsion.[30]

But whereas for Plato the reason which rules in the perfect state makes the laws which regulate the second-best state unnecessary, the Stoics shift the analogies which relate reason to virtue and find the basis of human knowledge and of political laws in the Law of Nature. The universe then becomes a country; men and gods become fellow-citizens; Zeus becomes the father of all, and all men are therefore brothers, kinsmen, and friends. The true freedom of the wise man is contrasted to the false freedom of the slave, and the freedom of the wise man who

29. *Republic* x. 617E.

30. Cicero, *Paradoxa Stoicorum* v. 34; cf. Diogenes Laertius *Lives of Eminent Philosophers, Zeno* vii. 121–22.

recognizes no country except the universe is contrasted to the freedom of the statesman who reluctantly assumes the duties of office. Diogenes and Socrates followed the first course of freedom,[31] and even Marcus Aurelius, who exemplified the second, thought Alexander, Julius Caesar, and Pompeius slaves in contrast to Diogenes, Heraclitus, and Socrates.[32] Moreover, the necessity which binds all things together is also the basis of a history of cyclical change, and the philosophers say

that this universe is but a single state, that the substance out of which it has been fashioned is single, and it needs must be that there is a certain periodic change and giving place of one thing to another, and that some things must be dissolved and others come into being, some things to remain in the same place and others to be removed.[33]

The movements of the wise man under the pressure of that concatenation are in response to needs or in appreciation of the spectacle of periodical growth and destruction which governs nature and the institutions of men. But in addition to this determination of the course of history which the wise man employs his wisdom in contemplating, the Stoic conception of freedom has a second consequence in the conception of history which brings the art of the statesman into close relation with the art of the historian. Cicero presents his friends urging him, in

31. *Arrians's Discourses of Epictetus* iv. 1. 152–70.
32. Marcus Aurelius *Meditations* viii. 3. Ralph Barton Perry makes use of the resources of the English language—which has two words, "freedom" and "liberty," to express what most languages express in one, but only one word "law" to express what other languages distinguish by means of two terms which continue the distinction between *"lex"* and *"jus"*—to reinforce the distinction between rightness of choice and absence of restraining circumstances by calling the one "freedom" and the other "liberty." Cf. "A Definition of the Humanities," *The Meaning of the Humanities,* ed. T. M. Greene (Princeton, N.J., 1938), pp. 4–6: "By freedom I mean enlightened choice. I mean the action in which habit, reflex or suggestion are superseded by an individual's fundamental judgments of good and evil; the action whose premises are explicit; the action which proceeds from personal reflection and integration. . . . By enlightened choice, I do not mean effective choice. For that I should prefer to reserve the term "liberty." Thus a man who chooses to roam abroad may be compelled to remain where he is, restrained by prison bars or lack of means. His choice may be enlightened, though he be deprived of the means of execution. I recognize the fact that freedom and liberty interact upon one another. External compulsion sets limits to choice, and conditions its degree of enlightenment. But unless the prisoner *chooses* to roam abroad his imprisonment does not deprive him of liberty— there is no clash between his will and his circumstances. Choice determines whether compulsion shall be gladly accepted, or turned to good use, or circumvented, or helplessly resented. Liberty has to do with the action of circumstances upon the man, freedom with man's action on circumstances."
33. Epictetus iii. 24. 9–12.

one of his philosophic dialogues, to undertake the writing of the history of Rome, on the grounds that the art of oratory and the art of history are the same, and statesmen have written history since his time, and historians have sought experience in government, on the assumption that experience and skill in affairs of state provide insight for the interpretation of historical occurrences.

According to Spinoza, who joins to a dialectical conception of freedom as wisdom a logistic conception of freedom as self-determined action, only the wise man is free, and human bondage consists in lack of power in moderating and checking the emotions. Book IV of the *Ethics* treats "Of Human Bondage or of the Strength of the Emotions" while Book V, "Concerning the Power of the Intellect or Human Freedom" proceeds to "the manner or way which leads to Liberty," to the power of reason over the emotions, and to the nature of "mental liberty or blessedness" (*mentis libertas seu beatitudo*).[34]

Liberty is a virtue or excellence or power. Freedom is not contingency but the use of reason for the preservation of one's own existence in accordance with the laws of human nature; God, who exists in absolute freedom, also understands and operates of necessity, that is, exists, understands, and operates according to the necessity of his own nature.[35] The rights of man, however, are not determined by sound reason but by desire and power, and whatever anyone has the power to do, he does by natural right. Consequently man can secure greater freedom if he respects the laws of his country and obeys the commands of his sovereign than if he relies only on his own powers. The freedom of the wise man is contrasted to the slavery of the man of passions; it is a mistake to define slavery as obeying commands and freedom as doing what one likes, for "the true slave is he who is led away by his pleasures and can neither see what is good for him nor act accordingly: he alone is free who lives with free consent under the entire guidance of reason."[36] But the freedom of the wise man is also contrasted to the freedom of private civil right, which is limited by the edicts of the sovereign and preserved only by the power of the sovereign. The state, like the individual, may be more or less free, and the free state is one whose laws are founded on sound reason.[37]

34. Spinoza *Ethics,* Book V, Preface.
35. *Tractatus politicus,* cap. ii, 7.
36. *Tractatus theologico-politicus,* cap. xvi.
37. *Ibid.*

The coincidence of wisdom and freedom led Plato to the delineation of an ideal state as a model for existing states, while short of the ideal, a good constitution depends on freedom conjoined with right regulation. It inspired in the Stoics a vision of the wise man, who attains freedom through duty and necessity, a sense of the brotherhood of man, and an indifference to suffering and the turns of fortune. It turned Spinoza to the task of setting forth the supreme importance of freedom of thought and expression. The final chapter of the *Tractatus theologico-politicus* is devoted to an eloquent demonstration that these freedoms cannot be taken from men, that they afford no danger to peace and security, and that, on the contrary, their abrogation is a grave danger to piety and public peace. This conception of freedom in the wisdom of the individual and in the laws of the state has its implications for history, too, since the method by which Spinoza undertook to combat superstition is the "historical analysis" of Scripture,[38] which has had a profound influence not only on Biblical criticism but also on the historical study of all kinds of documents.

4. The Logistic Analysis of Freedom and History

In logistic, the problems of freedom are problems of the nature and universality of scientific laws in general and of the laws governing human action in particular. Logistic historians seek to make history a science or to base it on the sciences. The research historian working with a multitude of documents, analyzing a complex mass of evidence, and selecting among a vast number of facts, tends to an unacknowledged or a conscious logistic conception of history since he seeks lines of relation, relevance, influence, and cause by which to relate the facts bearing on a restricted area of investigation, whereas the philosopher seeking concrete embodiment of his ideas in events and processes, or the historian seeking a universal context and extension of historical occurrences, recorded by many historians, tends to dialectical conceptions of history. Discussion of the philosophy of history therefore is usually "dialectical," while discussion of the methodology of history is usually "scientific." The problem of freedom enters into the problems of science, conceived according to the logistic method as the problem of the relation of contingency or indeterminacy to necessity; and from an-

38. *Ibid.*, cap. vii.

tiquity to the present that problem has been treated either by finding a place for contingency in the operation of necessary natural laws, or by demonstrating that the laws of nature, including human nature, are themselves contingent. The results are the same in the treatment of freedom, for whether freedom is based on the contingency which results from the interplay of many causal sequences or on the indeterminacy which results from the interplay of internal causes (or the nature of the thing) and external causes, freedom is found in the calculations of probability rather than in the precepts of wisdom, which are the sources of dialectical freedom. The "science of man," which is a consequence and ideal culmination of the logistic method, should afford explanations of human action according to laws stated in terms of causes or of probabilities.

The problems of history are therefore scientific problems both in the sense that history treats of events which exemplify the laws of human action and uses laws of action to explain the development of institutions, societies, and civilization in general, and also in the sense of employing scientific methods to examine the credibility and significance of testimony and evidence. The dialectical method tends to find the essence of man in freedom or in some human power, rational or irrational, which places him in harmonious relation with the universe and universal processes, and therefore tends to treat history as the evolution of conditions by which men have been able to perfect that power and approximate full adjustment with the necessities of the rational and the good. The logistic method, on the contrary, tends to find the explanation of human actions in laws of operation and reaction, and freedom emerges first, either in the power of internal causes to resist the influence of external causes, or in the contingencies of the circumstances in which man acts and, second, in the knowledge of causes and probabilities, which becomes an internal cause employed to resist the force of superstition, fear, and oppression; and history tends to become the account of the actual operation of those causes in past events. Dialectical history therefore finds its basic laws in some system of periods or of succession which determines all human action and knowledge, including morals, science, and philosophy, and history consists in disclosing the homogeneity of all expressions of human nature appropriate to that stage of development or culture. Logistic history, on the contrary, finds its basic laws in a science of human action which is the same for all men, at all times, and in all places, and which explains the differences which mankind develops historically in different periods, peoples, and cultures.

The diversity of dialectical analyses of freedom and of dialectical developments of history results from the variety of dialectical possibilities of relating freedom of choice to some basis of true freedom and from the consequent variety of dialectical grounds for marking off the stages of advance in the acquisition of true freedom. The different logistic analyses of freedom result, not from a similar dialectic of freedom and slavery, but from the choice of different elements and different causal relations by which to explain change; and the different forms of logistic or causal history are differentiated according to the elements made basic, the causes and probabilities thought applicable to those elements, and the sciences employed or envisaged as needed, though not yet developed, to trace the operation of causes and probabilities. Whatever the elements and whatever the causes of their motions in the sequences and wholes they constitute, the laws of their motions encounter some form of the classical problem of determinism conceived as a relation of necessity and contingency, of external determination and self-determination. Aristotle accused Democritus, thus, of reducing all sublunar motions to concatenations of necessary motions of atoms and of being forced therefore to find the origins of motion and the universe in chance. Locke, beginning with simple ideas rather than with simple bodies, treats liberty under the idea of "power" and finds the origin of the idea of power in the mind's observation of the alteration of simple ideas in things, inasmuch as the mind observes in one thing the possibility of having its simple ideas changed and in another the possibility of making that change: "so that the idea of liberty is the idea of a power in any agent to do or forbear any particular action, according to the determination of thought or the mind, whereby either of them is preferred to the other; where either of them is not in the power of the agent, to be produced by him according to his volition, there he is not at liberty, that agent is under necessity."[39] Hume finds the basic idea of necessity and causation in the uniformity observable in the operations of nature, and defines liberty as the power of acting or not acting according to the determinations of the will. Cournot, examining the grounds on which scientific laws are established, differentiates and re-

___

39. Locke, *An Essay concerning Human Understanding*, Bk. II, chap. 21, par. 8.

lates the ideas of chance and the irrational and the ideas of order and the rational. Boutroux finds the laws of nature themselves involved in contingency. The formulation of the principle of indeterminacy has been the starting point of much contemporary speculation concerning the natural bases of freedom. History has frequently taken the form of tracing the numerous series of long converging lines of causes, as Polybius presents the divergent and apparently unrelated events that were essential to the establishment and growth of Rome. The relation of history to science has been conceived as the relation of concrete processes to the general laws which state the regularity and principles of processes. With the theory of evolution and the theory of relativity, an historical dimension has become prominent in science. Spencer identified history with natural evolution, while Huxley argued that social progress is possible only by flying in the face of natural law; Henry Adams set forth in *The Tendency of History* the consequences he saw for historical processes in the principle of the dissipation of energy expressed in the second law of thermodynamics; Bury argued that history is a science, no less and no more, and, on later reconsideration of the nature of the science of history, subordinated history to sociology or anthropology.

Hume's attempt to introduce the experimental method of reasoning into moral subjects led him to the discovery of a fundamental identity between the causes of natural motions and of human actions. Necessity is an essential part of causation, and liberty is identical with chance which is nothing but a secret and concealed cause. Hume's historical researches are therefore an extension of his philosophic inquiries into the principles of human understanding and morals, since in both he treats of the same causal relations. History reveals a uniformity in the actions of men which underlies the possibility of using past experience to regulate future conduct as well as speculation and to mount to the knowledge of men's inclinations and motives from their actions, expressions, and even gestures, and again descend to the interpretation of their actions from our knowledge of their motives and inclinations.

It is universally acknowledged that there is a great uniformity among the actions of men, in all nations and ages, and that human nature remains the same, in its principles and operations. The same motives always produce the same action: The same events follow from the same causes. Ambition, avarice, self-love, vanity, friendship, generosity, public spirit: these passions, mixed in various degrees, and distributed through society have been, from the beginning of the world, and still are, the source of all the actions and enterprises, which have ever been observed among mankind. Would you know the sentiments, inclinations, and the course of life of the Greeks and the Romans? Study well the temper and actions of the French and the English: You cannot be much mistaken in transferring to the former *most* of the observations which you have made with regard to the latter. Mankind are so much the same, in all times and places, that history informs us of nothing new or strange in this particular. Its chief use is only to discover the constant and universal principles of human nature, by showing men in all varieties of circumstances and situations, and furnishing us with materials from which we may form our observations and become acquainted with the regular springs of human action and behaviour. These records of wars, intrigues, factions, and revolutions, are so many collections of experiments, by which the politician or moral philosopher fixes the principles of his science, in the same manner as the physician or natural philosopher becomes acquainted with the nature of plants, minerals, and other external objects, by the experiments which he forms concerning them. Nor are the earth, water and other elements, examined by Aristotle and Hippocrates more like those which at present lie under our observation than the men described by Polybius and Tacitus are to those who now govern the world.[40]

Philosophers establish on the observation of parallel instances a maxim that the connection between all causes is equally necessary, and that the seeming uncertainty of that connection in some instances proceeds from the secret opposition of contrary causes. The conjunction between motives and voluntary actions is as regular and uniform as that between cause and effect in any part of nature, and in this obvious sense all mankind have always agreed in the doctrine of necessity. Politics, morals, and literary criticism as well as history depend on recognizing that necessity, and the work of the historian consists precisely in the reconstruction of the long chains of causes and arguments by which actions are explained.

Two kinds of causes or arguments, both of them reticulated in long chains, are involved in historical studies: the connections of cause and effect following the laws of human nature which are the basis of the actions of men and the connections of cause and effect followed in argument and inference which are the basis of belief, on present evidence, concerning the character of past personages and the nature of the events in which they were involved. The former are the same as all other connections of cause and effect in natural processes; the latter exemplify the reasoning of the mind from causes to effects which, since our infer-

40. Hume, *An Enquiry concerning Human Understanding*, Sect. VIII, Part. 1, par. 65.

ences cannot proceed *ad infinitum,* must stop at an impression of memory or of the senses.

To give an instance of this, we may chuse any point of history and consider for what reason we either believe or reject it. Thus we believe that Caesar was kill'd in the senate-house on the *ides of March;* and that because this fact is establish'd on the unanimous testimony of historians, who agree to assign this precise time and place to that event. Here are certain characters and letters present either to our memory or senses; which characters we likewise remember to have been us'd as the signs of certain ideas; and these ideas were either in the minds of such as were immediately present at that action, and receiv'd the ideas directly from its existence; or they were deriv'd from the testimony of others, and that again from another testimony, by a visible gradation, 'till we arrive at those who were eye-witnesses and spectators of the event. 'Tis obvious all this chain of argument or connexion of causes and effects, is at first founded on these characters or letters, which are seen or remember'd, and that without the authority either of the memory or senses our whole reasoning wou'd be chimerical and without foundation. Every link of the chain wou'd in that case hang upon another; but there wou'd not be any thing fix'd to one end of it, capable of sustaining the whole; and consequently there wou'd be no belief nor evidence. And this actually is the case with all *hypothetical* arguments, or reasonings upon a supposition; there being in them, neither any present impression, nor belief of a real existence.[41]

Human reason is distinguished into three kinds according to the several degrees of evidence: reasoning from knowledge, from proofs, and from probabilities. Knowledge is the assurance arising from the comparison of ideas; proofs are arguments which are derived from the relation of cause and effect and which are entirely free from doubt and uncertainty; probability is evidence which is still attended with uncertainty. Probability, in turn, is of two kinds, that which is founded on chance and that which arises from causes, and chance is nothing in nature but a secret and concealed cause. Neither liberty nor, what is the same thing, chance exists in the sense of an absence of causation and necessity, and

41. Hume, *A Treatise of Human Nature.* Bk. I, part iii, Sec. 4. Cf. *Ibid.* Sect. 13, where Hume uses the same example as a possible objection to his analysis since the chain of reason or arguments is "of almost an innumerable length" in the case of ancient history. Since the steps of the argument and the links of causes are basically the same, the vivacity of the belief is not diminished: "If all the long chain of causes and effects, which connect any past event with any volume of history, were compos'd of parts different from each other, and which 'twere necessary for the mind distinctly to conceive, 'tis impossible we shou'd preserve to the end any belief or evidence. But as most of these proofs are perfectly resembling, the mind runs easily through along them, jumps from one part to another with facility, and forms but a confus'd and general notion of each link."

Hume therefore makes use of the distinction between liberty of spontaneity (which is opposed to violence and external causation) and liberty of indifference (which means a negation of necessity and causes) to express his conviction that the former is the most common sense of the word.[42] "Will" he defines as "the internal impression we feel and are conscious of, when we knowingly give rise to any new motion of our body, or new perception of our mind."[43] The only acceptable definition of liberty, therefore, is "a power of acting or not acting, according to the determinations of the will; that is, if we choose to remain at rest, we may; if we choose to move, also we may."[44] This "hypothetical liberty" Hume finds to be universally allowed as is likewise the doctrine of necessity.

When H. T. Buckle formed his plans to write a scientific history of civilization, he found two causes which had retarded the formation of the science of history: the inferior ability of historians as contrasted to investigators of nature and the greater complexity of the social phenomena with which they are concerned.[45] The discovery of the laws of nature and the extension of their application is itself a part of history of civilization, and the progress of civilization is marked by the same oppositions of the doctrines of chance and necessity which have given rise to subsequent dogmas of free will (which is founded on a metaphysical hypothesis) and predestination (which is founded on a theological hypothesis). The believer in the possibility of a science of history is not called upon to hold either doctrine, and Buckle expresses his conviction that metaphysics will never be raised to a science by the ordinary process of observing individual minds and that "its study can only be successfully prosecuted by the deductive application of laws which must be discovered historically, that is to say, which must be evolved by an examination of the whole of those vast phenomena which the long course of human affairs presents to our view."[46] All that is required as a basis for the science of history is recognition that motives have antecedents which obey laws of movement. The operation of those laws is a balance and opposition of internal and external causes.

42. *Ibid.,* Bk. II, Part iii, Sec. 2.
43. *Ibid.,* Sect. 1.
44. *An Enquiry concerning Human Understanding,* Sect. VIII, Part i, par. 73.
45. H. T. Buckle, *History of Civilization in England* ("World Classics," London, 1903), p. 7.
46. *Ibid.,* p. 15.

Rejecting, then, the metaphysical dogma of free will, and the theological dogma of predestined events, we are driven to the conclusion that the actions of men being determined solely by their antecedents, must have a character of uniformity, that is to say, must, under precisely the same circumstances, always issue in precisely the same results. And as all antecedents are either in the mind or out of it, we clearly see that all the variations in the results, in other words, all the changes of which history is full, all the vicissitudes of the human race, their progress and their decay, must be the fruit of a double action; an action of external phenomena upon the mind, and another action of the mind upon the phenomena.[47]

The materials out of which a philosophic history can be constructed are, on the one hand, the human mind obeying the laws of its own existence and developing itself, when uncontrolled by external agents, according to the conditions of its organization and, on the other hand, Nature, obeying likewise its laws, but incessantly coming into contact with the minds of men, exciting their passions, and therefore giving to their actions a direction which they would not have taken without such disturbance. All events spring necessarily from the reciprocal influence of man modifying nature and man modifying man.

Buckle therefore formulates two sets of laws: *physical laws,* which are classified under four heads, namely, climate, food, soil, and the general aspect of nature, that is, the appearances which give rise to different habits of national thought, and *mental laws,* which are divided into moral and intellectual.[48] The progress of civilization in Europe has been

47. *Ibid.,* p. 17.
48. *Ibid.,* p. 30. The characters attributed to periods, peoples, nations, and races, which assume a fundamental place in dialectical history, are explained in logistic or causal history by basic and universal causes. According to dialectical historians the "essence" of man is determined by the freedom he has achieved or by the relations of production which characterize him in any period. According to Buckle the general aspect of nature produces its principal results by exciting the imagination and by suggesting superstitions which are the great obstacles to advancing knowledge, and since the power of superstitions is supreme in the infancy of a people, they have caused corresponding varieties in the popular character and have imparted to the national religion peculiarities which, under certain circumstances, it is impossible to efface. Hypothetical distinctions of race, on the other hand, are explained by climate, food, and soil. Buckle quotes Mill in support of these conclusions: "of all vulgar modes of escaping from the consideration of the effect of social and moral influence on the human mind, the most vulgar is that of attributing the diversities of conduct and character to inherent natural differences" (*Principles of Political Economy,* vol. I, p. 390). According to Hume, national characteristics are to be explained rather by the principle of sympathy applied to the members of a group: "To this principle we ought to ascribe the great uniformity we may observe in the humours and turn of thinking of those of the same nation; and 'tis much more probable, that this resemblance arises from sympathy, than from any influence of the soil and climate, which,

marked by the diminishing influence of the external world. This is due to the fact that the powers of nature are limited and stationary, whereas the powers of man are unlimited and progressive.

The first premiss is, that we are in possession of no evidence that the powers of nature have ever been permanently increased; and we have no reason to expect that any such increase can take place. The other premiss is, that we have abundant evidence that the resources of the human mind have become more powerful, more numerous, and more able to grapple with the difficulties of the external world; because every fresh accession to our knowledge supplies fresh means, with which we can either control the operations of nature, or, failing in that, can foresee the consequences, and thus avoid what is impossible to prevent; in both instances, diminishing the pressure exercised on us by external agents.[49]

Among mental laws, the intellectual take precedence over the moral, since intellectual truths have been progressive whereas moral truths have been stationary. Progress is measured by control of external nature and by the diminution of the two greatest evils with which men have contrived to inflict their fellow men: religious persecution and war. The changes in every civilized people are dependent solely on three things: (1) the amount of knowledge possessed by their ablest men, (2) the direction taken by that knowledge, that is, the sort of subjects to which it refers, and (3), what is most important, the extent to which the knowledge is diffused, and the freedom with which it pervades all classes of society.[50] The importance of the history of a country depends, not upon the splendor of its exploits, but upon the degree to which its actions are due to causes springing out of itself.[51] The triumph of mental laws over physical and of intellectual laws over moral, in which the progress of civilization is summarized,[52] means the predominance of internal causes of human actions over external conditions, natural or human, achieved through the acquisition of fresh knowledge made possible by skepticism and tolerance.

---

tho' they continue invariably the same, are not able to preserve the character of a nation the same for a century together" (*A Treatise of Human Nature*, Bk. II, Part I, Sec. 11), but he also classifies under the species of unphilosophical probability one derived from general rules, which is the source of prejudice and which manifests itself in attributing characteristics to peoples which are unaffected by instances or evidence to the contrary (*ibid.*, Bk. I Part iii, sect. 13).

49. *Ibid.*, pp. 118–19; cf. also pp. 39–40.
50. *Ibid.*, p. 177.
51. *Ibid.*, p. 185.
52. *Ibid.*, pp. 180–181.

Buckle does not discuss progress or civilization in terms of freedom, but he discovers the marks of progress in the extension of what other writers have called freedom from want, from superstition, and from fear. Such freedom results from knowledge identified not with wisdom, but with liberation from external determination. Buckle had originally planned a history of general civilization, but since the materials prepared by historians were inadequate for that task, he wrote the history of a single people, choosing England because the history of civilization has followed a more orderly course there than in any other European country. The reasons for this judgment constitute a list of freedoms, conceived as self-determination rather than determination from outside.

. . . Of all European countries, England is the one where, during the longest period, the government has been most quiescent, and the people most active; where popular freedom has been settled on the widest basis; where each man is most able to say what he likes, and to do what he likes; where everyone can follow his own bent, and propagate his own opinions; where religious persecution being little known, the play and flow of the human mind may be clearly seen unchecked by those restraints to which it is elsewhere subjected; where the profession of heresy is least dangerous and the practice of dissent most common; where hostile creeds flourish side by side, and rise and decay without disturbance, according to the wants of the people, unaffected by the wishes of the Church; where all interests, and all classes, both spiritual and temporal, are most left to take care of themselves; where that meddlesome doctrine called Protection was first attacked, and where alone it has been destroyed; and where, in a word, those dangerous extremes to which interference gives rise having been avoided, despotism and rebellion are equally rare, and concession being recognized as the groundwork of policy, the national progress has been least disturbed by the power of privileged classes, by the influence of particular sects, or by the violence of arbitrary rulers.[53]

Logistic freedom is found in an order of elements, and it is protected by knowledge that insures initiative of action and cures diseases that threaten it.

What makes the history of England so valuable is, that nowhere else has the national progress been so little interfered with, either for good or for evil. But the mere fact that our civilization has, by this means, been preserved in a more natural and healthy state, renders it incumbent on us to study the diseases to which it is liable, by observing those other countries where social disease is more rife. The security and durability of civilization must depend on the regularity with which its elements are combined, and on the harmony with which

53. *Ibid.*, 186.

they work. If any one element is too active, the whole composition will be in danger. Hence it is, that although the laws of the composition of the elements will be the best ascertained wherever we can find the composition most complete, we must, nevertheless, search for the laws of each separate element, wherever we find the element itself most active.[54]

Progress results from the acquisition of fresh knowledge. The conditions requisite, however, for that knowledge and science, are found in freedom conceived as absence of constraint to agree, rather than in freedom conceived as truth or wisdom constraining agreement—but removing other constraints. Freedom from external interference depends on knowledge and science; not on a science dialectically warranted to be certain, but on a science of causes and laws of action; and it is achieved, not by the necessary stages of a dialectical succession of ages, but by the acquisition of fresh knowledge, for which the requisite conditions are found in skepticism and tolerance.[55]

A. A. Cournot found still other ways to relate freedom and history to science by means of causes and probabilities. The basic ideas of the philosophy of the sciences and the philosophy of history are the related ideas of chance and reason, of the irrational and order, for which Cournot established a theoretic basis and an instrument for calculation in his *Exposition de la théorie des Chances et des Probabilités*. The distinction between the necessary and the fortuitous, the essential and the accidental is found in nature and is indispensable for true history. Chance or hazard is not a phantom invented to disguise our ignorance nor an idea relative to the variable and always imperfect state of our knowledge, but a natural fact which consists "in the mutual *independence* of several series of causes and effects which concur *accidentally* to produce a given phenomenon, to lead to a given conjunction, to determine a given event, which for that reason is called *fortuitous;* and this independence among particular chains in no way excludes the idea of a common suspension of all the chains from a single primordial link, beyond the limits, or even within the limits, to which our reasonings and our observations can attain."[56] Statistics is the key to the philosophy of history—which Cournot prefers to call historical etiology—understanding by that the analysis and discussion of the causes or of the concatenation of

54. *Ibid.,* 204.
55. *Ibid.,* pp. 270–71, 291.
56. A. A. Cournot, *Considérations sur la Marche des Idées et des Evènements dans les Temps Modernes,* ed. F. Mentré (Paris, 1934), vol. I, pp. 1–2.

causes which have concurred to lead to the events of which history presents the tableau and which should be studied from the point of view of their independence or their solidarity. The recognition that the accidental is real does not imply, however, either the absurd hypothesis of an effect without cause, or the idea of a fact which human wisdom might have prevented or at least foreseen, or, on the contrary, the idea of a fact which escapes all prevision. The etiology or the philosophy of history seeks the cause, or more precisely the reason, of events, for in some cases hazard may intervene to invert, modify, or suppress a long chain of events, and in others there is a necessary and inevitable result when the essential data of the situation must finally prevail over all the fortuitous accidents. These are considerations which lead, not to the science of history, for scientific demonstration is not applicable to these questions, but to the philosophy of history which is obliged, like all philosophy, to be content with analogies, inductions, and probabilities. They are also the reasons for Cournot's suspicions of historical laws, and his preference for the statement of facts, general as well as particular. Even history must in the long run manifest the theoretic subordination of the particular to the general.[57]

The philosophy of history is distinct from history, even from the history of civilization. The purpose of the philosophy of history is to discern in the ensemble of historical events those general and dominant

---

57. *Ibid.* Préface, pp. xxvi-xxviii: "L'histoire même se charge de manifester à la longue la subordination théorique du particulier au général . . . Ces premières réflexions, aussi bien que le titre de notre livre, annoncent assez qu'il appartient, non au genre de la composition historique, mais à ce que l'on est convenu appeler 'la philosophie de l'histoire.' Or, celà nous oblige, pour ne pas affronter trop de préventions à la fois, de dire en quoi notre philosophie de l'histoire diffère essentiellement de celle de beaucoup d'autres, qui ont eu la prétention de découvrir des *lois* dans l'histoire. Qu'il y ait ou qu'il n'y ait pas de lois dans l'histoire, il suffit qu'il y ait des *faits,* et que ces faits soient, tantôt subordonnés les uns aux autres, tantôt indépendants les uns des autres, pour qu'il y ait lieu à une critique dont le but est de démêler, ici la subordination, là l'indépendance. Et comme cette critique ne peut pas prétendre à des démonstrations irrésistibles, de la nature de celles qui donnent la certitude scientifique, mais que son rôle se borne à faire valoir des analogies, des inductions, du genre de celles dont il faut que la philosophie se contente (sans quoi ce serait une science, comme tant de gens l'ont rêvé, mais toujours vainement, et ce ne serait plus la philosophie), il s'ensuit que l'on est parfaitement en droit de donner à la critique dont il s'agit, si attrayante malgré ses incertitudes, le nom de 'philosophie de l'histoire.' Il en est à cet égard de l'histoire des peuples comme de l'histoire de la Nature, qu'il ne faut pas confondre avec la science de la Nature, parce qu'elles ont principalement pour objet, l'une des lois, l'autre des faits, mais des faits qui peuvent acquérir une si vaste proportion, avoir des conséquences si vastes et si durables, qu'ils nous paraissent avoir et qu'ils ont effectivement la même importance que des lois."

facts which form its framework and skeleton and to show how other facts, down to particular facts of detail, are subordinated to these general and primary facts. The part played by chance is much greater in political history than in the history of sciences and of industry. As scientific work is organized, as the number of workers increases, and as the means of communication among the workers is perfected, chance is eliminated more and more and the sciences emerge from what can be called their historical phase. The history of languages, religions, arts, and civil institutions resembles political history in this respect, while the history of civilization resembles the history of the sciences, for although the civilization proper to a given people can decline, there is a common foundation of civilization which always progresses in the manner of the sciences and of industry.[58] Statistics, history, and the philosophy of history do not militate against the freedom of man or his moral responsibility, for they provide no basis for judgment of the intrinsic nature of the efficient causes, and the philosophy of history is no more "jansenist" than "molinist," no more indulgent than severe. Historical naturalism, even though it inclines toward historical fatalism, does nothing to restrain the liberty of the human person, to discharge him of obligation and moral responsibilities, or to repugn the intervention of Providence, in the government of moral beings by ordinary or by extraordinary means. Man in his individuality, the human person belongs to the priest, to the judge, to the ascetic, to the moralist, to the poet, to the novelist: science seeks less elevated regions and firmer ground. That which forms the continuation of the science and history of Nature is the science and history, not of man, but of human societies: man, in the plenitude of his intellectual faculties and his moral attributes, is another subject of contemplation and study.[59] The economic transformation of societies and industrial progress has led to social leveling and to democracy, but it has not been favorable to freedom, in spite of the fact that civil and political freedoms have been guaranteed in modern civilization by more stable institutions.[60] Much of history must therefore be recounted rather than reasoned, precisely because the political element is prior and supplies the framework of the history. The order of historical priority of causes and effects does not agree with the order of importance and final predominance of the data and of the

58. *Ibid.*, p. 12.
59. *Ibid.*, vol. II, p. 179.
60. *Ibid.*, vol. II, pp. 206–9, 233.

results which reason conceives and which the sequence of events ought to make evident: there is one order for the use of history and another for the use of the philosophy of history.[61]

5. The Problematic Analysis of Freedom and History

The literal sense of the word "history" is inquiry, examination, study of facts, and in the study and use of history according to the problematic method or the method of inquiry, history retains that sense of an assemblage and examination of facts. History is neither a dialectic nor a science. The historian encounters in his inquiries neither the organic necessities of dialectical reasons which reconcile existing contraries nor the linear necessities of efficient causation which forms chains of causes and effects. History is inquiry concerning data assembled relative to any set of problems or any subject matter, including the human actions associated by the common problems they treat or by the common groupings of men in action. If the historian speculating on the relations of cultures and on the characteristics of a given culture or period tends to write dialectical or epochal history, and if the historian working with data and documents and with their generalized significance in the progress of civilization tends to write logistic or causal history, the historian assembling what men have said and thought concerning any subject and relevant to the treatment of any problem, including dialectic and logistic, tends to write problematic or disciplinary history. Freedom in that context is neither a dialectical knowledge or power of choosing the right, set in contrast to a wrong use of choice, nor a science or power, dependent on the advancement of scientific knowledge, of acting by self-determination, set in contrast to external determination. Freedom has a political and social rather than a dialectical or physical context. It is limited to human action in a context of political and social circumstances which afford protection to the action of the individual. Freedom, in the definitions which it receives in applications of this method of inquiry, tends to be associated with democracy, in the sense of self-rule, and the knowledge requisite for freedom is understanding and communication adequate to serve as basis for agreement. The dialectical freedom of right choice and action based on truth, on the contrary, is dependent on the certainties of dialectical knowledge and dialectical processes. It may be realized in other political and social structures than

61. *Ibid.,* vol. II, pp. 255–56.

democracy, unless democracy is redefined to mean government for the good of the people rather than government by the people. The logistic freedom of intrinsic or self-determined action, unlike the other two varieties of freedom, is dependent on the advancement of scientific knowledge. It leads to the advancement of economic and social democracy and equality, but not necessarily to freedom in the sense of self-determined action, since industrial and scientific advance leads to increased external influences of nations, groups, and classes, to the routinization of the processes of life in uniform schedules and time-tables, and to the extension of government regulation and control.

The association between freedom and history is as close in the meanings given those terms by the application of reflexive principles in the method of inquiry as in the meanings which they receive from other principles and other methods. The meanings of freedom and history, according to the method of inquiry, are seen most sharply in the opposition which they induce to the conception of *freedom* as action in dialectical conformity with natural processes or as consequence of scientific knowledge and to the conception of *history* as science or as a development of freedom or as a pattern of inevitable progress. R. G. Collingwood is somewhat more critical of causal history than of epochal history for he argues, in his brief and abrupt treatment of philosophers and historians who think that history is or might be a science, that such a conception is based on a misconception of both history and science. He finds the connection between history and freedom in the distinction of both from natural science.

Historical thought, thought about rational activity, is free from the domination of natural science, and rational activity is free from the domination of nature. . . . For myself, I should welcome either of these two statements, as providing evidence that the person who made it has seen far enough into the nature of history to have discovered (a) that historical thought is free from the domination of natural science, and is an autonomous science, and (b) that rational activity is free from the domination of nature and builds its own world of human affairs, *Res Gestae,* at its own bidding and in its own way, (c) that there is an intimate connexion between these two propositions.[62]

In much the same fashion, the method of inquiry, applied to the facts of history, suggests doubts concerning the notion of history as a movement toward freedom. These doubts arise from an altered condition of the relation of history and reason according to which history traces the

62. Collingwood, *The Idea of History* (Oxford, 1946), p. 318.

consequences, not of the necessary operation of reason in nature nor of the operation of necessary scientific laws and causes in particular phenomena, but of the use of human reason from time to time in the solution of human problems. John Dewey expresses these doubts concerning the relations of history and freedom as prelude to a more sober conception of history.

By proper selection and arrangement, we can even make out a case for the idea that all past history has been a movement, at first unconscious and then conscious, to attain freedom. A more sober view of history discloses that it took a very fortunate conjunction of events to bring about the rapid and seemingly complete victory of democracy during the nineteenth century. The conclusion to be drawn is not the depressing one that it is now in danger of destruction because of an unfavorable conjunction of events. The conclusion is that what was won in a more or less external and accidental manner must now be achieved and sustained by deliberate and intelligent endeavor.[63]

If truth tends to triumph, it is only because errors are corrigible, and the connection between freedom and history is not that freedom is reason, which perforce prevails in the evolution of ages or which waxes and wanes in the successions of civilizations, nor that freedom results from science, which must in turn provide scientific means to prevent the misuse of the accomplishments of science, but rather that freedom provides the opportunity to put what purport to be the truths of wisdom and science to the test. John Stuart Mill, in spite of the influence, which he acknowledges, of the Saint-Simonian and Comtean periodizations of history on his own thought, argues that there is a preponderance among mankind of rational opinions and rational conduct because man is capable of rectifying his errors by discussion and experience, not because truth must triumph.

But, indeed, the dictum that truth always triumphs over persecution is one of those pleasant falsehoods which men repeat after one another, till they pass into commonplaces, but which all experience refutes. . . . It is a piece of idle sentimentality that truth, merely as truth, has any inherent power denied to error of prevailing against the dungeon and the stake. Men are not more zealous for truth than they often are for error, and a sufficient application of legal or even of social penalties will generally succeed in stopping the propagation of either. The real advantage which truth has, consists in this, that when an opinion is true, it may be extinguished once, twice, or many times, but in the course of ages there will generally be found persons to rediscover it, until some one of its reappearances falls upon a time when from favorable circumstances

63. Dewey, *Freedom and Culture* (New York, 1939), p. 173.

it escapes persecution until it has had such head as to withstand all subsequent attempts to suppress it.[64]

History makes its connection with freedom in the occurrence of circumstances in which freedom of thought and expression may have their effect on the expression of truth and the determination of action.

The actions of men, like the movements of bodies, exhibit regularities which are subject to scientific inquiry, and the method of history has been influenced by the refinements and extension of scientific method. Nonetheless there has been no evidence either to support the supposition that general laws or general facts are disclosed by history or to render plausible the analogy of history to the natural sciences. The history of man, in the large, reveals progress in the acquisition of knowledge and the extension of freedoms. Nonetheless there is no reason either to suppose that science will provide the solution to the practical problems which are incident to the history of the development of science or to justify the identification of history with the continuous development of freedom. Freedom has been a conquest of the human spirit, but the recognition of that truth affords neither meaning for the identification of the nature of man, nor of his spirit, with freedom, nor evidence for its truth. Freedom has been advanced by the deliberate and intelligent ordering of society and the state; but the extension of the scientific method to the regulation of society or the control of the state, no less than the dialectical identification of natural law, with civil law, and moral law, or dialectical analogies or balances among them, find little concrete meaning in the history of past actions or in the problems of action in the present. These oppositions in the conception and use of history are not simple and unambiguous distinctions, since they depend on varying conceptions of freedom based in turn on opposed conceptions of science. The freedom for which evidence can be found in problematic histories depends on knowledge, not in the sense of a dialectic of society or a science of human action and human relations, but in the sense of a practical knowledge of the variety of circumstances in which human action takes place and of the mutual understanding by which freedom is promoted and preserved.

The characteristic mark of the discussion of freedom according to

64. Mill, *On Liberty,* chap. ii, "On the Liberty of Thought and Expression." For a recent revival of this pleasant falsehood, cf. Bertrand Russell's B.B.C. lecture, "Why Fanaticism Always Brings Defeat," *The Listener,* XL (1948), pp. 452–53; reprinted in *University of Chicago Round Table Pamphlet,* No. 615 (January 1, 1950).

the method of inquiry has therefore been the moral-political setting which is substituted for the cosmological-historical setting of dialectical freedom and the mathematical-physical setting of logistic freedom. The history of the discussion of political theory is a history of recurrent arguments designed to show that not only the analogy of human communities to a concourse of atoms, a machine, a human body, or a society of insects, animals, or angels, but also the analogy of political states to kinship groups, voluntary associations, and economic institutions, misses the essence not only of the political but of the moral problem. Aristotle criticized Plato for analogizing the various forms of human association; Locke criticized Filmer for a like tendency; and Dewey criticized the use of similar analogies by his contemporaries. No less recurrent are the arguments designed to show that the sciences of morals and politics are distinct in method, subject matter, and mode of operation from the physical sciences; but also that virtue and justice are distinct from knowledge, since we may know the better course of action yet follow the worse and we may know what is just in general yet be unable to put that knowledge into operation in particular circumstances. The associations of men are based on equality, but there is an equality in a family or among friends that is distinct from the equality in a political state, and Aristotle found the basic errors of the communism of Plato's ideal state in the erroneous assumption that the unity of a state should be the same as the unity of a family. The actions of individual men are determined by their individual characters, but the individuality of men is determined neither by the essence of man nor by the laws of reaction to external stimuli, but by habits peculiar to individuals and their circumstances by which voluntary actions are distinguished from involuntary.

According to Aristotle, politics is a science based on the study of the constitutions of many states, and ethics is a part of politics. The study of individual action depends on the possibility of discriminating voluntary from involuntary actions and from passions which are due to compulsion or ignorance. An action is involuntary through ignorance, if it is ignorance, not of the advantageous (for mistaken purpose is wickedness), nor of the universal (for men are not blamed for lack of knowledge of universals), but of particulars, that is, of the circumstances of the action and the objects with which it is concerned—who one is, what one is doing, what or whom one is acting on, with what instruments, to what end, and how. These are the "circumstances" of moral theory and of rhetoric, and they have continued to be used in law to determine responsibility.[65] The study of the kinds of government depends on defining the state in terms of its functions which in turn are determined by the functions of the citizens who compose it: Aristotle defines the citizen by his participation in the deliberative or judicial administration of the state. This definition, he observes, is best adapted to the citizen of a democracy,[66] for in a democracy the free claim the right to rule, and the end of the state is freedom,[67] and in general the distinguishing mark of true as opposed to perverted forms of government is that they are cominunities of freemen.[68] The basic questions of the communities and the associations of men and of the freedom which makes them possible and which they in turn secure and preserve are questions of equality and justice. Equality enters in other forms of association besides political forms and into other bonds of association besides those of justice, for some form of equality is essential in common action and cooperation.

But equality does not seem to take the same form in acts of justice and in friendships; for an act of justice that is equal in the primary sense is that which is in proportion of merit, while quantitative equality is secondary, but in friendship quantitative equality is primary and proportion to merit is secondary.[69]

All men think justice to be a sort of equality, but the equality of justice is likewise of two sorts: the numerical equality of rectificatory justice and the proportionate equality of distributive justice. Equality or inequality are found in the operation of the rules of civil and criminal law as well as in the various claims presented for participation in the administration of the state, such as wealth, virtue, birth, and freedom. Under these circumstances freedom cannot be viewed as the essence of man, since some men are born free, while others are by nature slaves, nor is freedom simply the power of self-determination as opposed to external

65. Aristotle, *Nicomachean Ethics* iii. 1. 1110b28–1111a21. According to later rhetorical theory, controversies or "hypotheses," since they concern particular as opposed to universal problems, turn on the consideration of the seven "circumstances": "quis, quid, quando, ubi, cur, quem ad modum, quibus adminiculis." Cf. Pseudo-Augustine, *De rhetorica* 7 (C. Halm, *Rhetores Latini minores* (Leipzig, 1863), p. 141); Fortunatianus, *Ars rhetorica* ii, 1 (Halm, p. 102).

66. *Politics* iii. 1. 1275b5–7.

67. *Ibid.*, 12. 1283a16–23; 13. 1283a33–b20. *Rhetoric* i. 8. 1366a4–6.

68. *Politics* iii. 6. 1279a17–21.

69. *Nicomachean Ethics* viii. 7. 1158b29–33.

causation, for the power of a man is determined, and the exercise of his power is controlled, by political institutions.

The state is "natural," and man is by nature a "political" animal, not in some mysterious sense that depends on discovering either natural laws which govern the operation of the state or a social instinct or faculty or sympathy which govern man's participation in the state, but in the more obvious and natural sense that the ends of human life, that is, its "principles," cannot be attained except in a community. The limitations by which some men are by nature slaves are found in their lack of power in the circumstances of the community to rule themselves; and there are as many forms of "justice" or "equality" as there are actual kinds of government.

In the many forms of government which have sprung up there has always been an acknowledgment of justice and proportionate equality, although mankind fail in attaining them, as indeed I have already explained. Democracy, for example, arises out of the notion that those who are equal in any respect are equal in all respects; because men are equally free, they claim to be absolutely equal. Oligarchy is based on the notion that those who are unequal in one respect are in all respects unequal; being unequal, that is, in property, they suppose themselves to be unequal absolutely. The democrats think that as they are equal they ought to be equal in all things; while the oligarchs, under the idea that they are unequal, claim too much, which is one form of inequality.[70]

Inequality, moreover, is the cause of revolution everywhere, and revolutions are of two kinds, those which alter the principle of equality in the constitution and those which merely change the party in power without changing the form of government. Since there are two kinds of equality, numerical and proportional, there are, among the many forms of government and justice, two principal forms in actual states: democracy and oligarchy. Aristotle argues that it is not good for a state to be ordered, simply and wholly, according to either form of equality, and offers as proof the fact that such forms of government never last.[71]

Since freedom is the basis of equality in democratic states, two sets of problems arise with respect to freedom: those relative to the inequalities of wealth and those relative to chaos or anarchy. The inequalities of wealth transform the contrast between the oligarchical government of the rich and the democratic government of the free into a contest between rich and poor; most actual governments are either oligarchical

70. *Politics* v. 1. 1301a26–35.
71. *Ibid.*, 1302a–8.

or democratic, and in the warfare of rich and poor, men lose their concern for equality and seek dominion or, if conquered, become willing to submit.[72] Anarchy and equality are alternative principles proposed for the definition of liberty, anarchy being the principle of living as one likes and being ruled by none, equality the principle of all ruling and being ruled in turn.

The basis of a democratic state is liberty; which, according to the common opinion of men, can only be enjoyed in such a state;—this they affirm to be the great end of every democracy. One principle of liberty is for all to rule and be ruled in turn, and indeed democratic justice is the application of numerical not proportionate equality; whence it follows that the majority must be supreme, and that whatever the majority approve must be the end and the just. Every citizen, it is said, must have equality, and therefore in a democracy the poor have more power than the rich, because there are more of them, and the will of the majority is supreme. This, then, is one note of liberty which all democrats affirm to be the principle of their state. Another is that a man should live as he likes. This, they say, is the privilege of a freeman, since, on the other hand, not to live as a man likes is the mark of a slave. This is the second characteristic of democracy, whence has arisen the claim of men to be ruled by none, if possible, or, if this is impossible, to rule and be ruled in turns; and so it contributes to the freedom based on equality.[73]

Freedom becomes, in problematic analysis or inquiry, a political problem determined by constitutional forms and social conditions, while the difference among practicable or actual political constitutions and among the kinds of justice proper to them is determined by the oppositions of economic classes. History is an account of circumstances and an accumulation of data rather than a delineation of rational trends or an application of scientific laws, and the use of knowledge in the definition and acquisition of values consists in the calculation of what is best, not only in general and absolutely, but also under particular circumstances, and in the consideration of the means by which its attainment is possible.

John Stuart Mill begins his essay *On Liberty* (which he thought likely to survive longer than anything else he had written) by limiting his inquiry to civil or social liberty. His subject is not "the so-called liberty of the will, so unfortunately opposed to the misnamed doctrine of philosophical necessity," but civil or social liberty which had never been

72. *Ibid.,* iv. 4. 1290b17–20; 11. 1296a22–b2.
73. *Ibid.,* vi. 2. 1317a40–b17; cf. *ibid.* iv. 4. 1291b30–1292a38; 6. 1292b22–1293a10.

discussed in general terms and which, though so far from being new that it has divided mankind from the remotest ages, presents new conditions and requires different and more fundamental treatment due to the progress of civilization. Liberty, as a principle, has no application to any state of things anterior to the time when mankind have become capable of being improved by free and equal discussion.[74] The principle of individuality serves in the place of the principle of equality in Mill's definition of freedom: the sole end for which mankind are warranted, individually or collectively, in interfering with the liberty of action in one of their number, is self-protection. "The only part of the conduct of any one, for which he is amenable to society, is that which concerns others. In the part which merely concerns himself, his independence is, of right, absolute. Over himself, over his own body and mind, the individual is sovereign."[75] A free society is one in which these freedoms of the individual exist absolute and unqualified. Mill acknowledges his indebtedness to Wilhelm von Humboldt for the insight that the end of man, "the highest and most harmonious development of his powers to a complete and consistent whole" consists in "the individuality of power and development," and that for the realization of this end there are two requisites, "freedom and variety of situations."[76] The balance between the individual and the community, which is the chief subject of discussion in the essay, as accomplished partly by differentiating the realm of freedom from the realm of morals and law, and partly by distinguishing the basic freedoms of thought and discussion from the calculations of freedom of action. The distinction between individual and community involves many of the same commonplaces as the dialectical distinction between freedom and free choice and the logistic distinction between freedom as necessity or self-determination and freedom as contingency or external indeterminacy, but the problem of freedom is transformed as a result of the change. It is not a dialectical or metaphysical problem of determining what right choice or wisdom is and of finding means to assure its universal extension and the elimination of wrong choices, nor is it an anthropological or mathematical problem of determining the laws of human action and extrapolating the course of man's action in probable future situations and occurrences; it is a political and casuistic problem, which occupies Mill at great length,

74. Mill, *On Liberty* (New York, 1885), chap. i, "Introductory," pp. 9, 25.
75. *Ibid.*, p. 24.
76. *Ibid.*, chap. iii, "Of Individuality, as One of the Elements of Well-Being" p. 103.

of separating acts which affect only the agent, or need not affect others unless they like, from acts which may properly be punished either by law or by opinion.

In his *Autobiography* Mill recounts the transition by which he passed from the conviction that democracy is an absolute principle based on scientific theory to the conviction that the possibility and desirability of democracy depend on time, place, and circumstance. He presents the problems of political constitutions in terms of the relations of rich and poor which set socialism and democracy in opposition.

Again, in politics, though I no longer accepted the doctrine of the Essay on Government as a scientific theory; though I ceased to consider representative democracy as an absolute principle, and regarded it as a question of time, place, and circumstance; though I now looked upon the choice of political institutions as a moral and educational question more than one of material interests, thinking that it ought to be decided mainly by consideration, what great improvement in life and culture stands next in order for the people concerned, as the condition of their further progress, and what institutions are most likely to promote that; nevertheless this change in the premises of my political philosophy did not alter my practical creed as to the requirements of my own time and country. I was as much as ever a radical and democrat for Europe, and especially for England. I thought the predominance of the aristocratic classes, the noble and the rich, in the English Constitution, an evil worth any struggle to get rid of; not on account of taxes, or any such comparatively small inconvenience, but as the great demoralizing agency in the country. . . . On these grounds I was not only as ardent as ever for democratic institutions, but earnestly hoped that Owenite, St. Simonian, and all other anti-property doctrines might spread widely among the poorer classes; not that I thought these doctrines true, or desired that they should be acted on, but in order that the higher classes might be made to see that they had more to fear from the poor when uneducated, than when educated.[77]

The essay *On Liberty* therefore is the expression of a single truth, which the changes progressively taking place in modern society tend to bring into even stronger relief: the importance, to man and society, of a large variety in the types of character and of giving full freedom to human nature to expand itself in innumerable and conflicting directions. The doctrine of the rights of individuality and the claim of the moral nature

77. Mill, *Autobiography* (New York, 1924), chap. v. pp. 120–21. Cf. also *ibid.*, p. 113: "If I am asked, what system of political philosophy I substituted for that which, as a philosophy, I had abandoned, I answer, no system: only a conviction that the true system was something much more complex and many-sided than I previously had any idea of, and that its office was to supply, not a set of model institutions, but principles from which the institutions suitable to any given circumstances might be deduced."

to develop itself in its own way, though it has superficial resemblances
to some of the projects of the socialists, "is diametrically opposed to
them in principle, since it recognizes no authority whatever in Society
over the individual, except to enforce equal freedom of development
for all individualities."[78] The use which Aristotle and Mill make of the
method of inquiry in the treatment of moral and political problems
leads to the discussion of freedom in terms of political and social circumstances. The two kinds of freedom which Aristotle distinguishes—
to be ruled by none and to rule and be ruled in turn—reduce in practice
to the principle of ruling and being ruled which is the equality on
which democracy is based and by which the citizen is defined. Justice,
which men acknowledge to be a kind of equality, is the connecting link
between politics and morals. In its political signification, justice is the
bond which unites men in states, and there are as many forms of justice
or equality as there are kinds of constitutions. The problems of justice
are not problems of adjusting to the requirements of existing circumstances but problems of achieving the best in whatever sense of the best
is relevant to the circumstances of a particular people—the best absolutely conceived as the ideal, the best in general conceived as the normal
interplay of forces and balance of discussion, the best relative to particular circumstances, and the best relative to imminent and pressing
change or revolutions—but in actual states the opposed possibilities
tend to take the form of oppositions between the rule of the many and
the few, of the poor and the rich. Among the circumstances which determine the constitution and the justice of a state is the moral and intellectual character of its citizens, and the character of the citizens is
formed in turn by the mode of life determined by the political structure.
In its moral signification, justice is a virtue which assumes two forms:
universal justice, that is, the lawful (since laws are directed to the common advantage of all or of the best or of those in power and they supply
external motivations to desired actions which serve in the place of particular virtues) and particular justice, that is, the fair or the equal (which
is a particular virtue or habit). Justice conceived as a particular virtue is
relevant both to the functions which men exercise in the state and to
the protection which they receive in the state from the actions of others,
and it is therefore distinguished into distributive justice and rectificatory justice. Both forms of justice are defined in terms of equality or

78. *Ibid.*, chap. vii, pp. 177–79.

proportion: the equality or proportion of distributive justice being geometric in the ratio of men's merits and their contribution to the common end, and the equality or proportion of rectificatory justice being arithmetic and determined by the action without consideration of the person. Roughly, questions of distributive justice are constitutional questions of offices and functions of government, and questions of rectificatory justice are questions of adjudication under civil and criminal law. Mill likewise is concerned exclusively with liberty in its civil or social sense, and the same commonplaces which divided Aristotle's treatment into political and moral aspects reappear in quite different uses in Mill's differentiation of the individual and society. Aristotle treats the relation of citizen and state as a functional relation and finds as many forms of equality among the citizens as there are forms of government; Mill asserts an absolute freedom of the individual relative to the community. Aristotle defines the citizen in terms of the democratic form of equality of ruling and being ruled, although he considered democracy neither the best nor the necessary form of government, but rather one suited to certain circumstances; Mill moved from the conception of democracy as an absolute principle, scientifically established, to a conception of representative democracy as suited to particular circumstances which made it feasible and desirable. Aristotle opposed the communism of Plato on the ground that it introduced an undesirable and impossible form of equality and unity in the state, but he argued that in the oppositions among actual states and political constitutions, between democracies and oligarchies conceived respectively as the rule of the poor and the rule of the rich, the possibilities of improvement were to be found in mixed forms and constitutions: in the polity, which is a mixture of democracy and oligarchy inclining toward democracy, or in the aristocracy, which is a mixture of the two inclining toward oligarchy. Mill opposed the socialisms of his day on grounds which included the errors they commit as knowledge and the dangers they present to freedom, but he argued that in the common opposition of democracy and socialism to aristocracy and oligarchy, the doctrine of socialism is a force for the promotion of democracy.

In the philosophy of John Dewey these commonplaces, with the change of circumstances, reappear with new emphases and contents. Democracy tended to assume a basic position in the definition of political communities for Aristotle and Mill, although the question of its desirability or possibility had to be decided by consideration of the particular circumstances of given communities. According to Dewey, democracy as an idea is not an alternative to other principles of associated life: it is the idea of community life itself.[79] Problems of freedom, equality, and fraternity, no less than problems of democracy take on concrete meaning only in the circumstances of an actual community.

> Only when we start from a community as a fact, grasp the fact in thought so as to clarify and enhance its constituent elements, can we reach an idea of democracy which is not utopian. The conceptions and shibboleths which are traditionally associated with the idea of democracy take on a veridical and directive meaning only when they are construed as marks and traits of an association which realizes the defining characteristics of a community. Fraternity, liberty and equality isolated from the communal life are hopeless abstractions.[80]

Problems of freedom involve therefore the differentiation of political association from other forms of association and of the "public" from the numerous other groups of men in association. The question "of what transactions should be left as far as possible to voluntary initiative and agreement and what should come under the regulation of the public is a question of time, place, and concrete conditions that can be known only by careful observation," and any notion "that social 'evolution' has been either from collectivism to individualism or the reverse is sheer superstition."[81] Once the individual and the political community have been distinguished, problems of freedom are found to have been complicated, in the second place, by the history of the development and discussion of individualism in which two forms have developed: an individualism based on freedom from political control and an individualism which transfers notions of political equality to social and economic relations.

Fraternity, liberty, and equality isolated from communal life are hopeless abstractions leading either to sentimentalism or violence. They assume concrete significance and practical utility in an actual community.

In its just connection with communal experience, fraternity is another name for the consciously appreciated goods which accrue from an association in which all share, and which give direction to the conduct of each. Liberty is that secure release and fulfillment of personal potentialities which takes place only in rich and manifold association with others: the power to be an individualized

79. Dewey, *The Public and its Problems* (New York, 1927), p. 148.
80. *Ibid.,* p. 149.
81. *Ibid.,* p. 193.

self making a distinctive contribution and enjoying in its own way the fruits of association. Equality denotes the unhampered share which each individual member of the community has in the consequences of associated action. It is equitable because it is measured by need and capacity to utilize, not by extraneous factors which deprive one in order that another may take and have. . . . It denotes effective regard for what is distinctive and unique in each, irrespective of physical and psychological inequalities. It is not a natural possession but is a fruit of the community when its action is directed by its character as a community.[82]

Early theory and practice had assumed an inherent, and so to say pre-established harmony between liberty and equality, but as liberty has been practiced in industry and trade, the economic inequalities produced have reacted against the existence of equality of opportunity.[83] Among the results have been a growing distrust of the efficacy of parliamentary bodies and a growing complexity in the relations between the need for collective ownership and control and the continued operation of democratic processes. The misuse of the conception of individualism derives from the same situation. The traditional individualistic philosophy was wrong in setting authority and freedom in opposition. The older forms of organized power that had exercised authority were shown by that philosophy to be oppressive with respect to the new forces that operated through the medium of individuals and to be hostile, in consequence, to all important social changes. But the new philosophy, in turn, was so hostile to the very principle of authority as to deprive individuals of the direction and support indispensable both for the organic freedom of individuals and social stability.[84] The new philosophy, in asserting the principle of individual freedom, contributed to justifying the activities of a new form of concentrated power, the economic, which has consistently denied effective freedom to the economically underpowered and underprivileged.[85] If a new individualism

82. *Ibid.,* pp. 150–51.

83. Dewey, *Freedom and Culture,* pp. 65–66.

84. Dewey, "Authority and Resistance to Social Change," *Problems of Man* (New York, 1946), p. 100.

85. *Ibid.* Cf. "Liberty and Social Control," *ibid.* p. 117: "I refer to this particular instance merely by way of illustration, and to indicate how far away so-called Jeffersonian democracy has drifted from the original ideas and policies of any democracy whatever. The drift of nominal democracy from the conception of life which may be characterized as democratic has come about under the influence of a so-called rugged individualism that defines the liberty of individuals in terms of the inequality bred by existing economic-legal institutions."

is to be constructed, it must be by the operation of co-operative intelligence which in science affords a working model of the union of freedom and intelligence. Freedom is defined relative to the circumstances and conditions by which it is made possible, and it results in a political individualism which is reconciled to the requirements of economic experimentation and control.

6. Semantics, Philosophy, and Action

The oppositions among the conceptions of freedom and history which flow from the different methods and the different principles they employ are not necessarily opposed in their implications for human action when these implications are examined in semantic analysis of the concepts and their implications. But they are developed in polemical oppositions of philosophic doctrines and in political oppositions of practical action, and the different conceptions of science and of the practical which they entail yield paradoxes and absurdities in theoretic discussion and conflicts in practical application. In the analysis of practical action and in the history of cooperation in action, those paradoxes and conflicts are epitomized in the shifting meanings and order of priority relative to each other, assumed by the triad of terms: "freedom," "equality," and "fraternity."

The dialectical frame of discussion depends on likenesses and analogies, and since there are likenesses between the most unlike things, there is no reason why dialectical resolutions of differences should not be intelligible and defensible—however extreme the antitheses that are joined—provided the likenesses are clearly determined. Those likenesses are marshalled in different forms of a dialectical science dependent on different comprehensive principles, and freedom is then found in the operation of those comprehensive principles, for absence of restraint is achieved by the operation of the pure will, or the enlightened mind, or of mind and will, thought and action, in organic integration. Those comprehensive principles, found in wisdom or love, in the development of Spirit or the extension of ownership of the means of production, determine the forms of the association of men and their place in those associations as well as the individual actions of men when they are free. The bond uniting men in dialectical systems tends to be the same whether the group under consideration is a family, a class, a voluntary organization, a city, a nation, or a state. Terms like "fraternity," the "brotherhood of man," "friendship," "class solidarity," and "love" are used to express it, and dialectical utopias have been projected in societies based on common ownership. The place of the individual is determined by the same wisdom or love, for the individual assumes a place determined by functions and needs in an organic whole, and if the word "equality" is used, a functional equality is meant, determined by the institutional place of the individual in the group. The essence of the individual in a dialectical or organic system is found in the actions of the individual by which he realizes his own nature in accordance with the nature and conditions of the organic whole: the principles of such actions and therefore of individual essences may properly provide the definition of "freedom." But since men are not always wise, or good, or free, the concept of freedom is doubled in dialectical systems by the differentiation of free choice from freedom of the will in the right exercise of free choice, by the differentiation of freedom under law from the freedom of the wise man, or by the differentiation of subjective freedom or freedom under necessity from objective or true freedom. Dialectical discussions of freedom under actual conditions, therefore, continue some form of Plato's differentiation of the perfect state from existent or possible states and some form of his differentiation of the ends of second-best states into freedom (derived from the ideals of democracy), wisdom (derived from monarchy in lieu of equality), and friendship or love or mutuality (holding the two in relation in lieu of fraternity).

The logistic frame of discussion depends on simple elements and simple relations. Since complex things are understood and used only by differentiating least parts and their basic relations and operations, there is no reason why logistic constructions of systems should not be accurate and verifiable—however complex the interactions calculated—provided the elements and their relations are clearly defined. These systems are determined by different forms of logistic analysis dependent on different simple principles, and freedom is then found in the actions initiated by an element or system of elements in contrast to the actions suffered by it. Restraint is the action of external causes and absence of restraint is operation according to the laws of one's own nature. A body falls freely until it encounters obstructions; an electron or a particle moves freely until it encounters some other moving particle; a man acts freely until he encounters interference with his action.

Freedom is freedom of motion, and the simple principles of motions may be found in the relation of bodies, of ideas, or of symbols. Once the nature of the individual is determined analytically and the laws of its motion have been stated scientifically, the system within which the individual operates is subject to two forms of statement: the laws of motion and the long chains of causes which are necessary and the interactions of bodies which are contingent and subject to probability. The logistic discussion of freedom and of motion alternates between two extremes: between the statement of mechanical (though not necessarily mechanistic) laws of the motions of particles and the operation of forces in systematic relations compounded of simple interactions at one extreme, and the calculation of the probable interactions of forces in contingent relations which approach the complexity of landslides and revolutions at the other. At the one extreme, freedom approaches necessity, for a thing must operate according to the laws of its own nature and the concepts of cause and responsibility alike depend on the regularity of such actions; at the other extreme, freedom consists in the power to act or to abstain from action in particular circumstances, for a thing is not free when it operates under restraint. There is consequently a doubling of the conception of the systems or of the associations into which particles or individuals enter. Man in his actual relations may be said to operate with the same necessity as atoms; or conversely, electrons in their actual relations may be said to operate with the same freedom as man. The analogies of human society have been sought in the interactions of bodies operating according to the laws of mechanics, in the interplay and balance of the parts of a machine, in the functions of the parts of a living organism operating according to the laws of physiology, or in the division of labor of societies of ants, bees, or termites, and logistic utopias have been projected in societies based on the rule of scientific academies. Since freedom in this sense is directly affected by knowledge of necessities and probabilities, the progress of society and civilization is the progress of science: the problem of equality is the problem of extending the benefits of the progress of civilization uniformly; the problem of freedom is the problem of combatting ignorance, fear, superstition, insecurity, and aggression; and the problem of fraternity is the problem of discovering and imposing laws of human relationship to advance those equalities and liberties while preventing the misuse of knowledge and science.

The problematic frame of discussion depends on differentiating and distinguishing problems. Since there are differences even among things and problems which are closely comparable in their distinctive properties or ultimately reducible to the same material elements, there is no reason why the problems and hypotheses of problematic analysis should not be distinguishable and analyzable in reflection and testable in experience—however interdependent the parts of experience and the properties of things—provided the differences of situations and subjects are unambiguously isolated. The differences among sciences, problems, purposes, modes of expression, and subject matters are determined by different forms of problematic analysis or inquiry dependent on different reflexive principles, and freedom is then found in the operation of those reflexive principles in planning action. Absence of restraint is achieved among rational beings by determining the conditions of interrelations, associations, and cooperations which will permit a maximum place for reflection by the individual in the treatment of his own and of common problems. Freedom based on the method of inquiry is defined by basic human and social properties and relations which are without cosmological or physical analogues, and utopias have been projected by the method of inquiry in societies based on mutual tolerance and understanding.

In dialectical analysis, in which the basic principles are comprehensive, the individual and his actions are determined by the whole of which he is an organic part: the analogy between the individual and the community makes the bond of the community identical with the principle of wisdom, love, or production which determines the action of the individual; equality is a functional equality introduced by that principle in the relations of the parts of the community; and freedom is distinct from free choice since it is the right use of free choice in accordance with that principle. In logistic analysis, in which the basic principles are simple, freedom is found, not in the essence of the individual, but in the system of the whole which is determined by the relations and interactions of elements: the laws of motion of the individual, and the systems of relations in which those motions occur, introduce a basic distinction between internal and external causes or between necessity and contingency, which provides for the individual a double set of systems, determined respectively by the laws of motion and by the circumscribing conditions and stated respectively in terms of necessity and probability. Freedom, which is the operation of internal as opposed to external causes, is advanced by a knowledge of causes; and equality is achieved by the extension of the benefits of the operation of such knowledge. In problematic analysis, in which the basic principles are reflexive, the problem of freedom is neither to discover the conditions of individual action within an organic universe nor to discover the systems of forces and relations which condition the action of an individual, but to discover the form of political community in which men can participate in organizing the conditions which determine the mode of life.

The concepts of freedom, fraternity, and equality, in substance, are determined dialectically by distinguishing two senses of freedom: the freedom of choice and the freedom of the right use of free choice, while the forms of equality and community follow from the number and influence of the wise, the good, or the owners of the instruments of production and the mode of their action. They are determined logistically by distinguishing two senses of fraternity, community, causes, or interactions: the interrelations expressed in necessary laws and the interrelations found in contingent situations, closed systems, and random groups, while the forms of freedom and equality follow from the calculation of continuing courses of motion or states of rest and the impacts by which they are altered. They are determined in inquiry by distinguishing two senses of equality or individuality, a functional equality determined by the contribution of the individual to the community and expressed in terms of rights and duties and a literal equality determined by methods of adjudication and adjustment formulated in law and custom, while the differences in the constitutions of states are determined by differences in the forms of functional or proportional equality they employ, and freedom is the objective and the basis of one form of constitution, the democracy.

From the complex oppositions of theories about freedom and of actions in vindication of freedom a pattern of meanings emerges for freedom or absence of external restraint. Freedom consists in right choice when the conditions of freedom are determined dialectically relative to the organic whole of which man and his development are parts and it operates to control external restraints manifested in passions and self-alienation which prevent men from reaching, in freedom, the full realization of their essences. Freedom consists in action in accordance with the nature of the individual when the conditions of freedom are determined logistically relative to the contingent situation in which man is found, and it operates in opposition to restraints imposed by external causes which inhibit individual action and the development of power and knowledge. Freedom consists in the realization of individual

potentialities in individual communities when the conditions of freedom are determined problematically relative to concrete circumstances
and situations, and it operates in opposition to political and social restraints which inhibit liberty and in calculation of restraints required
for its protection. These three conceptions of freedom are not in contradiction, for they are the consequences and applications of principles
which are radically different but which are not opposed if their basic
assumptions and definitions are respected. Nonetheless, in the development of philosophic discussions of freedom and of history they have
been the sources of opposed doctrines and reiterated refutations.

The semantic analysis which lifts these doctrines and arguments out
of their doctrinal oppositions to set forth the related meanings which
they express may supplement the relations in which they are developed
in polemical opposition and may thereby enrich the meanings they explore. It does not, however, solve the problems presented by their oppositions, for even when they have been shown to involve no contradiction in either their principles or their conclusions, practical doctrines
and prescriptions for action derived from them may lead to opposed
and irreconcilable programs of action. The oppositions of philosophies
applied in action are not simple repetitions of the oppositions of their
theoretic arguments. Rather, philosophies are transformed in action to
forces in competition with other forces determining behavior. Those
transformations of philosophies as they become forces in action affect
both the statement of their objectives and the conception of the means
by which they may be achieved. Objectives tend to assume utopian
statement in the simplified form which is possible in practical situations, and utopias tend to assume three forms: utopias based on "having" and "possessing" in common, utopias based on the progress of
knowledge, and utopias based on understanding and the realization of
individual potentialities. Means tend to be conceived in simplified
terms of the requirements of joint action in practical situations, and the
place assigned to scientific and philosophic knowledge in the preparation and use of means tends to assume three forms: the formulation of
a common policy or line of action, the preparation of technical knowledge for application, and the provision of means of communication and
discussion.

These simplifications of ends and means cannot be removed by
either the philosophical examination of the bases of doctrines or the
semantic analysis of their relations, since further doctrinal elaboration

undergoes the same translation and simplification. The problems of philosophy as a force in action are basically problems of reconciling opposed ends and adjusting apparently incompatible means: if ends are conceived as ultimate ideals based on reason or necessity there is no direct dialectical means affecting the devotion of the party committed to their attainment; if ends are conceived as the achievements of the progress of knowledge there is no direct scientific means of providing the conditions requisite for scientific advance; if ends are conceived as the realization by agreement of the potentialities of particular situations there is no direct reflective means of securing agreement concerning the means of securing agreement and cooperation. As a result dialectics harden into universal prescriptions to be imposed if necessary, by force and subterfuge; logistics discover that even valid and effective sciences do not provide the devices by which to secure their acceptance and use in control of action; and inquiry encounters so many differences of circumstances that cooperation is rendered ineffective by the multiplication of the sectarian disputes.

8
Philosophic Semantics and Philosophic Inquiry

The nature and functions of philosophy, like those of any other enterprise, are determined by its subject-matter and its conditioning circumstances. In a broad, ambiguous sense, the subject-matter and circumstances of philosophy are the same, for they both range through the
processes of nature, the structure of the cosmos, the experiences of
men, and the institutions of societies. But in a narrower, more precise
sense, the forces of "nature" and the problems of "experience" which
condition philosophizing differ from the interpretations of "nature"
and "experience" which result from philosophizing as a material stim-
ulus differs from a theoretical product. The beginnings of philosophizing are prehistoric, in the broad sense that the earliest recorded stages
of religion, literature, history, political organization, and science pre-
suppose and even record prior speculation and prior problems. Philosophy is one of the marks of an advanced culture, in the narrow and
precise sense that the statement and examination of basic problems are
culminating points of theory, practice, and production. Philosophies
have borrowed from science, politics, and art; they have determined
the nature and organization of knowledge, society, and aesthetic experience. The enterprises and objects which have been both subject-matters and conditioning influences of a philosophy include other philosophies. As subject-matter, the reinterpretation or refutation of other
philosophies, past or contemporary, is a proper part of the statement of
any philosophy; as conditioning influence, the continuity of philosophies in history and in controversy makes any philosophy at once an
architectonic reorganization of what is sound in the statements of phi-

Unpublished contribution to the Illinois Philosophy Conference, held at Carbondale,
Illinois, 26 February 1966. Privately reproduced and distributed by the author. © 1987
by Zahava K. McKeon

losophers and a cathartic exposure of what is absurd. In the broad, ambiguous sense there are as many interpretations of the philosophy of Aristotle or of Wittgenstein as there are interpretations of nature; in the strict sense there is only one true interpretation of statements or things.

The basic ambiguity of philosophic statement and discussion is not peculiar to philosophy. It is common to all discourse and to reflective inquiry in all fields. One of the tasks which has always been an inseparable or irresistible adjunct to philosophical speculation is the clarification of ambiguities. Ambiguities and contradictions are treated in two ways in inquiry: they are removed by choosing one of the several meanings of an ambiguous term or statement and by showing the others are absurd or irrelevant, or they are used by distinguishing the several senses and the appropriate regions of their application. Communication and presentation depend on unambiguous definition in basic statements and on consequential consistency in discursively related statements; discussion and inquiry depend on productive ambiguity in the interpretation of common problems and suggestive inconsistency in the assumptions proposed to resolve them. The statement of the solution of a problem moves from undifferentiated ambiguity to literal precision. Philosophic semantics is an examination of different solutions of philosophic problems; philosophic inquiry is an examination of common issues to which different philosophic resolutions may be found. The unambiguous resolution of a fundamental problem often leads to new ambiguous problems; semantics and inquiry are therefore stages in the ongoing process of philosophy. If they are differentiated, the relations among philosophies may be stated unambiguously and the recurrence of philosophic problems may be distinguished from the progress of philosophic resolutions.

The semantic interpretation of philosophies will never yield unique, adequate, or universally accepted interpretations of any philosophy, but philosophic semantics may provide schemata by which to make unambiguously clear the meanings that are attributed in a proposed interpretation to statements made in any philosophy. There is no simple relation between distinct philosophic positions nor is a comprehensive or sequential translation possible from one to another, but different philosophies are significantly related by the common problems they treat, and philosophic inquiry may provide modes by which to relate the stages of different solutions based on different interpretations of common problems. There is a variety of ways in which the schemata of semantics have been set up in the history of philosophy, and the distinctions have been employed in a variety of modes of philosophic inquiry. The semantic distinctions have accumulated a mass of ambiguities from which they are rescued periodically by the precisions of a great philosopher engaged in one of the modes of inquiry and the modes of inquiry, in the doctrines of a school, are reduced to precise repetitions from which they are rescued periodically by the controversial reformulations of common problems in the mode of a rival school. The precisions of philosophic semantics may be preserved by connections established by the modes of inquiry, and the communications among modes of inquiry may be preserved by precisions established by the distinctions of semantics.

Among the numerous semantic schemes that have been used in philosophy, one persistent and useful organization has been built about differences of method. For all their ambiguity the differences between dialogue or the dialectical method, debate or the operational method, proof or the logistic method, and inquiry or the problematic method were stated in ancient philosophy, have run through histories of restatement and modification, and are still operative in contemporary philosophy. The ambiguities arise in part because each of the methods assumes the functions of the others: dialectic is dialogue, but it is also debate, proof, and inquiry, and the same is true of each of the other methods; but they assume the functions of opposed methods by changing the method they borrow, and the transformation is therefore ambiguous and subject to clarification. The ambiguities arise in part also because a method is a discursive process which has a beginning or principles, and an end or conclusions; and the conclusions have constituent parts or categories. Four inclusive main heads of philosophic semantics may be set up—Principles, Methods, Interpretations, and Selections—but the differentiation of methods, and the relations of the methods to principles, interpretations, and selections can be rendered precise only by reference to common problems and to the modes of philosophic inquiry.

The common problems of the modes of inquiry which use such a semantics built on methods are problems of things, thoughts, facts, and simples. The modes of inquiry may be differentiated under any of these four heads, and there is a strict equivalence of the modes in their operation on the common problems which fall under each of the heads. The distinctions of the semantic scheme may therefore be established by consideration of the modes of thought. Even in non-technical considerations of thinking, four modes of thought may be distinguished: it is a process by which parts are put together, or englobing truths are approximated, or problems are solved, or arbitrary formulations are interpreted. The four are formally exhaustive of possibilities: the assumption of least parts, but no whole except by composition; the assumption of an ontological unifying principle, but no absolute least parts; the rejection of least parts and separated wholes, and the assumption of problems and natures encountered in the middle region; and the assumption that all distinctions are initially arbitrary. The four modes of thought are mutually exclusive and exhaustive of possible modes. Each of the modes has two moments and each makes use of a basic assumption: construction and decomposition make use of constituents; assimilation and exemplification of models; resolution and question of causes; and discrimination and postulation of theses.

The four methods distinguished in philosophic semantics may be differentiated unambiguously by the four modes of thought, and the characteristic operations of each as a method may be clarified by the mode of thought used to define it. Since there is a strict equivalence between the modes of thought and the modes of things, facts, and simples, the differentiation by the modes of thought may be translated into differentiations by modes of things, facts, and simples. The logistic method is proof by construction and decomposition dependent on indivisible elements; the dialectical method is dialogue by assimilation and exemplification dependent on changeless models; the problematic method is inquiry by resolution and questions dependent on discoverable causes; the operational method is debate by discrimination and postulation dependent on theses and rules. So defined, an important difference is observable in the four methods: two, the dialectical and the operational methods, are universal methods applicable to all problems and all subject-matters, and they do not require indemonstrable first principles or univocal terms; the other two, the logistic and the problematic methods, are particular methods, which require distinct methodological procedures for different problems or subject-matters, each with its own indemonstrable first principles and univocal definitions.

The principles which are employed in conjunction with one of the methods need not be determined by the same mode of thought as the

method. Nonetheless, the kinds of principles may be distinguished
from each other, as the methods were, by use of the modes of thought.
Moreover, principles are beginnings, and beginnings may be found
either in determinative wholes or in generative parts; and two modes
of thought lead back to holoscopic principles, while two modes lead
back to meroscopic principles. Comprehensive principles are holoscopic in that they assimilate all things, thoughts, symbols, and actions
into an inclusive whole formed by an englobing principle. Reflexive
principles are holoscopic in that they resolve problems into a plurality
of wholes formed by principles which are reflexively instances of themselves. Simple principles are meroscopic in that they decompose things,
thoughts, symbols, or actions into atoms, simple ideas, undefined
terms, or unconditioned impulses from which to construct what is
known to be and what is thought or felt or desired. Actional principles
are meroscopic in that they postulate distinctions by which to discriminate into kinds what is said, done, or made.

The propositions which are established as conclusions and the actions which are determined as consequences of principles and methods
need not be determined by the same mode of thought as the principles
or the methods. The kinds of interpretations may, nonetheless, be determined, as the methods and principles were, by use of the modes of
thought. Moreover, conclusions or consequences are found to be of
two kinds: they may derive their character from a reality assumed to
transcend or to underlie phenomena and statements, or they may reduce reality and values to aspects or consequences of phenomena. Ontological interpretations are ontic in that they assimilate what seems to
be the case to a reality which transcends and corrects appearances. Entitative interpretations are ontic in that they construct secondary qualities, perceptions, emotions, and other appearances from a nature
which underlies phenomena. Essentialistic interpretations are phenomenal in that they resolve problems by seeking properties and causes
which are natural functions or acquired conditionings. Existentialistic
interpretations are phenomenal in that they discriminate statements and
meanings which may be used to produce knowledge or attitudes or
satisfactions.

The rigidities of doctrine and the ambiguities of problem for which
philosophy is sometimes taxed are removed by the interplay of philosophic semantics and philosophic inquiry. A philosophic problem is
ambiguous. Philosophic discussion of a problem explores a broad, am-

biguous answer to a question; and in the interpretation of the question, different meanings are used to form opposed hypotheses which guide the resolutions of the problem in different modes of inquiry. In controversy the resulting reformulations of the original ambiguous answer are placed in opposition as if they were univocal and as if the choice between them were a simple problem of logic involving little more than the resolution of contradictions. The different meanings and references of the statements thought to be contradictory are examined in philosophic semantics; and their adequacy, their relations to each other, and the new problems they may raise are subjects for philosophic inquiry.

The question, What is freedom? is one of the recurrent ambiguous questions of philosophy which has opened up new dimensions in contemporary thought and action. It is a significant question because the initial interpretation, "freedom is the absence of external impediments to action," focuses attention on the need to remove the ambiguities of "absence," "external," "impediment," and "action," and the growing host of ambiguities in each clarifying statement. The semantic scheme constructed from the modes of thought sets forth, thus far (see chart p. 253), three sets of determinations of the question, What is freedom? What is freedom in fact or interpretation, *What* things are free?; What is freedom in thought or method, *What* property do free things share?; What is freedom in being or principle, *What* are the grounds of the possibility or the actuality of freedom? The question takes on a vast scope of meanings under these distinctions; and since a complete interpretation of the question makes use of all four semantic headings, the number is increased by the number of possible combinations of the four. The indefinitely large number of possible meanings is the source of the richness of philosophic inquiry, for each interpretation may be used as the hypothesis for further investigation.

What is freedom? treated as, What or who are free? is a question of interpretation. According to the entitative interpretation freedom is unimpeded motion, and external impediments are hindrances to motion; *bodies* are free. Human freedom is one instance of freedom to move: it is self-determination as opposed to restraint or coercion. According to the existentialist interpretation freedom is spontaneous or undetermined activity, and external impediments include psychological as well as physical hindrances and the fixities of automatic and habitual responses; *animate beings* are free. Human freedom is an instance of the freedom to originate: it is freedom of self-initiation or self-expression as opposed to conformity to the customary in action, opinion, or taste. According to the essentialist interpretation freedom is action in accordance with deliberative choice, and external impediments include lack of thought and decision as well as physical and psychological hindrances; *men* are free. Human freedom is self-adjustment or self-realization as opposed to reliance on nature, chance, or fortune for the achievement of values. According to the ontological interpretation freedom is autonomous thought and action, and external impediments include lack of wisdom as well as limitations of reason and will; in a strict sense only *God* is free and intelligent beings or wise men approximate to the divine freedom. Human freedom is self-perfection as opposed to determination by worldly, animal, or physical inclinations. In this large spread, from bodies to God, of interpretations of what or who is free, ontic interpretations are radically distinct from phenomenal interpretations: ontic freedoms consist in doing as one should—acting according to one's nature or according to wisdom—whether or not one pleases; while phenomenal freedoms consist in doing as one pleases—spontaneously or voluntarily—since freedom is a precondition of virtuous action, not an operation of nature or an effect of the good.

What is freedom? treated as, What is the freedom of the free, or what actions are free? is a question of method or of the use of thought in the recognition or achievement of freedom. Knowledge has a direct relation to freedom conceived according to the universal methods—one must have knowledge, in the form of knowledge appropriate to the method, to be free. The relation of knowledge to freedom is indirect in freedom achieved by the particular methods—one need not oneself possess the knowledge which is needed to secure and safeguard one's freedom. Universal freedoms depend on knowledge conceived as wisdom or on knowledge conceived as power. Free actions are wise actions; and hindrances in the way of freedom are removed *dialectically* by education and by development of knowledge leading to wisdom. Free actions are willed actions; and freedom is achieved and retained *operationally* by the acquisition and use of power and of knowledge which is power. Particular freedoms depend on knowledge conceived as science or on knowledge conceived as prudence. Free actions are actions in accordance with one's nature; and hindrances, inhibitions, and alienations may be removed to restore natural freedom by therapy performed by an expert in a *logistic* science of human nature and its diseases. Free actions are deliberate actions; and freedom is the precon-

dition and the effect *problematically* of democratic society, which operates according to prudence, or right reason, or the rule of law, without
the necessity that all free men be endowed with prudence or be expert
in jurisprudence.

What is freedom? treated as, What are the grounds of the possibility
or the actuality of freedom, or what decisions are free? is a question of
principles or of the groundings of freedom in being. The possibility of
freedom is grounded in the being of the universe or of man as holoscopic principles—practical decisions are cognitive if self-rule is possible by approximating one's actions to a rational structure in all being
or by establishing social institutions in which men are ruled by deliberations and decisions which they participate in and make. The actuality of freedom is grounded in agreements or conventions of men as
meroscopic principles—practical decisions are emotive and persuasive
if the end of action is to secure what one wants and if values are determined by agreement concerning desires to be satisfied and pleasures to
be secured. Society and justice are grounded in nature and being by
holoscopic principles, and transitions may be made in valid inference
from what is to what ought to be. Communities and right and wrong
are grounded in convention and agreement by meroscopic principles,
and no inference is possible from what is to what ought to be. Holoscopic principles place freedom in a rational universe or in human societies. Comprehensive principles, which establish a reflexive coincidence
between that which is and that which is intelligible, make freedom in
intelligent beings self-rule of inclinations and emotions by reason. Reflexive principles, which establish reflexive beginnings in separate inquiries and fields, limit freedom to the principles of ethics and politics
and make freedom self-rule in practical action. Meroscopic principles
place freedom in the pursuit of pleasure and the establishment of associations. Simple principles, which provide the elements from which to
construct what is real, seek the elements of value and communities in
preferences and agreements: freedom operates in the pursuit of pleasures and the establishment of preferences. Actional principles are arbitrary principles used in the formulation and interpretation of the real
and in the advancement of pleasure and the private and public good.

The semantic schema makes it possible to explore in precise detail
both the obvious fact that philosophers do not mean the same thing
when they talk about freedom and also the less frequently recognized
fact that the different meanings have been explored in implications and

applications which emerge only rarely in comparable sequences or in conclusions which can be placed in simple correlation. Philosophic semantics yields unambiguous philosophies which are related to each other in ambiguous controversy on common problems. The semantic schema has been constructed by giving precise meanings to kinds of methods, interpretations, and principles by defining each by a mode of thought—assimilation, discrimination, construction, and resolution. An ambiguous statement, like the initial definition of freedom, can then be given unambiguous meanings determined by methods, interpretations, and principles. The unambiguous resolutions of a problem, like the problem of freedom, may be seen in their ambiguous relations to each other by transforming the schema to show how the basic terms used to analyze knowing—knowledge, knower, known, and knowable—are transformed in their meanings from analysis to analysis.

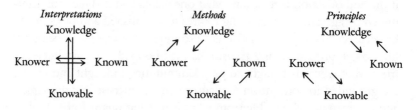

Ontic interpretations set up relations between knowledge and the knowable: ontological interpretations assimilate the knowable to knowledge; entitative interpretations construct knowledge from the elements of the knowable. Existentialist interpretations present the known (nature, society, man, and art) as products of the discrimination and activity of the knower; essentialist interpretations resolve the problems encountered in the known in theory, practice, and production to reconstitute the known in a new form. In the dialectical method knowledge is the objective which the knower seeks and approximates; in the operational method the knower makes knowledge. In the logistic method the knowable is transformed into the known; in the problematic method the known is used to inquire into the knowable. Holoscopic principles provide beginnings which are a coincidence of knowledge and known: comprehensive principles set up inclusive coincidences of that which is most truly and that which is most intelligible; reflexive principles seek a plurality of subject matters which are marked off by instances of knowledge which is self-instantiating and by beings which are self-caused or first causes. Meroscopic principles provide beginnings in which the contributions of the knower and the knowable are separated from each other and from influence one on the other: actional principles provide beginnings in uninterpreted terms set in fixed but undefined relations by thesis or postulation before they are interpreted to produce knowledge and values; simple terms provide beginnings which have no parts and therefore no possible error from which composite things and images and conventions can be formed without error in simple steps.

The ambiguities of the problems of philosophy and the precisions of the statements of philosophy fix the problems of defining the fourth and last column of the semantic schema, Selections. Simples can be enumerated, but explanation of their natures and uses requires statement or interpretation which is established by use of method and principles. Simples are employed in forming the constitutive parts of propositions, the terms and connectives of methods, and the simplicities of principles. The modes of thought may be translated into the modes of simplicity to define the kinds of selection. Simples of assimilation are categories of thought—ideas and presentations which are modes of being or of phenomena; they are set forth in selection in hierarchies ordered to a transcendent idea or being. Simples of discrimination are categories of language or action—symbols (or intentions) and rules of operation (or execution); they are set forth in selection in types ordered by perspectives of orientation (or purpose). Simples of construction are categories of things—discerned by cognition and emotion; they are set forth in selection by matters or objects to which other arrangements of processes and materials may be transformed by reduction. Simples of resolution are categories of terms—natures and dispositions; they are set forth in selection as functions by which natures may be defined and classified. The statement of a philosophy involves a particular selection of categories, which is colored by the general selection characteristic of the philosophic communication of a period, making the primary use and determination of categories sometimes metaphysical for the clarification of principles (after a revolt against sophistry and empiricism), sometimes epistemological for the ordering of judgments and consequences critically and methodologically (after a revolt against dogmatism and theoretical metaphysics), sometimes semantic and pragmatic for the establishment of warranted statements and effective actions (after a revolt against idealisms and psychologisms). The ambiguous question, What is freedom? takes its fourth determination from the selection of categories, *what* are we talking about when we talk about freedom and how do we fix our meanings? There are four possible determinations of what has meaning and what is meant: basic thoughts and approximations to them; arbitrary orderings of experience interpreted by assigning significances to the words in which it is expressed; constructs composed of things known or images perceived; and natures and dispositions signified and denoted by terms.

The interaction of the modes of philosophic inquiry and the schema of philosophic semantics is apparent both in framing of common problems for interpretation and investigation in different philosophies and in developing particular philosophies in distinction from and opposition to other philosophies. The interdependent structures are set forth in parallel form in the following chart:

The basic equivalence of the modes of being, thought, fact, and simple is indicated in the chart of the modes of inquiry by the lines connecting the modes. The principles, methods, interpretations, and selections which employ a single mode are likewise connected in the semantic chart by lines which trace paths from the inclusive to the simple kinds. The basic divisions of philosophy tabulated below the two charts take their origin from the dominant mode under which they are classified. The division into theoretic, practical and poetic has a metaphysical foundation and was developed by Aristotle in controversial treatment of the problems of philosophy and the positions of philosophers. The division into physics, ethics, and logic has a Hellenistic origin; Aristotle uses it in the *Topics* as a classification of dialectical questions. The distinction philosophy, poetry, and history is made when the emphasis is on modes of fact and statement, and Aristotle uses it to determine the proper nature of poetry. Philosophy becomes logic, rhetoric, or grammar when questions of structure and categorial parts become central. The basic problems listed in the final tabulation arise in the differentiation of principles, methods, interpretations, and terms under which they are tabulated.

The discussion of philosophical positions is a discussion of facts about philosophies; the discussion of philosophical problems is a discussion of issues between philosophies. Philosophic semantics is a method to secure precision in the statement and investigation of philosophical positions; philosophic inquiry is a method to introduce flexibility into the statement and investigation of philosophical problems. They supplement each other, since philosophic semantics becomes rigid

MODES OF PHILOSOPHIC INQUIRY

Modes of Being *Being*	Modes of Thought *That which is*	Modes of Fact *Existence*	Modes of Simplicity *Experience*
Being and Becoming	Assimilation and Exemplification (models)	Reality and Approximation	Categories of Thought (Ideas and presentations)
Phenomena and Projections	Discrimination and Postulation	Process and Frame	Categories of Language and Action (Symbols and rules)
Elements and Composites	Construction and Decomposition (constituents)	Object and Impression	Categories of Things (Cognition and Emotion)
Actuality and Potentiality	Resolution and Question (causes)	Substance and Accident	Categories of Terms

SCHEMA OF PHILOSOPHIC SEMANTICS

Principles	*Methods*	*Interpretations*	*Selections*
Holoscopic	*Universal*	*Ontic*	
Comprehensive	Dialectical	Ontological	Hierarchies (transcendental)
Reflexive	Operational	Entitative	Matters (reductive)
Meroscopic	*Particular*	*Phenomenal*	
Simple	Logistic	Existentialist	Types (perspective)
Actional	Problematic	Essentialist	Kinds (functional)

BASIC DIVISIONS OF PHILOSOPHY

Theoretic	Physics	Philosophy	Logic
Practical	Ethics	Poetry	Rhetoric
Poetic	Logic	History	Grammar

BASIC PROBLEMS

Universal	Reality	One
Particular	Process	Many
Whole		
Part		

and doctrinaire if it loses contact with the problems to which the positions are solutions, and philosophic inquiry becomes abstract and sectarian if it cuts off communication with other positions and other interpretations of the problem.

The semantic schema does not provide a final determination of what is meant by a philosophic statement, but rather a means of isolating successive aspects of proposed meanings for consideration and development. Its use may be illustrated by sketching some of the high points of the meanings that have been taken on by the four methods listed. Philosophies have not frequently followed the lines traced on the chart by which methods are related to principles, interpretations, and selections determined by the same mode of thought; and one aspect of the diversification of methods arises from the innovations introduced by altering principles, interpretations or selections.

The metamorphoses of the dialectical method range from the synoptic method which Plato used to discuss all problems, to the skepticism of the Academy, to the transcendentalism and mysticism of the Neoplatonists, to Christian creationism and mysticism, to Marxist materialism. Plato combined the dialectical method with comprehensive principles and ontological interpretation; the dialectical method was retained in Academic skepticism but was used with actional principles and existentialist interpretation; Plotinus restored the ontological interpretation with dialectic but used simple principles; Augustine combined the dialectical method and ontological interpretation with actional principles; Hegel used the dialectical method with reflexive principles and entitative interpretation; Marx turned Hegel upside down by retaining the dialectical method and entitative interpretation but substituting actional for reflexive principles.

The logistic method was used by Democritus and Euclid in antiquity and by Hobbes, Newton, Locke, Descartes, Spinoza, and Leibniz in the seventeenth century and by Peirce and Santayana in recent times. The influence of Descartes or Newton is difficult to trace without semantic distinctions: thus, Descartes used the logistic method with reflexive principles and existentialist interpretation; Spinoza's criticisms and modifications centered on the interpretation, and he therefore retained the method and principles but substituted the ontological for the existentialist interpretation.

The operational method was the method of the Sophists, the Pyrrhonian Skeptics, and Cicero in antiquity, and of Galileo, Bacon, Berkeley, and Hume in the seventeenth and eighteenth centuries, and of Kant and John Stuart Mill. Mill expressed admiration for the ethics of Kant and undertook to show that the categorical imperative can be grounded only by utilitarian consideration of consequences; Kant used a combination of operational method (he observed that his method was the method of skepticism) and reflexive principles with an ontological interpretation; Mill used the same method (which he professed to derive from Cicero) and principles with an existentialist interpretation.

The problematic method was used by Aristotle in antiquity, by Thomas Aquinas and some other scholastics of the thirteenth and fourteenth centuries, and by William James and John Dewey. Aristotle used a problematic method, reflexive principles, and essentialist interpretation; Aquinas retained the method and principles but substituted an ontological for the essentialist interpretation. James thought that pragmatism was a continuation of Mill's utilitarianism: Mill used an operational method with reflexive principles and an existentialist interpretation; James retained the interpretation but used a problematic method and actional principles; Dewey continued the problematic method and actional principles but used an essentialist interpretation.

The modes of philosophic inquiry do not provide a fixed list of the persistent or perennial problems of philosophy, but rather a structure for the formation of hypotheses concerning a common question viewed from the orientation of different modes of inquiry. Interpretation of the structure of different modes yields questions that have been asked or that might be asked and develops a context of related questions. The four modes of inquiry, thus, take particular form in the four scientific questions raised by Aristotle at the beginning of the second book of the *Posterior Analytics*—experience is the concern of the question, whether it is; existence is the concern of, what it is; that which is answers the question, of what sort it is; and being is the source of answers to, why it is. The same four questions became the four *constitutiones* of the Roman rhetoricians, whence they entered into legal and political philosophy. They provide a basis for the reformulation of metaphysical problems which I once tried in an essay called, "Being, Existence, and That Which Is."* They serve to relate, in a rich variety of ways, the categories which are modes of simples and the transcendentals which are predicated reflexively of each other and which are modes of being.

* Published in *Review of Metaphysics* 13, no. 4 (June 1960): 539–54.

The distinction between things better known to us and things better known in nature and the prolix progeny of that distinction, which includes the distinction between *a posteriori* and *a priori,* explore the relations between the modes of experience and the modes of being. The modes of inquiry serve to unravel the tangled history of the methods of induction and deduction, analysis and synthesis, discovery and proof, which first emerged from distinct modes and were variously merged with each other and inverted.

The modes of inquiry serve, finally, to separate continuing structures of problems from structures of suggestive innovation, and they suggest the rich possibilities which are opened when the dominant selection is the modes of fact and existence which turn to problems of concreteness of action and statement. It has been the hope of many recent philosophers that to begin with the concrete is to avoid false problems and meaningless controversy. That expectation has encountered the difficulty that the particular philosophies which have undertaken to be architectonic have faced controversial oppositions. Too little attention has been paid to the fact that common problems have been treated in different ways or to the possibility that the accord of philosophies is not to be found in a common ideology or a common language but in a common enterprise to which different philosophies make supplementary contributions.**

**When Richard McKeon first presented "Philosophic Semantics and Philosophic Inquiry," it concluded with the following passage:

> "Facts, Categories, and Experience" is a delineation and a contribution to that kind of common philosophy. It will be treated controversially, in whatever consideration it receives, in accordance with the rival possibilities provided by semantic schemata, but the problems it raises may shift attention from the position taken to issues between that position and other possible positions and to the discussion and investigation of possible changes in the concrete situation and in the problems.

"Facts, Categories, and Experience" is the overall title of the three Paul Carus Foundation Lectures that McKeon delivered at the Sixty-second Annual Meeting of the American Philosophical Association Eastern Division, held in New York City from 27 December through 29 December 1965. When McKeon presented "Philosophic Semantics and Philosophic Inquiry" scarcely two months later, he intended to expand the earlier paper for publication by the Carus Foundation in book form, as is customary.

In fact, the lectures remain in their original draft version, unpublished; consequently, I felt it best to omit the passage above from the body of the later paper. However, the unpublished paper, "Facts, Categories, and Experience" will appear in a forthcoming volume of the collected works of Richard P. McKeon, to be published by the University of Chicago Press. [Zahava K. McKeon]

Author-Title Index

Subject Index

Abstractions embalmed, 14
Accord of philosophies, 256
Accountability, 51, 61, 65, 69–70, 81
Action: historical, 152; indicative, 58; involuntary, 225; language and, 161; programs of, 170
Actions: communication and, 101–2; free, 248; freedom and, 236; interdependence of, 4; thoughts and, 5
Adventure, 3, 24
Ages, 88–91, 127, 160, 182
Ambiguities: of common speech, 163; of methods, two sources, 244; philosophic, 53; productive, 56; removal, 137; removed or used, 243
Ambiguity: agreement, differences and, 49; all discourse and inquiry, 243; "cold war" and, 95; discussion and, 93; inescapable, 136–37; inquiry and, 243; productive, 41, 243; semantics and, 163, 181, 244, 250; of statement, 253; useful or productive, 41, 49, 56, 93, 243
America (United States), 10, 11, 13, 95, 100, 168–69
Analysis of Ideas and Study of Methods, Committee on, 16
Analysis today, 160–61
Antitheses, great, 49
Argument, (see Method; Inquiry; Semantics; Principle; Interpretation)
Art needed today, 94
Assumptions: of four modes of thought, 245; of nature of man, 163; philosophic, 104, 148; postulates and purposes, 167; reserved from discussion, 95; varieties of history, 188
Attitudes of mind, 168–69
Authority and freedom, 234
Autobiography, 4, 5

Basic: approaches, 89; assumptions, 163, 188, 245; attitudes, 176; considerations, 99; contingency, 189; differences, 166, 169; distinctions and subject matters, 164; divisions of philosophy, 252; equivalence of modes, 252; force, 197; freedoms of thought and discussion, 229; historical law, 188; ideas, 45, 63, 218; philosophic issues, 117; philosophic orientations, 60; principles, 6, 14, 161, 163, 174, 186; problems, 3, 85, 89–97, 99, 125, 132, 167, 188, 242, 243, 252, 253, 255; questions, 161, 226; terms, 49–50, 60, 95, 250; theory, 160, 184
Biography: metaphysics and, 5; spiritual, 4
Blacks in the United States, 59

Canon law, 165–66
Categories, 251
Causes, 153, 211
Censorship problem, how to solve, 99–100
Chains of causes or arguments, 212, 218
CHART of Modes of Inquiry and Semantic Schema, 253 (see also DIAGRAM)

263